CE

techno
textiles 2

techno textiles 2

Sarah E. Braddock Clarke and Marie O'Mahony

With 337 colour illustrations

Thames & Hudson

First published in the United Kingdom in 1998 with
the title *Techno Textiles* by Thames & Hudson Ltd,
181A High Holborn, London WC1V 7QX

www.thamesandhudson.com

This completely revised edition
© 2005 Sarah E. Braddock Clarke and Marie O'Mahony

British Library Cataloguing-in-Publication Data
A catalogue record for this book is available from
the British Library

ISBN-13: 978-0-500-51245-6
ISBN-10: 0-500-51245-0

Printed and bound in China by CS Graphics

1 (half-title)
RYOKO YAMANAKA
Strata 2 (detail). 2001
see p. 23

2 (opposite title page)
SARAH TAYLOR
Rhythm & Blues (detail). 2002
240 (height) x 120 (width) x 15
(depth) cm

Interactive light-emitting material
installation with sound. This is a
sensor-activated piece which uses
polymer optical fibre, coloured
enamelled copper wire and
polyamide monofilament together
with sensors, a Midicreator © (York
Electronics Centre), speakers, an
amplifier and sounds (Immersive
Media Spaces Ltd). Eleven woven
optical fibre circles contain bundles
of optical fibre. The main lighting
creates pulsating polychromatic
effects in blue, magenta and white.
Interaction causes individual
percussion sounds and illuminates
the bundles. It is lit by two tungsten
halide light projectors and light-
emitting diodes (LEDs). This work
was exhibited at the Jerwood
Applied Arts Prize: 2002 Textiles at
the Crafts Council, London.

3 (title page)
ANN RICHARDS
Pleat-Stripe. 2004

A softly pleated handwoven textile
uses a yarn that is a blend of linen
(87 per cent) and stainless steel (13
per cent) called Irony from Linificio
e Canapificio. This is used with
spun silk in the warp. The weft yarn
is normal twist spun silk, but much
finer than that used for the warp.
The pleating in this fabric is caused
by the weave structure, combined
with the size relationships between
the warp and weft yarns. Ann
Richards uses a computer weave
drafting programme to develop and
visualize weave structures and then
samples on the loom to assess the
physical properties of various
materials in different structures.
The resulting textile has a unique
texture and a temporary memory
for further effects. It is intended for
use in clothing and accessories.

5 (contents page)
**SAVITHRI BARTLETT & KAREN
SPURGIN**
**Detail of layers of laser-cut fabrics
with sequinned embellishment**

See p. 113

CONTENTS

Introduction

above and opposite below
SAVITHRI BARTLETT
Detail of layers of laser-cut fabrics

Textile designer Savithri Bartlett
hand-dyed and laser cut 45 metres
(150 feet) of fabric (opaque habotai
silk and translucent resin-coated
paper nylon) in seven colour ways
for a collaborative garment (see
p. 113) made for the exhibition
Great Expectations in New York,
October 2001 hosted by the Design
Council, UK. Collaborators were
haute couture designer, Deborah
Milner and textile embellisher,
Karen Spurgin. Savithri Bartlett
found that cutting a series of holes
and lines in fabric and offsetting
them by less than 30 degrees
creates a moiré effect. Using two
to three bright colours further
confuses the eye.

Never has there been a more exciting time to work with advanced textiles. There have been periods of great creative output, and also times of important technical developments, but what we are seeing in these early years of the twenty-first century is a combination of the creative and scientific as never before.

Since the first edition of *Techno Textiles* was published in 1998, much has changed. Many of the examples used in the original book were then only at research or prototype stage; others were limited to small or one-off production runs. Now we can follow their progress into reality. Techniques such as thermo-forming and three-dimensional weaving and knitting have become more widespread. There are even examples of fabrics produced using nanotechnology, something that was only talked about at the time of the first edition, while the issue of sustainability deserves more consideration. Included here are several new practitioners using sophisticated technologies, whose research indicates the future for advanced

textiles. We have tracked down a huge number of fresh images (over 80 per cent are new since the first edition) and the text has been updated and revised throughout.

Part 1 of the book examines innovations in the world of textiles: how the latest textiles are dreamt up and made. The whole lexicon of what is and what is not textile is subject to debate. Practitioners are increasingly using combinations of textile and non-textile; mixing hard and soft materials to invent hybrids; and developing composites, where two or more materials are brought together to create a new one with enhanced performance characteristics. The term 'textile' has come to be applied to a whole host of media – not only those that are flexible, but also some that are rigid or with strength to match steel. The use of new textile machinery and processes for metal and ceramic means that we now see knitted metal and ceramic foam.

Fabrics are bringing the worlds of art, design, engineering and science ever closer. Digitizing construction and imagery, laminating and coating fabrics have become the tools of the artist as much as the fashion designer and textile engineer. The results are dramatically different and impact on one another. Silicone, to take one typical example, was originally used as a purely functional coating to provide protection against the environment. It was simply applied as a uniform covering at the required thickness and was usually colourless. The textile designer, however, now adds colour and prints directly with the rubber instead, instantly giving it a visual appeal as well as fabric texture. Industry takes note and we see them add an aesthetic quality to the functionality already provided. The result: blue, red and yellow coated glass fibre.

Synthetics can now be made to take on a variety of guises. They can be heat-set, using their inherent thermoplastic properties, to create subtle changes in relief surface or even dramatic three-dimensional forms. A chemical finish such as dévoré can deconstruct a cloth to create a new and interesting surface. Many of the new finishing treatments, such as water-resistant coatings and holographic laminates, stem from advanced research into high-performance textiles. These have now filtered down and become available for applications from product design to fashion and interiors. Such sophisticated fabrics are judged on their own merits, unlike the early synthetics that were

often seen as cheaper alternatives to silk. The new pliant materials demonstrate the extraordinary breadth of application of textiles today and in the future.

Technology and tradition can work superbly well together. Textile designers are continually taking traditional techniques and updating them to offer a new aesthetic. Some designers have a different approach, working with the latest digital technologies, lasers and ultrasound. These techniques usually signify large-scale production. It is precisely with this in mind that designers and artists choose to work with them. By adding handmade elements such as stitch or appliqué, the subversion of both tradition and technology is emphasized. There is a strong interest in collaboration between industry and craft: a number of initiatives in America and Europe have fostered a mutual respect and eagerness to learn from each other's working practice.

Part 2 of the book is devoted to looking at how fashion designers, product designers, architects and artists use these innovations. Most fashion designers are alert to the recent development in fibres and fabrics and the importance of the right choice for their collections. Techno textiles offer a look quite different to traditional, natural materials and do not work against them but alongside them instead. Many of the latest

developments have in-built performance characteristics desirable in professional sport; for fashion purposes, however, they will give a different look and expression of personal and contemporary style. Shown here is the work of several designers of fashion textiles and fashion designers who are known for their use of high-tech materials. It is increasingly apparent how interlocked the worlds of textiles and fashion are with many collaborations taking place.

Fashion designers might create the textiles themselves; others work closely with a textile designer who provides them with unique fabrics specially designed to be compatible with their ideas for clothing. Some might even have their collections sponsored by a large textile company. The shape of a garment is affected by the type of fabric chosen, and a pared down, contemporary silhouette can show the fabric off to advantage. The new ultra-stretch materials support, flatter and streamline the body and demonstrate their huge role in the world of fashion.

It is not only fashion designers who are making great use of the latest fabrics. Taking advantage of their higher performance and improved aesthetic, with greater accessibility to these materials, a new way of working means the designer is no longer an isolated individual, but one who calls on the input of manufacturers, engineers, craftspeople and artists as needed. The scientific community in Britain is also utilizing fibre and fabric expertise to demonstrate the potential of their technologies, in an ongoing relationship between textiles and science that is altogether appropriate in a country whose Industrial Revolution began in the textile mills. Today's architectural membranes are expected to be as reliable as conventional roofing structures, yet also be capable of innumerable variations. The challenge faces architects, engineers and membrane manufacturers. Single-skin temporary and mobile structures have given way to inflatable and more permanent examples. Artists are starting to use fabrics on a monumental scale

and work with architectural engineers to realize these ambitious new works.

Textile artists are experimenting widely with the latest technologies and using them as tools to make powerful comments on the world in which we live. Whether used towards an appreciation of nature or social comment, the concepts are as varied as the individuals: all the works shown here are engaged with new textile materials or textile techniques in various ways. Some embrace the latest materials, while others look to the processes to best communicate their ideas. Digital technology is especially favoured, either as a construction process with computer-aided weaving and computerized knitting machines or in the creation of a futuristic surface with digital printing. Since imagery can now be easily imported, manipulated and recreated,

there are possibilities for an entirely new approach to materiality. The physicality of textiles is still a crucial element in the creative process and cannot be replaced with screen-based technology, but a real understanding of 'textile' together with comprehensive knowledge of computers is a potent combination. The recent methodologies are suggesting that we rethink our aesthetic criteria. What is beautiful? What is real? This book shows some of the newest ways of thinking, working and communicating.

opposite top
ANISH KAPOOR
Installation in the Turbine Hall,
Tate Modern, London. 2004

opposite below
MAHARISHI
Gorscuba Futura jacket.
Autumn/Winter 2001/2002

Maharishi Gorscuba, Futura jacket, in the reflective 'Fu Splinter' camouflage pattern. From Hardy Blechman, *DPM: Disruptive Pattern Material, an Encyclopaedia of Camouflage*, 2005.

above
SONJA WEBER
Untitled. 2003
185 (height) x 290 (width) cm

Cotton warp and viscose weft. Inspired by nature and here by the constantly changing appearance of the sea, artist Sonja Weber takes photographs and then reworks and elaborates upon her imagery in a textile CAD programme. She then interprets the imagery by weaving the textile on an electronic Jacquard loom. This can achieve a photographic realism due to its ability to control the lifting of each individual thread. Light, dark, shade, depth and movement are all beautifully captured in her poetic work.

PART I

INNOVATIONS

1 The future of fibres and fabrics

Sarah E. Braddock Clarke

2 Electronic textiles

Marie O'Mahony

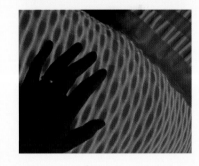

3 Engineered textiles

Marie O'Mahony

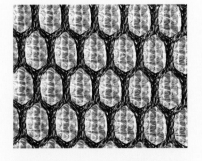

4 Textile finishes

Sarah E. Braddock Clarke

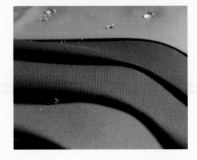

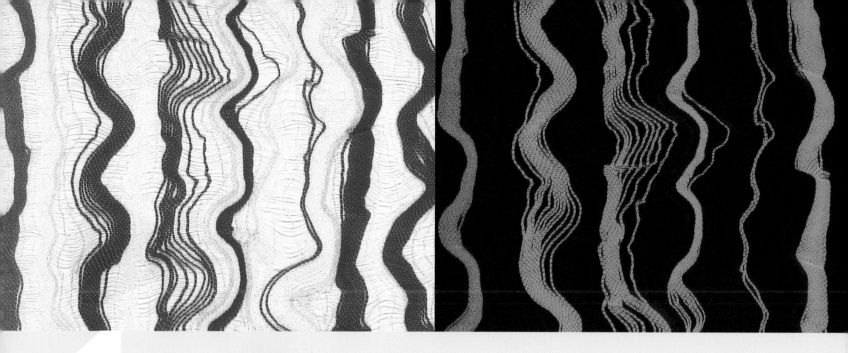

The future of fibres and fabrics

Sarah E. Braddock Clarke

SOPHIE ROET
Wandering Lines – Red. 2001
above left: in daylight
above right: glowing in the dark

Sophie Roet uses phosphorescent yarn (polyester/polyamide) in stripes together with brightly coloured silk in the warp. The weft is densely packed polyamide monofilament which gives an attractive crinkly texture. The look of this warp-designed fabric is very contemporary with its clashing colours. When shown to an intense light source for approximately two minutes, the phosphorescent yarn will absorb the light and glow in subdued lighting and gradually fade. Collection of the Victoria & Albert Museum, London.

right
PRADA WOMAN
Spring/Summer 2003

This top has a wonderful embossed shiny surface. It is teamed with shorts, both are trimmed with a technical material inspired by wetsuits. Accessories are a large plastic necklace and silver pointed flat shoes.

The future of textiles lies in the development of new fibres and fabrics. Recent advances have been truly innovative where aesthetic is as important as performance. Research into synthetics is crucial and there has been a huge change in the way these materials are perceived. Early synthetics often clung unattractively to the wearer due to static electricity, which also made the fabric collect dirt and pollution. The first chemically produced textiles were often uncomfortable as they did not allow the wearer's body to breathe. In comparison, highly sophisticated synthetics have none of these disadvantages and can create efficient barriers to rain, wind and snow while being totally breathable. Today's synthetics can be renamed to distinguish them from former inventions – for example, polyamide is often the preferred name for nylon.

Once developed to imitate natural fibres, synthetics with their unique characteristics are now being considered in their own right. The latest compare well with the best quality naturals, both in look and handle, and also bring with them super-enhanced performance. Synthetic filaments are produced by the extrusion of the chemical through fine holes. They are incredibly versatile and capable of being moulded into many different forms during the liquid stage of their manufacture. This flexibility means that fibres can be made to exact specifications. Some are ultra-lightweight and high-stretch, others are thin and light-reflective, while hollow fibres trap air to retain heat. A wide range of visual and tactile effects can be achieved. However, even when super-fine, transparent and fragile-looking, the new synthetics are still very strong, durable and easy to care for.

Natural fibres are often blended with synthetic to improve on performance qualities such as strength, crease-resistance and easy-care. Various combinations and percentages of blended fibres are tried: at least 50 per cent synthetic must be used if its properties are to be fully utilized, and in practice the percentage is often higher.

This chapter looks at some of the recent developments in the world of textiles and explores many in depth. From the latest ultra-microfibres and regenerated textiles to combinations of textile and non-textile materials, the new techno textiles are all designed to perform well, feel good and look beautiful. They offer excellent potential for sophisticated applications.

TRADITION AND TECHNOLOGY IN JAPAN

The world of textiles has a huge tradition and heritage from which to draw with inspiring examples from diverse cultures. Many textile practitioners think it is important to acknowledge this while also looking to the future. In Japan, where many exciting technological advances are taking place, an aesthetic pared down to its essence and a complete understanding and reverence for materials is intrinsic to Japanese craft. Unlike the West, the applied arts in Japan enjoy a high status equal to that of the fine arts. There, craft techniques, which enjoy an active rural tradition, are of major importance in developing and applying the new textile technologies. The result is that the traditional and the super-advanced co-exist in harmony.

Kyoto, once the imperial capital of Japan for over a thousand years (794–1868), has been famous for its textiles for centuries. Nishijin, an area of Kyoto, is particularly known for its woven fabrics, kimonos and obi. Following this tradition, today's fabrics from the Kyoto region combine handcraft with sophisticated materials and techniques. In this way textile

traditions are perpetuated and often labour-intensive methods can be updated and their potential extended by using technology. Japanese textile designers are often pioneers in the creative and scientific field of textiles; they push the aesthetic and practical boundaries of physical materials with their experimental fabric technology. Respect for tradition and the appreciation of materials is reflected in their textiles by strong avant-garde fashion and expressive textile art.

Reiko Sudo is the main designer and director of Nuno Corporation, a textile company based in Tokyo. The word *nuno* means functional textile, and their aim is to create beautiful fabrics for the contemporary world. Nuno respect the craft traditions of textiles while simultaneously developing the latest technologies. The design team use computers and industrial methods to produce designs that often look hand-woven. Layered-weave structures made on computer-assisted Jacquard looms allow for intricate constructions and reversibles. The fabrics are unique and innovative, with a quality superior to most of those that are mass-produced. Yarns are selected which are often rough, slub or highly twisted for interesting looks and handles. Most Nuno fabrics are woven, a process which lends itself well to the creation of abstract visual patterns and due to the use of character yarns, the tactile interest is often integral to the structure. Diverse materials are employed, such as metals and papers in combination with silks and polyesters. Nuno textiles often combine textile and non-textile

below left
**NUNO CORPORATION
REIKO SUDO (design)
Stainless Steel Sparkler. 1998**

Stainless steel, cotton, polyamide and polyurethane. The stainless steel fibre was developed by a Japanese tyre manufacturer in 1996 to increase the strength and durability of their product. Here it is woven with cotton and polyamide to create a soft and flexible cloth. The small polyurethane content enables a stretch metal textile with sparkling highlights.

below right
**NUNO CORPORATION
KEIJI OTANI (design)
Copper Quadrata. 1998**

Cotton, copper, polyamide and polyurethane are combined to create a wonderful metallic surface. Polyurethane is used to coat the copper in order to prevent the metal turning green and brittle through oxidation.

Previous pages:
page 10
BARBARA LAYNE
Light-emitting diodes (LEDs) embedded in handwoven linen. 2004

The LEDs woven into the textile present changing patterns and are programmable with interactive capabilities that can be controlled through sensors. Barbara Layne draws parallels between circuitry and the warp and weft of weaving, as x and y co-ordinates. She is mainly interested in them being used in creative arts practice and while she recognizes their commercial potential, sportswear and medical use, for example, she envisages them as interactive costumes for dance, theatre and expressive gallery textiles. See also p. 27.

page 11
Chapter 1
(left) **NUNO CORPORATION
REIKO SUDO (design)
Waterglass. 1997** – see p. 25
(right) **JAKOB SCHLAEPFER
Luminoso** – see p. 28

Chapter 2
(left) **VIBEKE RIISBERG
Digital print** – see p. 37
(right) **INTERACTIVE INSTITUTE
Pillows** – see p. 48

Chapter 3
(left) **HYBRIDS AND FUSION
Spacer fabrics** – see p. 71
(right) **HEATHCOAT
Military knit** – see p. 66

Chapter 4
(left) **SCHOELLER TEXTIL AG
3XDRY finish** – see p. 96
(right) **EUGÈNE VAN VELDHOVEN
Laser cutting on acetate. 2000** – see p. 83

materials and techniques – for example, incorporating metal or using techniques appropriated from Japan's car industry. There are some printed Nuno textiles but even these often give attention to texture with their raised surfaces. Some stitched and embellished fabrics are also included in their range. In all their textiles emphasis is given to the exploration and the interaction of the various characteristics of fibre and fabric. In Japan the essence of an artefact lies in its imperfection and individuality and an honest approach to the materials is still highly regarded. This philosophy has become an important part of artistic expression – a design or work of art is enhanced by evidence of the hand that created it. For Nuno this concept is fundamental.

Jun'ichi Arai, co-founder of Nuno with Reiko Sudo, has since left Nuno and is based in Kiryú (just north of Tokyo and known for its rich traditional past for textiles). He concentrates on the creation of one-off textiles and is fascinated with the new developments in textiles. He calls himself a 'textile planner', and has moved into making fabrics that have relief surface and even three-dimensional structure. Primarily interested in weaving, he has used the computer to create complex forms. He has also patented numerous metallic textiles – fusing tradition and technology to create beautifully fluid and shimmering material. Jun'ichi Arai works directly with yarns, manipulating and contrasting their inherent properties. He has no preference for either natural or synthetic fibres, but enjoys the play of their different qualities when they are combined. Travelling the world extensively, he collects and studies textiles from many cultures, including the traditional hand-woven, brightly coloured cloths of India and Indonesia. Adapting new technology, he reinvents traditional crafts, keeping them alive by his fresh vision.

MICROFIBRES

Using the latest in microtechnology scientists are building fabrics where the fibre itself is scrutinized in minute detail. Microfibres were developed by textile professionals who made close studies of microstructures in nature and took advantage of technological breakthroughs which allow the manipulation of molecules. By looking at a micro-world to create advanced materials, the potential is almost limitless, and the resulting microfibres are being developed to create fabrics with distinctive aesthetic, tactile and performance properties. Such materials were originally intended for space and military applications, but now designers are selecting them for their unique appeal.

A microfibre is by definition one in which the yarn is 1/60th the thickness of an average human hair, or less. Ultra-microfibres are now on the market which are infinitely fine – up to 1/200th of the same thickness. Because they are super-fine, specific qualities and functions can be built in. Generally, the thinner the fibre, the greater the possibilities – a soft, sheer appearance, delicate, attractive handle, ultra light in weight, crease-resistant, extremely strong, durable and with excellent draping qualities. Microfibre fabrics are easy to care for, are machine-washable and will not lose their shape. The fibres are so fine that it is possible to construct fabrics dense enough to be windproof and breathable, which means they can prevent the smallest drop of water from entering while allowing perspiration to pass through as water vapour. These fabrics can maintain an even body temperature in both hot and cold conditions, keeping the wearer comfortable.

Synthetic fibres' gain in appeal is partly due to the invention of microfibres. The main generic names of the synthetic fibre group are polyamide, polyester, polypropylene, acetate, acrylic, viscose and elastane, from which are derived many trade names. Most are derived from coal- and oil-based raw materials and offer easy-care and quick-drying fabrics. Polyamide 6.6 and polyester filament yarns fulfil the criteria necessary for the dense structure of a microfibre fabric (most are woven but some are knitted), and textile companies have generally been concentrating on these two synthetics.

Polyamide was the first successful entirely synthetic fibre, and was originally developed by DuPont in the USA in 1938. It is a very strong, durable fibre, resists wear and tear, absorbs dye and takes most finishes easily. This synthetic blends well with and improves the performance of both synthetic and natural fibres.

Polyester was invented in the 1940s by J. R. Whinfield and J. T. Dickson, and was first called Terylene by Imperial Chemical Industries (ICI). It has a smooth look and feel (it is compared to human skin, making it useful for surgery), is strong even when wet, naturally elastic and resilient and, like polyamide, takes dye and finishes well and improves the performance of the fibre it is blended with. The refinement of polyester into a microfibre gives a yarn which is slightly smoother and cheaper to produce than a polyamide one, and it therefore tends to dominate the market.

In order to offer optimum performance and protection, when microfibres were first introduced they were used in both the warp and the weft of a high density weave. A microfibre or even an ultra-microfibre is a very sophisticated textile – its light weight and its performance qualities offer distinct advantages in competitive sports, for example. As the fibre-engineering is integral, repeated washing will not affect it adversely. These pure microfibres are, however, expensive. An alternative is to select a microfibre yarn for either the warp or the weft of a woven textile. The end fabric still looks and feels good and generally performs well, often vastly improving on the yarn it is blended with.

Combinations of microfibres with regenerated yarns, cottons, linens, silks and other synthetics are often successful in creating new looks, handles and added performance. For example, a microfibre combined with cotton (chosen for its appearance and absorbency) gives the resulting textile a natural appeal with built-in technical properties.

Microfibres are also open to a range of finishing treatments. For example, crushed and wrinkled finishes can be used that are thermochromic (changing colour according to temperature), antibacterial, light-sensitive, deodorant or that block ultra-violet rays. Microfibres can be altered at any stage of their manufacture – from the fibre to the finishing of the fabric, and this is what makes them the real future of textiles.

MICROFIBRES ON THE MARKET

Research and development into high-performance textiles for extreme sportswear is where much investment has taken place. Clothing and accessories for the fast-growing area of sport, in all its guises, has meant the invention of a range of materials with incredible properties. As a result, sportswear and other high-performance clothing is where the majority of microfibre applications can be seen.

However, the creative potential in working with fabrics constructed with microfibres is extensive. The results of scientific research into microfibres eventually filters down to textile designers, fashion designers and textile artists. Today, microfibres are not only used for sportswear but also for interior fabrics and fashion and are even being incorporated into expressive work for gallery textiles. Blends are most commonly used where performance is less critical, and in both prêt-à-porter and haute couture fashion, the main criteria are the unique appearance and tactile quality which such fabrics offer.

DuPont are the leading producers of polyamide fibre worldwide, and their research into synthetics has a long history. Their best-known microfibre is Tactel, whose name emphasizes the importance of touch. This is a registered trademark of DuPont for its brand of speciality fibres with different aesthetic and tactile qualities. Tactel is expensive and in order to justify the cost the textile needs to offer distinctive looks, handles and superior performance. To reduce the price it can be blended with other fibres where it imparts a soft, fluid feel. Tactel describes a wide range of Polyamide 6.6 yarns which can be altered during their finishing processes to create many effects. There are a number of different categories of Tactel, all having their own aesthetic, texture and performance. For example, Tactel HT is extremely strong and abrasion-resistant and has been used for parachutes. Tactel texturals is used mainly for active sportswear and has a matt, rugged look. It is 30 per cent lighter than cotton, and protects from the elements without being bulky and heavy. Tactel aquator can be pure or blended with other fibres in the outer layer, an example being with very fine filaments of Tactel on the inside and cotton on the outside. The Tactel surface moves moisture away from the body to the outer cotton layer where it spreads over a large surface area and evaporates, leaving a dry fabric and ensuring the wearer keeps a consistent body temperature. This facility to manage moisture makes it eminently suitable for sportswear

opposite top
**NUNO CORPORATION
REIKO SUDO (design)
Patched Paper. 1997**

To create this lightweight fabric, strips of Mino washi (handmade paper) are woven into a sheer polyester organdy base. This paper is one of the strongest in Japan and traditionally used for shoji (sliding screens). The cloth is finished by a metal foil brocade specialist weaver to impart a soft lustre. Included in the Design Collection of the Museum of Modern Art, New York, 2000, the Metropolitan Museum of Art, 2000, the Museum of Fine Art, Houston, 2000, the Montreal Museum of Art, 2001 and the Baltimore Museum of Art, 2002.

opposite below
**GRETHE WITTROCK
ice@blue (detail). 2003**
400 (height) x 125 (width) cm

To create this textile, polyamide (warp) and paper (weft) were machine woven in Japan. It was then hand silkscreen printed using silver/grey mother-of-pearl paste. The source of inspiration comes from ice crystals. This is a one-off textile design for interiors. It can be used as a room-divider, a curtain in front of a large window or simply for pure decoration. This work was chosen to be exhibited at the Danish Biennale 2004.

left above
**IRENE VAN VLIET
Handwoven textile. 2000**

This textile has a warp of silver-look polyester with a weft of red silk and polyurethane. The combination of both natural and synthetic yarns and dramatic colour contrasts creates a striking fabric.

left
**I.E. UNIFORM
Autumn/Winter 2002/03**

The metallic top is given a finishing treatment to make the fabric emulate liquid mercury. A jersey fabric which uses Tactel by DuPont to make its handle particularly soft and fluid has layers of tiny gunmetal foil spots applied to its surface. Eventually they combine to give a consistent metallized finish. The Tactel allows the fabric to maintain its drape even after several applications of glue and foil which would otherwise have stiffened the fabric. This top has smocked sleeve detail which combines a traditional labour-intensive hand technique with a highly technical textile.

SCHOELLER TEXTIL AG
soft-shell fabrics

Innovative fabrics from Schoeller
using stretch technology
demonstrating their many years
of experience in this area. These
functional stretch woven textiles
have excellent shape-retention,
are light, soft, comfortable, hard-
wearing, extremely breathable and
both wind- and water-repellent.
They feel good next to the skin
and are ideal for sportswear,
and in fashion they can create
contemporary silhouettes.

and underwear. Tactel diabolo has a special
cross-sectional form to the fibre which gives
it lustre and good draping qualities, and is
marketed for fashion knitwear, swimwear and
underwear. Tactel multisoft is super-soft,
lightweight, strong and lustrous, ideal for
hosiery and underwear. Tactel ispira has a
cross-section resembling a spring which
makes it elastic while being strong. Tactel
micro provides an extremely luxurious textile
for hosiery; it can also be used for rainwear,
as it is water-repellent and yet breathable.
In addition to these, 6.6 Tactel was developed
to protect the body in temperatures as low as
-80°C (-112°F). The ability for a microfibre
such as Tactel to be modified to create
a variety of types has huge potential. Still
further categories can be added in response
to new consumer demands and this is where
the future lies.

Meryl Microfibre is made by Nylstar,
an Italian company and one of the largest
producers of Polyamide 6.6. It is marketed
as a high-performance textile, making water-
resistant, windproof and breathable fabrics
that are also ultra-soft and drape well. It
has many applications for the world of sport
where it offers superior properties – ideal
for swimming, sailing and athletics.

The Japanese company Kanebo
manufacture a high-density woven polyamide
and polyester fabric called Belseta. Made
from the microfibre, Belima-X, it is used for
both sportswear and fashion.

Akzo Nobel, a large company with
specialist divisions in the Netherlands,
Germany and France, have been producing
microfibres since 1983 when the preference
was for natural fibres. They make a polyester
microfibre, Diolen Micro, a super-fine
filament yarn which blends particularly well
with natural fibres such as cotton, linen and
wool. It can be given many finishes for a
variety of looks and textures, and is also
available as a staple fibre which is best used
in blends.

Hoechst High Chem, a German company,
launched Trevira Finesse in 1987, a polyester
microfibre intended for high-performance
clothing. A development from Trevira Finesse
is Trevira Micronesse, a polyester microfibre
three times finer than wool and half the
thickness of silk. It can be modified, for
example, to be transparent, opaque, smooth
or textured. This fibre also blends well with

others, such as cotton and viscose, making
it very versatile.

Terital Zero.4 is a polyester filament
microfibre developed by the Italian textile
company Montefibre/Enimont. They have
been producing fabric which has a silk-like
quality for a number of years and have used
this knowledge to create an extremely fine
microfibre. Originally developed for
sportswear, now applications are being seen
for fashion and lingerie. Montefibre/Enimont
have also developed an acrylic microfibre
called Myoliss to blend with wool and Leacril
Micro to blend with cotton. Both are highly
sophisticated yarns that make extremely soft
performance textiles.

Since 1964 the Japanese textile company
Kuraray have been developing textiles with
ultra-fine synthetic fibres as alternatives to
leather. The complex structure of leather was
studied carefully, and Kuraray's knowledge of
synthetic and polymer chemistry fully utilized.
Their products Clarino and Sofrina look good
and are strong, light, soft and water-resistant.
Since they are produced synthetically, a wide
range of effects can be achieved in surface
interest and thickness. Their fabrics are used
for sportswear, luggage and fashion.

Rojel is an ultra-microfibre fabric made by
Kolon Fibres. It also has the look and texture
of leather and is a warp-knitted textile. This
luxury material is high-performance and
easy-care due to its specific engineering.
There is much research and development
being undertaken worldwide into creating
materials which resemble leathers and
suedes but have improved performance
properties. They can also be marketed as
a more ethically sound product.

HEALTH-GIVING FABRICS

Microtechnology and health is a strong area
of research and development. So-called
'wellness' fibres and fabrics often begin
with fibre engineering. New textiles that can
look attractive, feel good and perform well
can now even benefit the wearer's health.
Microfibres are being engineered with
substances suspended in minute bubbles
that can be gradually released. These
microcapsules are hollow and can contain
a range of products, including medication,
natural remedies, vitamins, UV-blockers, anti-
bacterial/anti-microbial agents, mosquito and

insect repellents, moisturizers, essential oils and perfumes. These ingredients are invisible to the eye and yet can have a dramatic effect. Many of these microfibres were originally developed for use in space but are now being used in fashion and for the lingerie and hosiery markets. This is a fast-growing area, particularly in Japan where large textile companies are giving prominence to such research. The Japanese are even developing youth-giving textiles which encapsulate anti-ageing creams into fabrics worn next to the skin. In Europe, the company Rhovyl produce Rhovyl As fibres which contain an anti-bacterial agent in the solvent before being mixed with polymers. The agent fights against the micro-organisms to prevent the growth of bacteria. As it is engineered into the fibre it can withstand washing.

This microencapsulation technique works when the seals around the tiny capsules are broken by the fabric being creased or rubbed. The contents are absorbed slowly through the skin. Even the warmth of the body makes, for example, a fragrance incorporated into the material become stronger. The main disadvantage is that over time the substance will be used up: in some fabrics this added ingredient may last for around thirty washes.

In-built UV-ray protectors can make a fabric change colour when the wearer has had too much sun. Anti-bacterial substances can deodorize textiles so the wearer will stay comfortable and smell good all day, even when engaged in extreme sport. For example, the Japanese company Toray have slightly altered the chemical configuration of polyamide to create an anti-bacterial and anti-odour fabric called Dericana. Essential oils such as lavender can be incorporated and used for making nightwear or pillows for insomniacs. A daily dose of Vitamin C can be absorbed from hosiery or nutritional seaweed extracts incorporated into underwear.

Outlast, an American company, invented a textile called simply Outlast which uses microencapsulation with a phase-change material. There are many such materials which have the ability to change state depending on the surrounding temperature – solid when cool and liquid when warmed. A phase-change material will absorb excess heat, store it and then gradually release it later, ideal for control of body temperature when the wearer is engaged in sport.

In the early 1990s the Japanese company Kanebo introduced Esprit de Fleur, which uses a microencapsulation technique to release perfume from its fibres. Scented fabrics are being made into lingerie and hosiery and also used for fashion.

Welbeck Fabrics UK have worked in this area to create fragrance in fabrics which have been used by the Italian luxury lingerie/clothing company La Perla. Examples of the microencapsulated scents include lavender, lemon and vanilla. Welbeck Fabrics are also investigating ways of incorporating moisturizers such as aloe vera into textiles.

Seaweed's beneficial minerals, mainly calcium and magnesium, can be harnessed to create textiles which are useful to the wearer with a skin condition. Pulverized seaweed is being embedded into fibres such as cotton (to be effective the seaweed content needs to be at least 25 per cent). The minerals are made

SCHOELLER TEXTIL AG
schoeller-PCM

The phase change materials are contained within microcapsules and set at a specific temperature range. When either the body temperature of the wearer or the outside temperature rises these materials can store the excess heat, when the temperature falls again they release the previously stored heat. Shown below left is a jacket made with schoeller-PCM – it retains the heat (below left). The jacket without schoeller-PCM (below right) emits the heat which is demonstrated by the red areas. In this way increased comfort and optimum performance is achieved – ideal for the very active person or athlete.

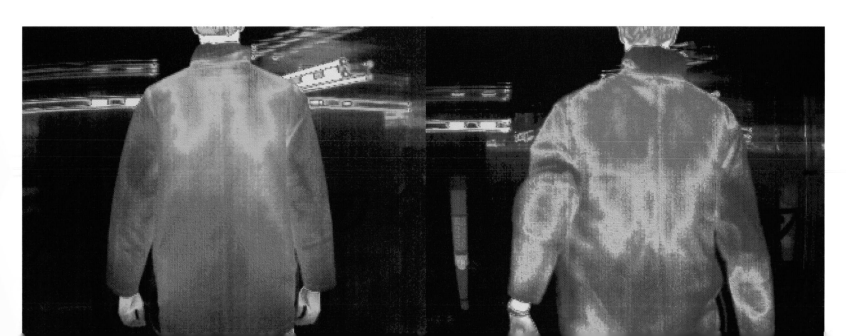

left
**NUNO CORPORATION
REIKO SUDO (design)**
Bincho Charcoal. 2001

Wool, silk, charcoal, polyamide and polyurethane. Charcoal is used for its health-giving properties as it absorbs chemical impurities in the air. Since the mid 1980s Japanese textile companies have invested much research time and money into development of new fibres from unusual source materials. An unconventional mixture of materials – the result is a cloth with a unique handle and beneficial properties.

below left
**NUNO CORPORATION
REIKO SUDO (design)**
Brush Bamboo. 2001

Bamboo has anti-bacterial and anti-odour properties. Residues from the manufacturing process of extracting a chemical from brush bamboo, to be used as a digestive medicine, are made into a natural fibre and used by Nuno to produce this new fabric. The fresh, cooling bamboo fibres are combined with rayon, silk, polyamide and polyurethane to create a textural effect which features subtle gathering in a repeat design.

opposite top
SOPHIE ROET
Paper Textile. 2004

Polyamide monofilament, paper and steel. This textile is intended for interior application and was commissioned for a château in France. A transparent polyamide warp has a paper/steel yarn as weft which creates a wonderful crinkly texture and sense of movement within the textile. The shiny surface of the monofilament allows the paper/steel yarn to be manipulated once woven to create an irregular movement of stripes. Collection of the Victoria & Albert Museum, London.

opposite bottom
IRENE VAN VLIET
Handwoven textile. 2000

This textile has a warp of polyester with a weft of viscose and iridescent yarn. A soft ethereal shimmer is created by the colour and light-reflecting qualities of the chosen yarns. The iridescent polyamide lurex is from the manufacturer Sildorex in France.

active by heat from the wearer's body and are gradually absorbed into their skin – not unlike the microencapsulation technique.

Peat can be used to make a textile, and Kultaturve, a company based in Finland, are combining this with another yarn, such as wool, to create a textile which has beneficial inherent properties. A resulting peat textile is anti-bacterial, absorbs radiation and prevents the build up of electrostatic charge.

Fabrics can be made of charcoal which will filter odour and pollution. Zorflex is the brand name made by the German company Charcoal Cloth International (CCI), a subsidiary of the US Calgon Carbon Corporation. This textile has mainly industrial and military applications but the scope could be even wider. Nuno, for example, have created a textile which contains charcoal blended with natural and synthetic yarns.

The Japanese company Omikenshi Co. Ltd have even developed a type of viscose made from crab shells. The yarn is called Crabyon, and is combined with cotton. It is promoted as being able to eliminate 90 per cent of known bacteria.

NATURAL CHEMICAL TEXTILES

Natural chemical or regenerated textiles begin with natural raw materials and chemically engineer them to create a whole new range of fabrics. Regenerated fabrics offer an alternative to synthetics, which, often being oil-based, use up finite resources and can take many years, even centuries, to biodegrade, if they do at all. Many companies have realized the advantages of these textiles and there has been a surge of interest in recent years.

Viscose rayon was the first regenerated fabric derived from wood pulp. In France as early as 1889 it was shown how viscose could be created from cellulose, and in 1892 three English chemists patented this textile. The rights to make viscose rayon were bought by Samuel Courtauld in 1904 and Courtaulds went on to produce this successful natural chemical fibre. The term 'viscose' comes from the word viscosity, used to describe the thickness of a liquid, and refers to its manufacturing process. Courtaulds, aware of ecological issues, chose a fast-growing tree species and the forestry is carefully monitored so that felled trees are replaced.

To create viscose rayon, wood pulp is dissolved in a chemical solvent which is then spun into cellulose. This is then forced through small holes to make fibres and through slits to make cellophane. Originally intended as a cheap substitute for silk and with similar qualities in look, handle and drape, viscose rayon was first known as artificial silk. It is absorbent and hard-wearing and can be blended successfully with both natural and synthetic fibres, giving softness and fluidity. Viscose is a very versatile fibre, accepting dyes and a wide range of finishes readily, including textured effects. It has many applications for industrial, interior and fashion textiles.

A development from this original regenerated fibre is a group of organically solvent spun cellulose fibres whose generic name is lyocell. A lyocell fibre, like a natural chemical one, is based on a vegetable source and the resulting fabric is totally recyclable and biodegradable.

Tencel is one such lyocell fibre and, like viscose, is made from wood pulp. Its main technical properties include strength when wet, durability and easy-care. Being a cellulose fibre, it breathes well and is absorbent (therefore taking dye well), and yet has a more silky appearance and a better drape than cotton. This fibre uses a simple, environmentally sound manufacturing process which produces no hazardous waste. In the creation of this fibre the molecules arrange themselves in microscopic fibrils and this is the key to its success. Early in Tencel's development the research team realized that this type of textile could be engineered to specification: for example, a round cross-section gives a lustrous appearance. Tencel can also withstand many chemical finishing treatments to give a wide range of aesthetic properties and weights of fabric, from super-lightweight to a medium weight. As it is a strong fibre, very fine and lightweight yarns can be produced, making ideal warp yarns for weaving. Natural Stretch is a fabric made from Tencel which will extend by up to 25 per cent, made possible by the fabric construction, so there is no need to incorporate a stretch yarn such as Lycra.

Unblended, Tencel comes into its own. In Japan interest has been in the development of Tencel for fashion, concentrating on pure Tencel, and also on the finishing treatments that can be applied to it. However, it can also be mixed successfully with both natural and synthetic fibres, which is where the interests of Europe tend to be.

Another company undertaking research into lyocell fibres is the Austrian textile company Lenzing. Since the mid-1980s they have developed advanced cellulose fibres. Like Tencel, Lenzing Lyocell is derived from a replenishable raw material, wood pulp; but the manufacturing differs – although it too is ecologically sound and the result fully biodegradable. Lenzing Lyocell has very desirable properties: it has high strength when wet and is hard-wearing, soft, breathable and easy to care for. In addition, different visual and tactile effects can be obtained by varying the finishing process, making it a versatile fibre for fashion fabrics.

Enka Viscose is a continuous filament yarn manufactured by the German division of the company Akzo Nobel. Again, its raw material is wood which is chemically treated; the raw materials are renewable and any manufacturing waste is recycled. The resulting fibre is available as staple yarn as well as continuous filament, opening up the range of textures which can be created – matt, hairy effects with staples and smooth, shiny ones with filaments. Fabrics made from Enka Viscose are fine, lustrous, strong and elastic. They drape beautifully, and take finishes such as dyeing and printing well. Applications include fashion textiles and good-quality linings.

SUPERNATURALS

Research has not been solely in the area of synthetics or natural chemicals, but also in further investigation of natural fibres. The public tend to like the look and feel of natural materials but are increasingly aware of the way a fibre such as wool or cotton can be combined with a synthetic or given an advanced finishing treatment to impart increased performance. Nature and science are being fused in a very positive way.

Wool is an important traditional fibre and research is being undertaken into new blends and finishes to alter its look, feel and capabilities. For example, a wool core covered with cotton has the crisp, tactile appeal of a cotton while the wool content gives warmth.

Nippon Keori Kaisha Ltd (NIKKE) is Japan's largest wool company. Together with the Commonwealth Scientific and Industrial Research Organization (CSIRO) and the Woolmark Company, NIKKE have developed a fibre called Odin Optim, a very fine soft wool which drapes superbly. To achieve this superior wool they altered the fibres' naturally circular cross-section to a crystal shape while keeping the scaly outer structure.

Research by the Italian textile-spinning company Zegna Baruffa-Lane Borgosesia Spa has led to new supernaturals. Their B Active line takes quality raw materials (such as wool) and treats them to high-tech processes to create fibres which look natural but whose performance is improved. Enhancement could make a fabric which is water-repellent, stain-resistant and totally easy-care. Trade names for yarns from the B Active range include Rain, Storm and Twister. The B-Exclusive line takes luxurious sources like merino wool or cashmere to make incredibly soft, light, elegant high-performance textiles.

Besides wool there are a number of raw natural materials being used to create textiles which offer specific benefits. Fabric made from bamboo, for example, is very popular in Japan; its fibre is lustrous, very soft and blends well with other fibres such as cotton. A fibre using nettles as its base is very soft and blends well, especially with other naturals. Textiles derived from banana stalks are environmentally friendly as the stalks are usually just thrown away. The fibre obtained from them is mixed with cotton in the yarn to create a very light and absorbent textile.

Soya beans from China have been processed in Italy by the textile spinners Marioboselli and by Zegna Baruffa. The result is similar to silk, being soft and draping beautifully. Soya bean oil is being used to create plastics which look very similar to the usual petroleum-based product but are much more environmentally friendly.

NEW FLEXIBLES

The latest technologies have yielded pliable materials which are adaptable. This area is very exciting and it appears that the developers of innovative flexibles have no preconceptions concerning the physical properties of materials. It is useful to think laterally and combine the unusual. The result

top left
NUNO CORPORATION
REIKO SUDO (design)
Rusted Silver. 1991

Cotton, rayon, lamé and polyester
are combined to create this stunning
metallic fabric with its sparkling
surface effects. Aluminium lamé
slit yarns are spun into polyester
monofilament yarns which makes
both the metal and the synthetic
more stable in weaving. This
technique makes reference to
traditional Japanese gold and silver
brocade threads. The metal content
gives a crunchy texture and a
malleable surface.

top right
IRENE VAN VLIET
Handwoven textile. 2000

This textile has a warp of Polyamide
6.6 with a copper weft. The
combination of synthetic and metal
creates a futuristic looking textile
with an unusual handle. The metal
content makes it malleable and
a variety of surfaces and structures
can be created.

middle left
ANN RICHARDS
Steel/Linen Pleat. 2004

Silk/steel (65 per cent silk, 35 per
cent stainless steel) from Loro Piana
and spun silk are used in the warp.
The weft yarns are crêpe silk and
linen. The steel yarn is combined with
spun silk to create a strong contrast
and impart texture to the handwoven
fabric. The rippling effect created is
due to the difference in elasticity
between the silk and the metallics.
Crêpe silk used as the weft is a very
high-twist yarn and, combined with
the weave structure, is responsible
for the pleats that run along the
length of the warp. The metal content
allows possibilities of shaping the
fabric to allow varieties of form
which can relate to the body.
Previously a biologist, Ann Richards
draws inspiration from nature and
of particular interest is the way
living things work as well as their
inherent beauty.

middle right
MEADOWBROOK INVENTIONS, INC.
Angelina® Silver Sparkle Hologram
Fibres

With this holographic effect, as the
viewing angle changes, different
spectrums of colour are made visible
which themselves vary according to
the lighting conditions and viewing
directions. The result is a futuristic-
looking effect which feels good to
touch.

is that many materials are now being used to create new types of fabric, including metals and papers. Research into textile and non-textile combinations is ensuring fresh possibilities with numerous applications.

METALLICS

Usually thought of as being tough and resilient, metals can be made to appear fluid, as when a very fine spattering of stainless steel, for example, is sprayed on to a base cloth. Thin sheet metal, slit into strips or drawn into fine wire, can be used to create a yarn used for weaving or for surface embellishment. More commonly the metal is wound tightly around a core such as cotton, to make it strong and flexible. For a woven metal fabric it is generally best to have the metallic in the weft (where there is less strain) but a cloth can also be made with metal exclusively in the warp and the weft. Pure metal fabrics are very malleable, allowing many different relief effects and three-dimensional forms. Metals can work successfully in combination with softer, more traditional textiles such as cotton, silk or wool. Metal textiles can even be elastic by utilizing a knitted construction or combining with an elastane yarn. The results of incorporating metals with textiles are distinctive visual, tactile and performance properties. One advantage in adding even a small percentage of metal into a fabric is it will give an anti-static property, which is particularly useful for synthetics.

Copper is a good choice for a pure metallic as it is strong and ductile. Other metals that have been woven to create metal textiles include stainless steel, brass and even platinum (but it is expensive). Historically, silver has been used for its medical and well-being properties; it is extremely effective at treating wounds because it prevents the growth of bacteria. About 15 per cent pure silver is needed to impart benefits which should not diminish over time. Such benefits include anti-static, anti-microbial, anti-odour, thermo-regulating and breathable qualities. Silver fabrics are being used in spun or filament yarns and in woven, nonwoven and knitted constructions. A fibre called X-Static is manufactured by Noble Fibre Technologies which uses silver and permanently bonds it to the surface of a fibre, such as wool (which retains its characteristics). X-Static has

numerous applications in the medical world where control of infection is paramount.

Angelina is a registered trademark of Meadowbrook Inventions Inc., USA. It is polyester-based and available in different deniers, staple lengths and colours. Meadowbrook's Angelina fibres have revolutionized the textile and nonwoven industries. The visual aspects of Angelina are very appealing: it is iridescent and comes in a fantastic range of colours, metallized or non-metallized, and even holographic (depending on the lighting and the viewer's position, entire spectrums of colour can be seen). Angelina Fibre's technical benefits include being breathable, super-soft and possessing the ability to be heat-bonded to other fibres. Angelina Copper Fibres use pure copper with its many health-giving properties, anti-microbial, anti-inflammatory and thermal-regulating. When blended they can add a rich colour to a range of other fibres and are suitable for fashion applications. Angelina Aluminum Fibres are both decorative and high-performance. The fibres are given a special epoxy coating (plain or pigmented) – coloured Angelina Aluminum Fibres can be made into eye-catching futuristic fabrics which may be crushed and pleated to give even greater variety. They also perform well and are breathable, anti-static and conductive; they regulate temperature by reflecting body heat, and offer protection from the environment by providing an electromagnetic shield. Angelina can be mixed with other fibres to create textiles with a high-tech appearance and function.

Reiko Sudo frequently combines metals with textiles to make innovative fabrics, borrowing from other disciplines and adapting the technology for her own purposes. She has used aluminium slit yarns, brass wire, copper telephone wire and stainless steel fibres developed by a tyre manufacturer. Even discarded wire is recycled and transformed into a beautiful material and stainless steel has been combined with polyurethane to create a cloth which stretches for dramatic effect.

NONWOVENS

This is a fast-growing area with applications ranging from industrial textiles to fabrics for avant-garde fashion. Nonwovens can be made

MARIA BLAISSE
Tube hat and bag. 2004

The designs for this hat (top) and bag (above) originated in rubber (from the Gomma series) and the abstract forms are translated into woollen felt. From the rubber shape of the tube hat Maria Blaisse made a wooden mould from which felt hats were made. The rubber prototype of the tube bag is transformed into spherical pieces of thick felt which allow many configurations.

from many fibres, natural, regenerated and synthetic, and the latter are often thermoplastic which enables them to be manipulated. The structure of a nonwoven has a cross-hatching of fibres going in all directions with the fibres being bonded together, often by heat and pressure or needlepunching. Nonwovens do not fray, so they can be perforated or subjected to complex cutting, including by lasers for extremely fine, lace-like textiles. Previously, nonwovens were used as invisible interlinings (adhesive and non-adhesive) to define areas of clothing such as collars and cuffs. Today, they are being used in their own right to offer a distinctive look. Because they are relatively inexpensive to produce, money can be spent on advanced finishing treatments to create a wide range of different effects. Like microfibres, nonwovens can be highly flexible and their production controlled from beginning to end to create fabrics for very specific applications.

Tyvek by DuPont is an example of a synthetic nonwoven. Made from polyethylene, it has high-tech properties such as being very lightweight, durable (rip-proof and resistant to many chemicals) and is machine-washable at 30°C (90°F).

Paper is a cellulosic nonwoven and therefore has similar characteristics to textiles such as cotton and viscose. Textiles made from it can be crisp, translucent, lightweight and often make a wonderful rustling sound when worn. As paper does not fray edges will not need finishing and it is recyclable for an environmentally sound material. It is extremely versatile: when knitted, paper can be pliable, and when densely woven it can hold its own shape. It is often backed with polyamide to provide strength. Paper was used in the 1960s as a disposable material for clothing but the new nonwovens and technological papers are being used by today's textile and fashion designers for interesting garments with unique looks and textures that can be worn many times. Research worldwide continues to create inexpensive, durable materials from nonwovens to give exciting new possibilities.

SYNTHETIC FOAMS, RUBBERS AND GELS

Most high-tech foams are made from synthetic polymers which means they are inherently adaptable. They are thermoplastic and can range from ultra-soft to extra tough while providing warmth and remaining light in weight. Foams can work well with other fabrics and give the resulting material strength and resiliency. These materials feel good next to the body and have an appealing tactile quality. Synthetic foams distribute weight evenly and absorb shock, stress and energy while rapidly returning to their original form when crushed. In addition, advanced synthetic foams can be CFC-free and fully recyclable. Such foams present an expansive field for exploration across the world of art and design.

Tempur is a high-tech foam originally developed by NASA and intended for astronaut seating where it would absorb the high G-forces experienced during take-off. This synthetic foam responds to body heat and pressure, spreading weight uniformly to give maximum comfort. It is manufactured by Benelux BV, a company based in the Netherlands.

The Dutch designer Maria Blaisse finds synthetic foams and rubbers ideal materials for her body-related works as they are lightweight, inherently flexible and able to be moulded. She has been researching industrial materials in depth for many years and extensively explores the three-dimensional possibilities of cutting in relation to the human form. Concave and convex volumes create infinite permutations. Often inspired by nature and its patterns of organic growth, she is interested in creating the essence of form and how many forms can originate from one. In doing this, she exploits the qualities of her chosen materials and develops them into

left
RYOKO YAMANAKA
Splashed Line. 2003
80 (height) x 80 (width) x
10 (depth) cm

Bonded polyurethane stitched with
electroluminescent fibres. This has
dual function as an art piece and
for design use. The light-emitting
fibres contrast with the black
bonded substrate – like a splashed
pattern, they make tracks.

below
RYOKO YAMANAKA
Strata 2. 2001
80 (height) x 80 (width) x
20 (depth) cm

This art work was commissioned
for the Miyuki Hospital in Yamagata
prefecture. It is woven by hand
using polyethylene foam tape and
set in an acrylic resin frame box
containing fluorescent lamps.
Different primary colours are mixed
and back-lit to create wonderful
variations in deep colour, texture
and light.

opposite right
LUISA CEVESE
**Riedizioni collection. Square
cushion**
30 (height) x 30 (width) cm

Textile designer Luisa Cevese uses
textile waste for her Riedizioni
(recycling) collection. Here, linen
selvedges (the edges of a woven
cloth which are usually cut off after
weaving and thrown away) and
Technogel, a revolutionary
polyurethane gel manufactured by
Technogel Italia are combined to
create this cushion. Technogel
properties include electrical
insulation, transparency, comfort
and a wonderful soft, tactile feel.

LIZA BRUCE
Swimwear

Liza Bruce's swimwear collections always use good quality textiles. Polyamide and a high percentage of Lycra is used for a stretch material which supports and flatters the female form. Cut to follow the curves, the shaping of the fabric and its inherent characteristics work together to create strong, sculptural shapes that are simultaneously powerful and sensual.

right
I.E.UNIFORM
Autumn/Winter 2002/03

DuPont were the main sponsor for this collection by i.e. uniform. Lesley Sealey is the textile designer and Roger Lee the fashion designer behind this London-based label. The pleated high-collared jacket is made of a stretch leather by DuPont. This new development involves leather being backed with a Lycra jersey.

minimal but expressive pieces which comment on nature's rich variation. Maria Blaisse works eclectically across many disciplines including fashion, fashion accessories and costumes for live performances. Her works demonstrate the sequence of emerging new forms and the fascinating possibilities and potential for a wide variety of applications.

Stretch is a very important property in today's fashion fabrics, providing support, comfort and a flattering fit. Wool has a natural crimp which gives elasticity but synthetics can have this built in and varied according to need. Some stretch synthetics can extend by up to 500 per cent and also recover very quickly. The combination of a lightweight microfibre with an elastane is increasingly popular.

Natural rubber has inherent elasticity but synthetic rubber is an attractive alternative and widely used. Its tactile appeal makes it ideal for wearing close to the body; an important ecological consideration is that both natural and synthetic rubber are recyclable. Synthetic rubber can be mixed with a variety of other materials to vary aesthetic, texture and performance. Only a small amount is needed to improve comfort and flexibility while a high percentage will give a more significant result. Neoprene, for instance, can be combined with knitted and elastane textiles to provide interesting fabrics for sportswear and fashion. Louis Vuitton and Chanel have included neoprene in past collections, creating flattering garments with an edge to them.

Lycra is the registered trademark of DuPont for their premium stretch synthetic fibre and fabric. It is almost a byword for elastic. Lycra has excellent stretch recovery, is light in weight, strong, porous while drying quickly, and is used to impart a crease-resistant and stretch finish to garments. It is extremely versatile and blends well with a whole range of fibres from naturals to synthetics. DuPont also manufacture a low-power stretch fibre called Lycra T4090 which has a percentage of Lycra to achieve a comfort stretch to support and flatter the body but is not designed to be super-elastic. Using Lycra, tailored looks with flattering, comfortable and lean silhouettes are made possible without the need for complex cutting. And one-size clothing is feasible with this revolutionary fibre. Today,

Lycra is used in all types of garments from under to outerwear and from day to evening wear. DuPont have sponsored many fashion designers to use this revolutionary textile to project sporty images, make glamorous and supportive evening knitwear and create sexy, functional swimwear.

DuPont joined forces with The Woolmark Company to make Wool Stretch, a combination of natural and synthetic yarns to give a yarn with added stretch and bounce. It is available in both knitted and woven constructions and possesses stretch capabilities lengthways and widthways.

With the aim of improving on the unique properties of leather, DuPont have combined leather or suede with their revolutionary stretch fibre. By bringing together technology with nature they have created an elastic material with wide-ranging applications from outerwear to fashion accessories. Leather or suede is fused with Lycra using laminating technology and its subsequent stretch and recovery properties are excellent (pure leather or suede does stretch but will not recover). This takes Lycra into a whole new dimension as skins are very different to a constructed textile.

The company Jitrois have created a stretch leather for garments and accessories including footwear. The natural product is enhanced and a thin, lightweight, elastic leather is made which works with the wearer's body and feels fantastic. These super-fine, supple leathers can be manipulated in much the same way as a fabric, for example gathering or ruching them to create a variety of relief surfaces.

Many of the new gel materials were originally developed for medical applications. Technogel by Technogel Italia feels wonderful to touch as it yields under pressure and distributes stress evenly. It is thick, soft and pliable and will conform to fit many shapes such as the human form. This gel will not harden over time as it does not contain any plasticizers. Technogel can be injected directly into a mould using an advanced vacuum system which allows it to be covered with a range of materials. Such materials have far-reaching possibilities and will be sought out by designers – ever on the search for something new and attracted by their high performance, appearance and attractive handle.

CARBON, GLASS, FIBRE OPTIC AND CERAMIC

These are materials not usually associated with textiles but are surprisingly versatile. Carbon fibre was first on the market in 1960 and is made by modifying rayon or acrylic or as a by-product of petrol. First used in the car industry and for sportswear, it is now being used for fashion and interiors. Carbon fibre is extremely strong, durable (resisting abrasion and fire), lightweight, has anti-static and anti-stress properties and blends well with other fibres. The registered trademark textile Kevlar by DuPont is an example of a carbon fibre and has been mixed with many textiles including denim for, it is claimed, an indestructible cloth – Kevlar Denim is made by UCO, a large denim producer.

Glass fibre fabrics can be used for interior textiles as they do not deteriorate with exposure to sunlight; they reflect and filter light. It is also believed that they can filter X- and Gamma-rays. Glass fibre is fire-retardant and resists mould and moths. All these properties make it ideal for long-lasting curtains in public buildings. In addition, recycled glass can be used for an ecologically friendly material. One serious disadvantage, however, is that glass fibre fabrics can irritate the skin making them unsuitable for fashion fabrics.

Reflective textiles occupy a growing area and have many applications, including as trim on sportswear garments and on accessories (headgear and footwear) to ensure good visibility at all times. The fashion world has also taken up the look and the latest reflective technical textiles have been seen for both prêt-à-porter and haute couture, proving that functional can also be decorative. Most reflectives work on the same principle as cats' eyes in the middle of the road: they bounce light back to its source. Reflective panels can be printed on a substrate or a textile can be constructed with a reflective yarn. The Swiss company Schoeller Textil AG is famous for its technological textiles whose applications include sportswear and fashion. Their 'reflex' materials use tiny glass beads which reflect the light and a special weave surrounds and protects them.

top right
NUNO CORPORATION
REIKO SUDO (design)
Waterglass. 1997

Polyester slit yarns are woven with a small proportion of carbon which prevents static electricity from building up which can cause snags in the cloth. A beautiful transparent, glistening fabric is achieved and the pleating in fine ripples as a finishing effect gives the look of light shining across water. Reiko Sudo's innovative fabrics constantly astound in their creativity, beauty and their ability to expand our notion of what a textile is and can be.

middle right
SCHOELLER TEXTIL AG
schoeller-reflex

This protective textile by Schoeller looks good as well as imparting safety to its wearer. It uses Cordura (DuPont) and Scotchlite (3M). In the case of some of the individual innovations the reflex yarn woven into the fabric is no longer visible in daylight. It is elastic in its length to give an additional function. This fabric is ideal for sportswear applications as it offers good visibility.

bottom right
ANN RICHARDS
Reflex. 2004

A polyester reflective yarn gives a gentle shimmer to the handwoven textile which varies according to the lighting conditions. The warp yarns used are silk/steel (65 per cent silk, 35 per cent stainless steel) from Loro Piana and spun silk. The weft yarns are crêpe silk and Reflecta, a polyester reflective yarn manufactured in Germany by Fuesers Garne GmbH. The use of a high-twist silk crêpe silk yarn creates a lively texture and, combined with the weave structure produces the lengthwise pleating, which the cloth will always retain.

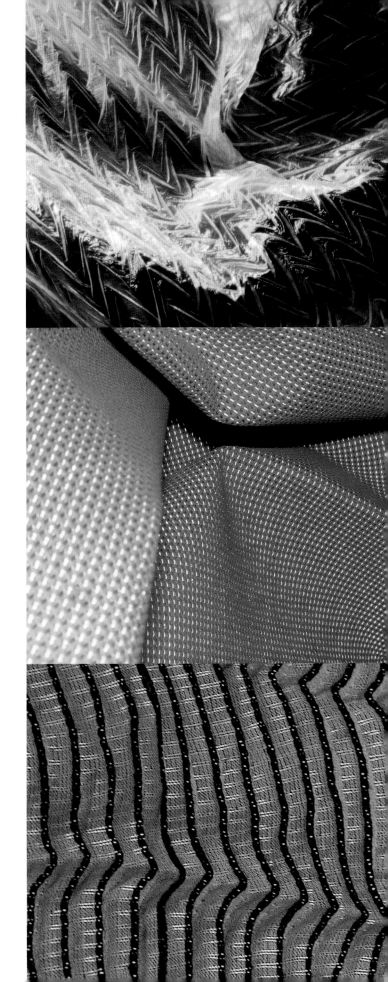

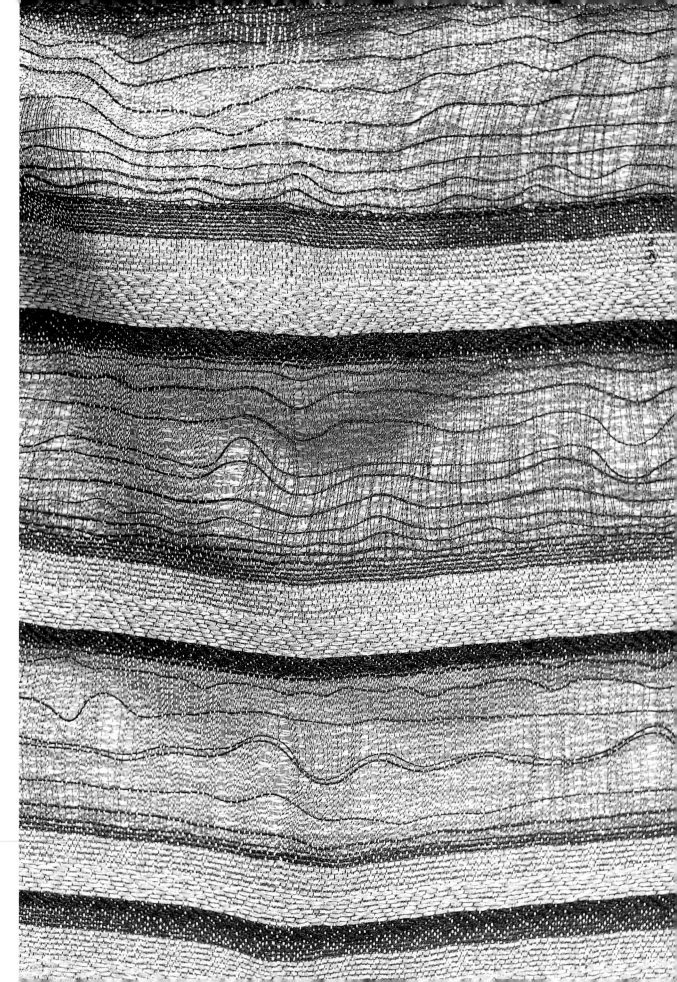

right
IRENE VAN VLIET
Handwoven textile. 2000

This textile has a warp of polyester with a weft of wool, polyamide and the reflective yarn Chromoflex from Ledal Torino in Italy. Beautiful variations are created in this textile which respond to various lighting conditions.

opposite
BARBARA LAYNE
Light Emitting Diodes (LEDs) with wire wrapping technique. 2004

Barbara Layne embeds microcontrollers and LEDs into the structure of handwoven fabric to create dynamic textiles (see pp. 10 and 13). Shown here are the flexible wires which are woven into the cloth alongside the traditional yarns. Each LED is individually embedded into the circuitry grid through soldering or a wire wrapping technique.

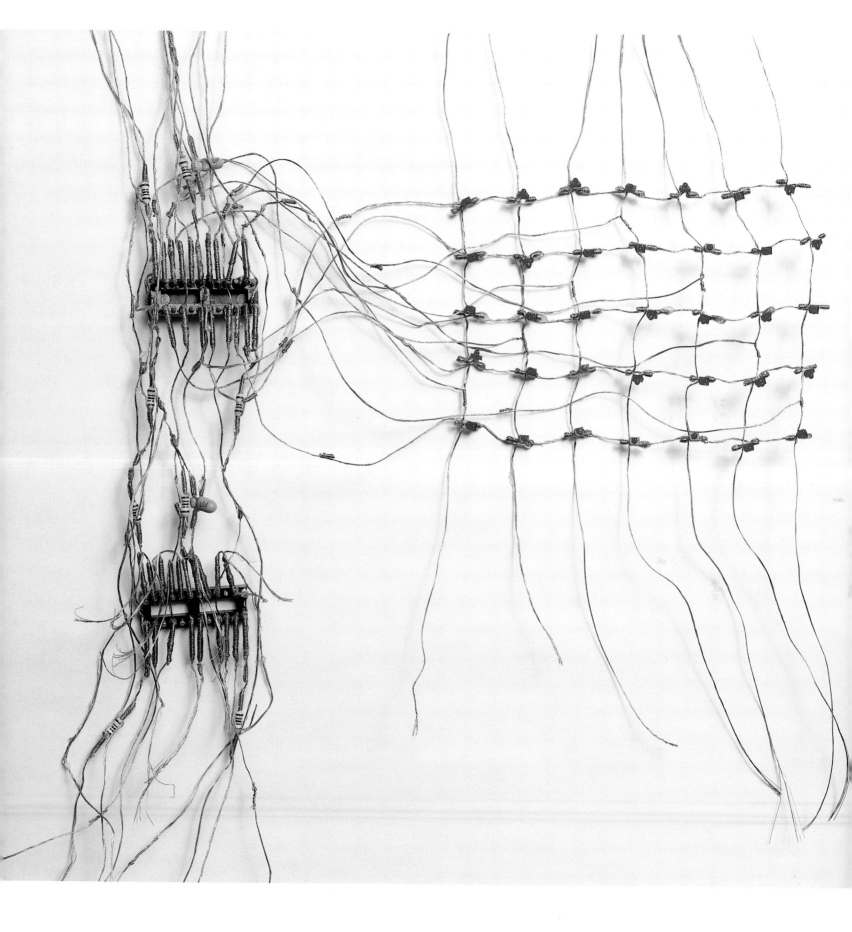

opposite left and right
JAKOB SCHLAEPFER
Luminoso

Fibre optic textile from their
Décor collection design for the
Swiss interior textile company
Création Baumann. The beautiful,
shimmering textile shown here
intended for curtain fabric includes
a fibre optic material which is
woven into a base fabric.

right
SARAH TAYLOR
Interactive Fibre Optic Panel. 2000
100 (height) x 120 (width) x 80
(depth) cm

Interactive fibre optic panel
incorporating sound. This piece
uses polymer optical fibre, sensors,
a Midicreator© (York Electronics
Centre), speakers, an amplifier and
sounds (Immersive Media Spaces
Ltd). The work exploits the tactile
qualities of fibre optics with colour
and the use of a midicreator
introduces elements of sound. It is
lit by three tungsten halide light
projectors. This work was exhibited
at the *Coming to Our Senses* – a
national touring multisensory crafts
exhibition organized by Craftspace
Touring, Birmingham (2000–2002).

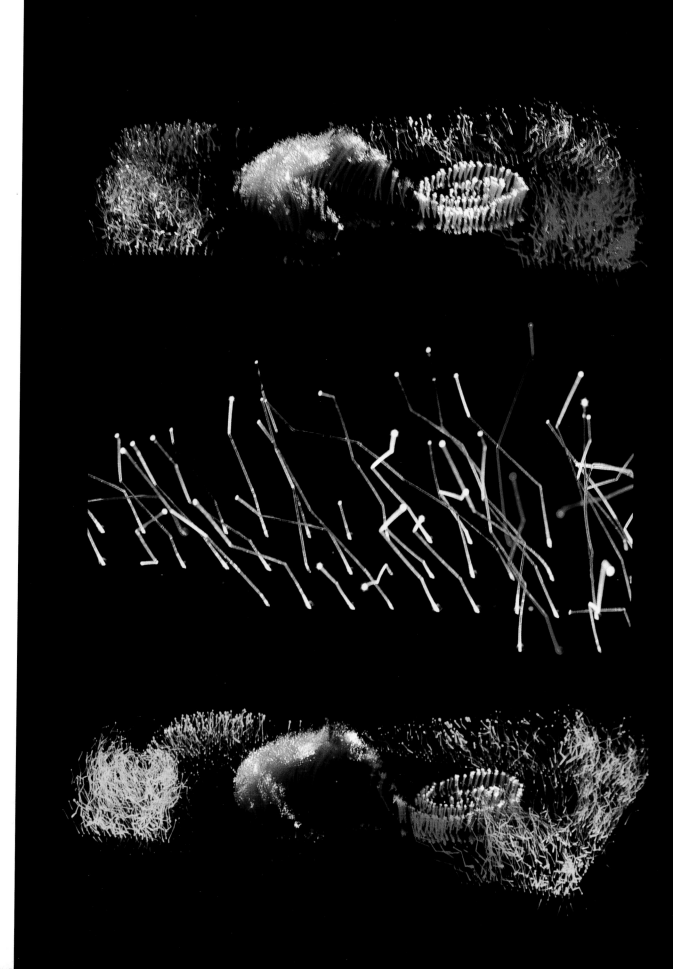

Fibre optics are also generating much interest. Originally used by the communications industry, many textile companies are investing in this technology and there are many potential applications. Either thin glass or plastic fibre is used through which light can be transmitted. Pulses of light contained in the fibre are capable of sending digital visual and written information over vast distances. Generally light is emitted from the end of the fibre, but if its surface is treated, light can also be emitted from along its length. Woven fibre optics can give out coloured light and transmit images and text in powerful ways. Like microfibres, the key to advances in this technology lies in the fineness of the fibre. Fibre optics provide a fascinating medium for transmitting information and optical data which is proving to be an interesting and challenging material in both textile design and gallery textiles.

Jakob Schlaepfer Co. AG is a textile company based in St Gallen, Switzerland. They have used unusual materials including fibre optics in many collections for both prêt-à-porter and haute couture fashion and also for interior textiles. Schlaepfer have combined fibre optics with traditional textile materials, the result being a precious cloth which shimmers beautifully in the light.

Combined with a textile, ceramic can offer distinctly advantageous properties. Ceramic textiles offer sun protection from both UVA and UVB light and are resistant to high temperatures. They are often used with polyester due to this fibre's inherent UV screening.

ECOLOGICAL CONCERNS

Today, textile companies are very aware of potentially harmful effects to the environment and work within strict guidelines with ecology often being a main concern. They understand that the world's resources will soon be depleted if we do not make major changes. The needs both of the consumer and the environment are being more closely considered with textiles being developed from renewable sources and manufactured with minimum impact on the environment.

Existing production processes are analysed in order to reduce air pollution, toxic chemicals are replaced by non-pollutant alternatives and waste products are increasingly being recycled and put to positive use. Research is also ongoing into ways of making textiles biodegrade more quickly as some synthetics can take hundreds of years. Central to many international textile company's approach and marketing are energy-saving and economic methods of production and a serious concern for ecology.

Nuno Corporation have taken corn starch to create their Green Fabric. A maize-based fibre has been developed by Japanese manufacturers Mitsui Chemical and Kanebo Synthetics. Nuno overspin this fibre to make a lively crêpe fabric. It biodegrades well, as after its useful life the fibres are broken down by micro-organisms in the soil into water and carbon dioxide, in harmony with nature.

Natural fibres are not necessarily all good and synthetics bad: the availability and quality of a natural fibre, for example, can be unpredictable. Pesticides, fungicides and fertilizers are often used to grow them, and bleaching, dyeing and other finishing processes can cause pollution. Even natural dyes can be harmful and produce waste. Chemical dyers are investigating methods of colouring microfibres in line with their supplier's ecological concerns.

Regenerated fibres, on the other hand, are made from natural, renewable sources, and the manufacturers of the new types are often ecologically aware in their choice of production. Tencel's raw material is wood pulp, a renewable source, and is manufactured using a system which recycles any waste products and effluents. Marketed as an exclusive textile, Tencel combines care for the environment with sophisticated technology.

Synthetics are extremely versatile and their fibres can be modified in terms of denier and cross-section and offered in a choice of staple or filament. Since the characteristics of a fibre can be pre-determined there is often no need for additional finishing treatments, reducing potential environmental damage. If a finish is required, there are chemicals for dyeing which are less damaging and inks and coatings can be water-based. Transfer and digital printing eliminate the need for screens. High-performance synthetic fleece (often made from waste products such as recycled glass and plastic) offers less bulk and weight than traditional materials while keeping the wearer warm and dry. And sophisticated ultra-microfibres and advanced textile finishes reduce the need for dry cleaning, meaning less harm to our world.

Textile designer Luisa Cevese uses industrial textile waste and transforms it into material used to create very desirable fashion accessories, interior products and textiles for exhibition. Her interest in recycling began in the 1980s when she was Director of Research for Mantero Seta, a large Italian textile company in Como, Italy, famous for its quality woven silk scarves and ties. She saw the huge amount of waste that was being made (selvedges, off-cuts and seconds, etc.) and considered creative ways of using it. Whereas at Mantero Seta the recycling was a sideline, her ongoing Riedizioni project is a main concern. She has sourced textiles from Scottish mills and collaborated with designers and companies such as Georgina von Etzdorf and Nuno Corporation. To transform the raw materials, Luisa Cevese bonds the waste with polyurethane which gives stability and strength as well as providing an easily washable surface. She then designs the end product – bags of various sizes from small cosmetic to large travel ones, raincoats, aprons and cushions. This Riedizioni series is very eye-catching and popular, they are all one-offs – being made from waste no two can be exactly the same. They vary in colour and pattern; some have frayed edges, while others use the tightly woven edge of the fabric. The result is an individual product which is manufactured on a commercial scale and sold through stores worldwide. Preserving antique textiles is also of interest to Luisa Cevese: she takes often fragile pieces of cloth and submerges them in plastic, contrasting the old and the new. These are frequently shown as gallery textiles and demonstrate her fascination with both traditional, artisanal hand-crafts and industrial technology.

Conscious of the dangers of the worldwide accumulation of waste, many designers and artists are using recyclable materials or those which return to nature by being fully biodegradable. Microfibres answer part of the question and may perhaps help to solve the world's ecological problems. The increasing diversity of advanced synthetics and supernaturals opens up new possibilities and challenges.

Consumer research has to be made alongside the development of advanced textiles. The customer wants products which are adaptable to our ever-changing lifestyles which means they need to be highly portable, multi-functional, protective, comfortable, attractive and affordable. These are huge demands. Emerging from intensive research, however, are revolutionary materials which answer such needs and are making their way into our everyday lives. Technology will take us into a very different world.

opposite top
NUNO CORPORATION
REIKO SUDO (design)
Green Fabric. 2001

This is made of a biodegradable fibre which is the result of research into cornstarch and other grain by-products. Working with overspun yarn experts in Kyoto using twisting and dyeing techniques this fabric with a wonderful texture is created. It is very sensitive to heat and when warmed smells slightly of roasted corn.

opposite bottom
SCHOELLER TEXTIL AG
bluesign textiles

Attractive and functional, these polyamide textiles have been given the bluesign (registered trademark for Bluesign Technologies AG) for the world's highest standard for safe and sustainable textile production. This guarantees the greatest possible exclusion of harmful substances to both humans and the environment and the most economical use of resources.

LUISA CEVESE
Riedizioni collection.
below left: **Small bag**
below right: **Very small bag**

Fashion accessories and domestic products from the Riedizioni collection are made from textile waste. Luisa Cevese combines Indian sari silk with polyurethane for the small bag. For the very small bag she uses coloured pieces of silk spread out and combined with polyurethane. The plastic gives durability, strength, structure, flexibility and makes the product waterproof. Unique pieces, similar, but never quite the same, are created due to the recycled materials used.

Electronic textiles

Marie O'Mahony

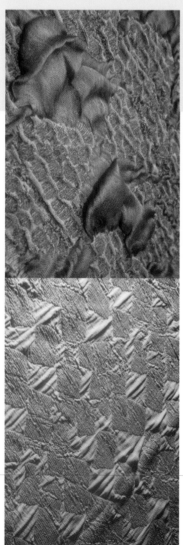

above
GRETHE SORENSEN
Interference 2

Grethe Sorensen's Interference 2
is part of an ongoing body of work
that treats the computerized images
as stills of an optical phenomenon.
The digitally generated images are
reconstructions of the physical
characteristics of perforated panels
and their interaction. Working with
the computer allowed the artist to
work in layers with the patterns –
turning, staggering, scaling
and changing angles to control
the interference and follow the
development of the huge moiré
pattern.

right, above and below
ANKE HENNIG

Fabric by German designer Anke
Hennig woven on a computer-aided
Jacquard loom using multiple warp
and weft constructions. Yarns
include silk, linen, polyester and
cotton.

It seems eons ago that the head of IBM estimated that the world would need four or five computers at most. Today computers are omnipresent, affecting every aspect of our lives. Textiles have not escaped their influence which we can see everywhere, from the use of computer-aided design (CAD) for structural or decorative purposes, to the Internet as a tool for sales and communication. Coupled with this is the development of wearable technology that includes the computer, but goes far beyond it. Embedded electronics, 'wearables' or 'wearable technology' are various terms used to refer to such systems. The intention is to allow the wearer to communicate with people and interact with the environment with greater ease. Effectively, such systems act as extensions of the senses and serve to create cyborgs. Though they did not consciously begin with any decorative element, this area has developed a strong design aesthetic that is readily recognizable.

The versatility of the computer medium is apparent in the ease with which it is used to produce fabrics for the catwalk and high street shops alike. Textile designers have little difficulty in making the medium their own. Conversely, the familiarity of a common tool also draws product and interactive designers to work with fabrics. Many of the designers discussed here use standard software systems, yet the finished textiles retain their individual identity. This is partly due to the simple fact that every designer has a particular way of using a tool. It can also be attributed to the care with which the designer selects the base fabric, printing inks and finishing treatments. There is one CAD area where uniformity is desirable, however – when the system is used to test safety features, function comes before aesthetic considerations. Hence the similarity of many protective products such as car driver airbags.

Textiles are ideal as a flexible conduit, particularly where the product is designed to be worn. Electronics can be incorporated into the fabric structure or surface that can change with greater speed and ease than more rigid surfaces. The term cyborg encompasses the concept of an enhanced

man that is part-human, part-machine. The monster in Mary Shelley's *Frankenstein* (1818) is one of the earliest examples of the cyborg in science fiction. More recently, Ian Gibson's cyberpunk novel *Neuromancer* (1984) highlights the dangers and desirability of a cyborg age where there is little to distinguish between what is real and what is virtual. A long-term goal of space exploration is to enable humans to live in an extra-terrestrial environment. Plans have already been drawn up for the development of a spaceplane and hotel complex for the first interplanetary holidays. A more immediate goal is to make astronauts' spacewalks more comfortable. Since the end of the Cold War many of these technologies have been made available for commercial purposes. The result is a more human-centred design that takes greater account of what it is like to wear these devices, what it is to be a cyborg.

COMPUTER-AIDED DESIGN (CAD)

The influence of the computer on textiles begins at the textile design stage and continues through manufacturing, marketing and eventual sale of products to the consumer. CAD has revolutionized the design process, introducing a sense of

above left and right
CHRISTINE KELLER
Light Content – Points of View

Christine Keller's Light Content – Points of View uses two superimposed images that have been digitally manipulated in Photoshop. She has used a double Jacquard weave with cotton, polyester, black wire and a retroreflective yarn. The artwork was done at the Centre for Contemporary Textiles in Montreal, Canada.

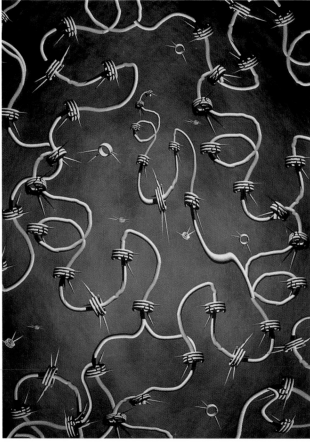

three-dimensional space into two-dimensional design and bringing with it a whole new visual aesthetic. The intensity of the computer's light-based colour spectrum is matched by the manufacturers of dyes and inks for textiles, closing the gap between the screen image and the finished fabric. From a marketing point of view, the Internet allows users to browse through designer collections in the comfort of their own home. The time taken to download an image or movie clip remains an issue. As reductions in the cost of computers and Internet services continue to trickle down, they are becoming more widely used, supplementing and even replacing the paintbrush as the designer's main tool.

A common use of CAD is in the design of surface pattern for fashion and furnishing fabrics. The system allows complex designs to be completed in a relatively short period, and a variety of colour schemes can be created without having to redo the entire design each time. Alterations, which could take hours to do manually, can now be made with the click of a button. As software packages are increasingly specialized, it is becoming easier for designers to move between a number of programmes with a single design. This makes the medium even more flexible. Speed is one of the great benefits of CAD, but it is also the designer's most common complaint. In computer terms, speed translates as power, or the system's ability to perform tasks to a particular standard within a certain timeframe. While most design instructions for printed textiles take seconds or minutes to render, more complex instructions may have to be left overnight before they appear on the monitor.

The Apple Macintosh computer heralded the use of computers as a design tool for the textile industry. It introduced the first 'user-friendly' interface for which common sense rather than computer literacy was required. Menu options displayed self-explanatory terms such as 'open' or 'print', allowing many first-time users to teach themselves. The popularity of the Mac has led rival computer manufacturers to adopt a more user-friendly interface so that most now operate on an intuitive level. Software programmes offer a set of tools specific to the medium, rotating, subdividing and manipulating design elements to recreate the dynamics of a three-dimensional image in two-dimensional space.

British designer Garry Martin uses Infini-D to design fabric lengths for fashion. He adds to the three-dimensional effect by using a reactive ink in the printing process. Printed on silk, the colours have a rich, almost metallic lustre. The three-dimensional effect is heightened with distance. Martin uses Stork TCP jet printers which apply the dye in a fine jet of small droplets, thousands per second. The cloth is secured on a rotating drum while the printhead moves along the drum in a horizontal direction. The colours are then fixed in a special fixation unit that looks a little like a microwave oven. The fabric is then washed, dried and ready for use.

Danish designer Vibeke Riisberg uses colour to highlight optical characteristics. She takes full advantage of the light-based colour on her computer monitor, pitching her designs at a greater intensity than many pigment-based colour tools would allow. She designs fabric lengths for the textile company Kvadrat as well as her own one-off designs. Her fabric lengths are usually designed in series, using different colour combinations to provide various optical effects. Through careful selection of colour, the pattern can appear in the foreground, or recede into the background. Although most of her designs have a formal geometric base and an identifiable colour selection, Riisberg's work is most distinctive for its visual wit.

Robert Mew has adopted many of the computer-based techniques used in film and television, extending them into textile design as an alternative to traditional CAD design methodology. His interest is in the computer as designer, where the human designer is relegated to the role of facilitator and editor. Mew does not go so far as to claim an Artificial Intelligence or creativity for the computer; instead he concentrates on Chaos Theory as a working method. Using genetic algorithms to create fractal patterns, Mew uses a single programming sequence to produce several patterns. Choosing an image from the series, he transfers it to a paint programme for editing. The final stage sees the design transferred to a Moratronik knitting machine, producing a fabric suitable for garments. The issue of creativity and the computer is controversial. There is a strong argument that the computer is not, and can

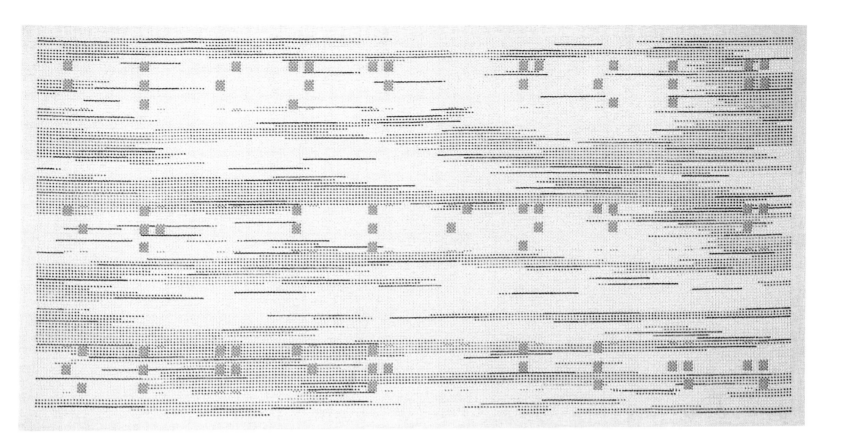

never be, creative because all its calculations are based on computing, or assembling information. But designs produced using a fractal system are undoubtedly very beautiful and unrepeatable.

Specially programmed CAD systems are increasingly being used as a means of testing new designs. This is vitally important for fabrics if they are to pass health and safety tests. How will an architectural membrane wear after ten years of heavy snowloads in winter and strong ultra-violet light in summer? If architects are to use new materials they have to prove they are fit for purpose and will stand wear over time. The Advanced Technology unit at Ove Arup and Partners have developed a software system designed for crash-testing vehicles. The benefit is that tests can be carried out at an early stage in the design process rather than waiting until prototype stage, saving both time and money. The focus of the software is the effect of impact on the occupants. A simulated family group is tested for injuries during side and front impact, allowing the performance of the airbags and seat belts to be assessed.

The sportswear company Speedo have utilized computer software more usually seen in the car industry in the design of the FASTSKIN FSII. Computational Fluid Dynamics (CFD) is generally applied to Formula One cars to see how they behave in wind tests at different speeds. It has been applied in competitive sports for skiers and cyclists to optimize their posture ergonomically so as to create the least possible drag. However, this uses the same wind tunnel testing facilities as the car industry with little modification. What Speedo and Fluent (a leading CFD software company) have done is to apply this technology to water. This has allowed researchers to see how the swimmer moves through water and identifies the greatest areas of friction drag. Dr Keith Hanna, Director of Marketing and Communications at Fluent is in doubt as to its importance for the sports industry: 'What Speedo has achieved by transforming motor-racing technical design methodologies to the hydrodynamics of swimming and swimsuits is probably a first for an Olympic discipline, and certainly a milestone of applied engineering.'

opposite top
JOHANNA MILLS ROSE
Collage

Textile artist Johanna Mills Rose's collage uses patterns that have first been scanned using Photoshop software, then printed and hand cut to form the collage.

opposite bottom
GARY MARTIN
Malice

The images for Gary Martin's Malice series of printed textiles use a variety of CAD programmes including Infini-D. The fabric is computer inkjet printed by Stork BV in the Netherlands using reactive dyes. Designed as a fashion fabric, both sides of the silk twill print can be used.

above
ANE HENRIKSEN
The Blind Following the Blind

The title for Ane Henriksen's *The Blind Following the Blind* is taken from a painting by Pieter Bruegel. In a contemporary setting, the artist's fears are of genetic engineering and manipulation in the hands of the scientist. The initial photograph of trees has been digitally manipulated in Photoshop. The strikingly digital appearance is deliberate and reflects the mediumused to create the image as well as Braille text and lists of DNA sequencing.

right
MACHI UE
Doughnuts

The original stereogram for
Muchi Ue's Doughnuts has been
computer designed before being
digitally printed on a cotton fabric.

opposite top left
VIBEKE RIISBERG
Digital Files

Vibeke Riisberg's digital print is
part of the Digital Files series
which considers changes in
perception and optical illusions.
Based on the eye motif, the image
becomes a repeat pattern in the
distance but on closer inspection
the eye can be clearly seen. The
reverse of the fabric is a mirror foil
to reflect the image of the viewer.

opposite bottom left
VIBEKE RIISBERG

A digital print by Danish designer
Vibeke Riisberg on cotton poplin
using a Mimaki Textile Jet 1,600
using ciba reactive inks. The
imagery is based on the eye motif
which can be seen close-up but not
at a distance where it takes on the
appearance of an overall repeat
pattern. The reverse of the fabric
uses a mirror foil.

opposite far right
LEE LAPTHORNE
Fleece

For the Fleece installation, artist
Lee Lapthorne has taken images
of sheep fleece and digitally
manipulated them before printing
onto a crêpe de chine. The
hangings were shown at the
Barbican chapel in London.

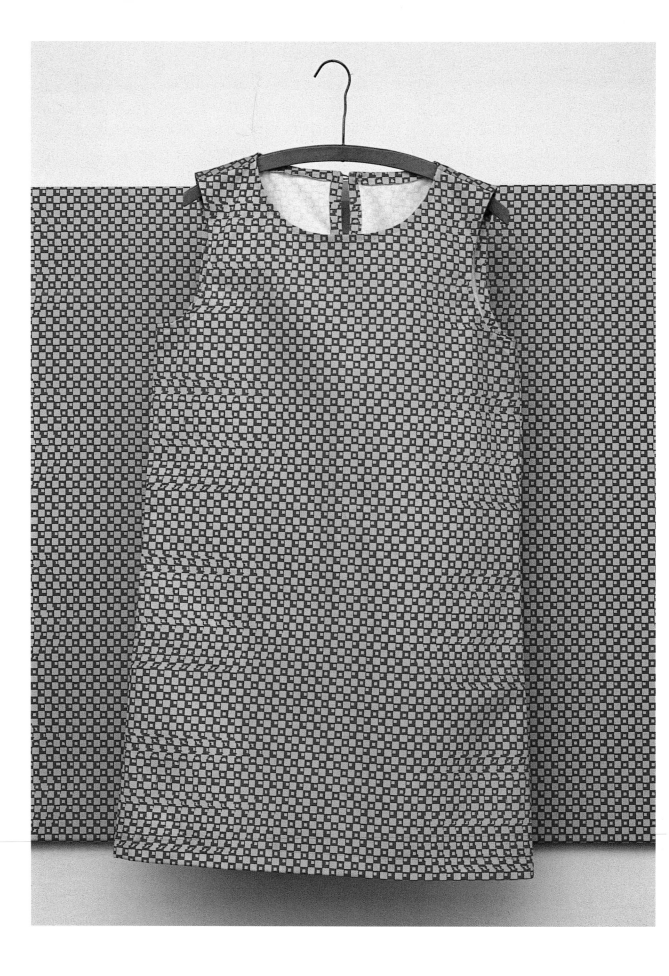

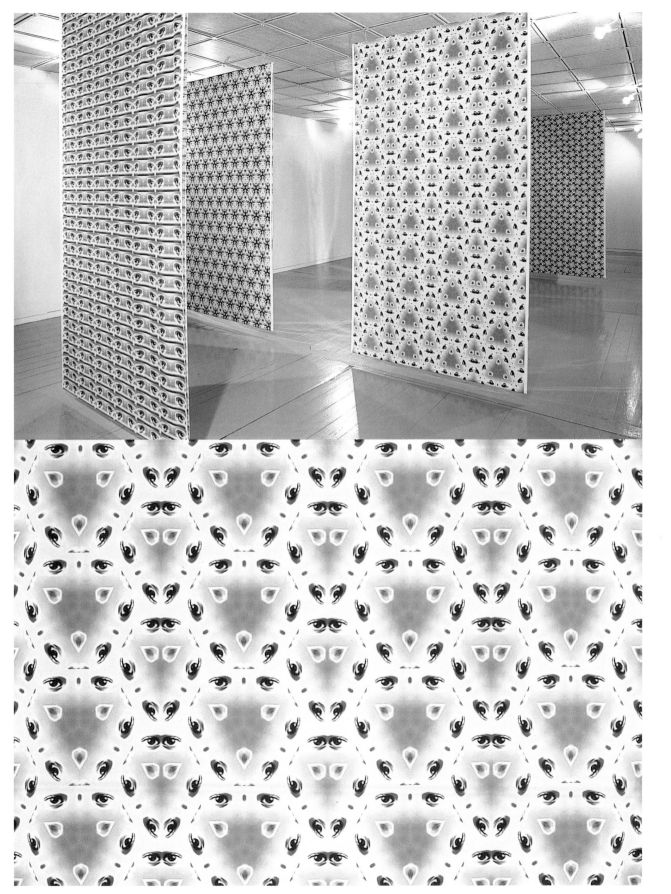

opposite
MICHIKO KOSHINO

London based fashion designer
Michiko Koshino has created a
hypernature by manipulating these
floral images on computer. The
impact is exotic, intense luxury,
the promise of a fantasy.

above left
HUSSEIN CHALAYAN
Spring/Summer 2000

Fashion designer Hussein Chalayan
worked with architectural engineers
b consultants to create a
computerized environment that he
could move through. Stills were then
selected from the wireframe urban
landscape and silkscreen printed
onto silk dresses (shown here) and
cotton T-shirts.

above right
HUSSEIN CHALAYAN
Pixellated cotton dress with fabric
designed by Eley Kishimoto
Spring/Summer 1996

Photocopies of hand-drawn flowers
were scanned into a computer to
enhance colour and accentuate
pixellation. The design appears
either animated or flat according
to the fabric it is printed on.

right
OVE ARUP AND PARTNERS
Inland Revenue Centre, Nottingham

It is vitally important for architects and engineers to know how membrane structures are likely to behave over time and under difficult weather conditions. A specially designed CAD programme has been used by architectural engineers Ove Arup and Partners to see how architect Michael Hopkins and Partners' design for the Amenities building at the Inland Revenue Centre in Nottingham would behave under snow loading.

below
SPEEDO

Specially adapted computer software using Computational Fluid Dynamics has allowed Speedo to see exactly how water moves over the body and identify problem areas of friction drag. In the world of competitive swimming, fractions of seconds can mean the difference between an Olympic gold and bronze.

opposite left
W&LT by WALTER VAN BEIRENDONCK
Killer/Astral Travel/4D-Hi-D
Spring/Summer 1996

This overall and gloves are from the Killer/Astral Travel/4D-Hi-D series W&LT by Walter van Beirendonck. An optical print has been used. The main garment is made from a neoprene fabric and the gloves use polyamide.

opposite right
W&LT by WALTER VAN BEIRENDONCK
Welcome Little Stranger
Spring/Summer 1997

The dress uses a nonwoven fabric with a photographically printed paper-like material embroidered onto the surface of the dress.

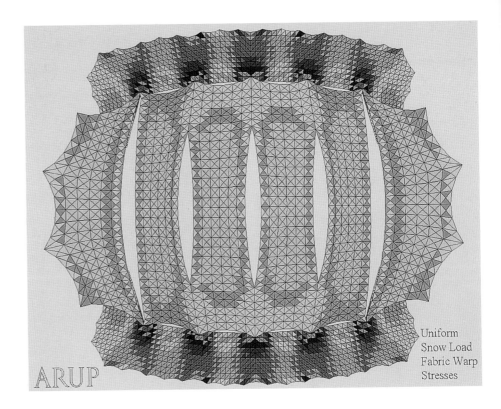

Uniform
Snow Load
Fabric Warp
Stresses

ARUP

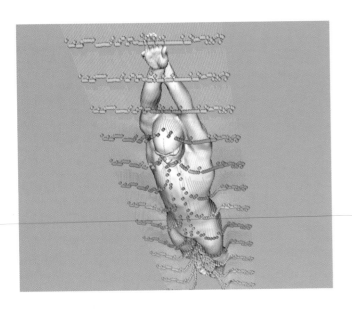

THE INTERNET

Used by designers and manufacturers not as a design tool, but as a means of research, marketing and sales, the Internet, or World Wide Web, has proved an invaluable tool. On the plus side, everything is infinitely more accessible saving time and money. A designer can sit in his or her studio in central London and see the Carnival in Rio as it happens, check the latest international news headlines or buy books. The fact that anyone can post information on a website means that there is a truly vast quantity of information available. The downside of this is that the information can also be wrong. Looking up 'Gutenburg' on the Internet I found three different birth dates for the inventor of the movable-type printing press. We have become so used to being fed a viewpoint through television, newspapers and magazines, it is good to be reminded of the need to check a source and question information.

Large manufacturers, designers and retailers tend to use the Internet as a direct sales tool. A standard format is to provide a basic profile with the lead page, then links to products and finally contact information for queries or purchasing goods. This works well for booking hotels or buying CDs but not so well for buying clothes or shoes. Part of the reason is fit. Five women who regularly buy size 12 clothes could stand in a row and be so utterly different in height and build that it would be impossible for any one garment to fit all five. Returns on mail-order and by extension on web-purchased garments is high. It is the sheer volume that makes it worthwhile in certain sectors. Few would spend serious money on a designer outfit without touching the fabric and trying it on. The better designers have recognized this and use the Internet as a marketing tool or simply a way to have some fun.

The Belgian fashion designer Walter van Beirendonck treats the medium as his plaything (www.waltervanbeirendonck.com). He manages to put the same creative energy into his websites, which constantly change, as his collections. At the time of writing, the website has a home page showing cartoon drawings like paper cutouts of the designer naked with his trademark Santa Claus beard. The figures are brightly coloured, like jelly baby sweets. When the user clicks on one of the functions the figure immediately above changes colour to black (the best jelly baby flavour), his outstretched arms lower by his

side and then he winks just before linking to the new page. All the information needed from a website is there, but it is given in a fun entertaining way.

The British designer Griffin likewise takes an unorthodox approach to their website. Clothes from the current collection are available to purchase and there is information about his shops in London and Tokyo. Along with quirky photos, the site also offers the chance to become a member with the promise that 'only nice things will be sent by email'.

DESIGN AND VIRTUAL REALITY

In Aldous Huxley's *Brave New World*, published in 1932, people experiencing 'the feelies' can feel every one of their senses. In reality we know that it is not always possible clearly to define each of our senses. Much of what we 'taste', for instance, is actually dictated by our sense of smell. Early research by the National Aeronautics and Space Administration (NASA) into flight simulation led to what we now refer to as Virtual Reality. The technology quickly found its way into the commercial world and is now being used in a range of industries, including entertainment and design. Users wear a helmet with two wide screens in front of the eyes, so close that they appear to be a single screen. The computer recreates an image on each screen, giving the user a feeling of being inside the stereoscopic image. When the wearer's head moves, the computer senses this and updates the image on the screens, allowing the user to look around his or her virtual environment.

Touch and manipulation of virtual objects are made possible by the use of gloves such as PowerGlove and CyberGlove. Again, these are linked to the computer, and the glove can actually be seen through the screens. The Dataglove and PowerGlove were two important developments in the late 1980s. The Dataglove used a Lycra-based fabric for comfort and flexibility. It was fitted with specially treated optical fibres which ran along the backs of the fingers, sending signals to a central processor. The glove could monitor ten finger joints as well as hand position and orientation. In the late 1980s the PowerGlove was developed by the Mattel Toy Company for Nintendo home video games. It used a moulded plastic gauntlet with a flexible

Lycra-based fabric in the palm area. What the glove lacked in comfort it made up for in its low cost. Resistive-ink flexible sensors were embedded in the plastic on the backs of the fingers. These registered finger movement while acoustic trackers located the glove in space. Games were specially designed for the PowerGlove, exploiting its 'grab and throw' facilities.

Immersion Corporation's CyberTouch instrumented glove offers the wearer tactile feedback via a series of small vibrotactile stimulators on each finger and the palm of the glove. Each can be individually programmed to vary from simple sensations such as pulses or sustained vibration, to complex tactile feedback patterns. CyberForce is a whole-hand force feedback system. Both left and right hand gloves can be used as part of the company's Haptic Workstation. The system can be used by the designer in a standing or seated position. Haptic Workstation reduces the reliance on physical prototypes in product development by providing real-time two-handed evaluation of the ergonomics, ease of assembly, and maintenance of the CAD design.

ADAPTING TO THE ELECTRONIC ENVIRONMENT

In 2004 it was estimated that in the UK alone 50 million people owned a mobile phone and to meet this demand 35,000 masts have been erected across the country. Few question what effect this has on the health of the people living or working in close proximity to the masts, and those who do complain are often dismissed as cranks.

Doctors sometimes diagnose 'total allergy syndrome' in patients who have mysterious symptoms that they cannot explain. Sufferers blame their ill health on a variety of factors, from pollution and food additives, to perfumes and tap water. In Todd Haynes's film *Safe*, Carol White claims allergies to the packaging on fruit, newsprint and even her new sofa. Seeking professional advice from alternative practitioners, she is encouraged to create an oasis, a 'toxic-free zone'. The final frame of the film finds Carol content at last, living in an airtight bubble-chamber with her face mask and oxygen cylinder. Ironically, she is escaping from the twentieth century through technology which has only become generally

available during this century. The plot for this mid-1990s film may seem far-fetched, but less than ten years on some people are actually living this nightmare.

Faisal Khawaja used to live 50 metres (165 feet) from a mobile phone mast. As soon as it was erected he reported symptoms such as dizziness, loss of concentration and memory, headaches and a clicking and high-pitched sound in his ears. He was forced to move house. Geraldine Attridge also suffered health problems when one was erected on top of her tower block. When she distributed a questionnaire to other people living in the flats she got an astonishing six hundred replies. Eight hundred people lived in the block. The image of such people in the media is of cranks and oddities. One taxi driver was photographed for an article in a national broadsheet wearing his home-made protective headgear – a sort of chickenwire cage with red gaffer tape holding it together. While at-risk workplaces have long been protected against the dangers of electromagnetic rays, little has been done to look at potential risks in the greater environment. The evidence tends to be anecdotal and litigation is rare.

The issue is being addressed by designers and artists on the basis that there is little point waiting for government or corporate protection to take action so it is up to the individual to protect themselves. Wearable mechanisms are now being developed which will allow us to protect ourselves and adapt to the changes in our environment. Daniel Cooper has designed a Chameleon Jacket that monitors and protects the wearer from pollution. The jacket can be worn in a 'passive' or 'aggressive' state, depending on pollution levels. This makes the function the main aesthetic focus. The front panels are made from a nylon fabric. Built-in detectors monitor nitrogen oxide, sulphur dioxide and ozone, changing from blue where there is little or no pollution, to orange for serious pollution levels. When the jacket is worn to protect against pollution, a neoprene face mask can be worn over the mouth and nose, providing the wearer with further protection. Air is inhaled through a charcoal-impregnated felt filter sandwiched between the neoprene and face, while two small valves allow air to be exhaled.

THE CYBORG

In the late 1950s a white laboratory rat at New York's Rockland State Hospital had a small osmotic pump implanted in its body to inject chemicals at a controlled rate, altering its physiological parameters. It was the first being to be referred to as a cyborg.

The term cyborg was coined by Manfred E. Clynes and Nathan S. Kline, in reference to an enhanced human being who would be able to

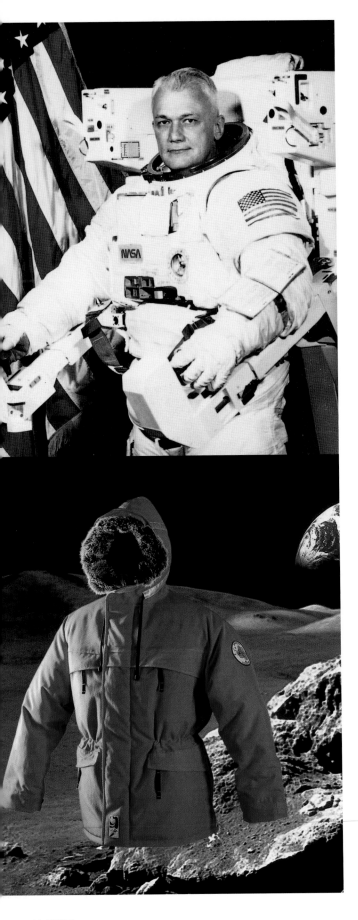

adapt to extraterrestrial environments. From the early 1960s the space industry took special interest in the idea. In the long term, it offers the possibility for humans to live on another planet. More immediately, it provided a design focus for the development of spacesuits. An early interest in the subject can be found in medicine, when oxygen apparatus was developed to help rescue workers in search of miners trapped below ground. In science fiction, the monster in Mary Shelley's *Frankenstein* represents technology out of control. Written in 1818 when industrial technology was new and mistrusted, the novel was a reflection of popular opinion at the time. In the 1930s Marvel Comics were responsible for introducing a range of cyborg characters such as Captain America and the X-Men. The graphic style of the early strips broke new ground. Images were dynamic, seeming to leap off the page. The cyborg has frequently served as a barometer of public concern about machines, war and the environment. Spiderman was created by exposure to radiation, while Ridley Scott's 1982 film *Blade Runner* (based on Philip K. Dick's 1968 book *Do Androids Dream of Electric Sheep?*) mirrors anxiety about a future with cyborgs so sophisticated that they are indistinguishable from humans.

As the miniaturization of technology has developed, the man–machine interface has become an important focus for garment and product designers alike. Our increasing ease with machines becomes more apparent as cyborg culture continues to become part of a design aesthetic.

LIVING IN AN EXTREME ENVIRONMENT

Man has always struggled to live and work at the extremities of our natural environment. Clothing has been adapted to allow us to survive and move with a degree of ease and comfort through difficult terrain. The rigorous demands of areas such as the Antarctic, with its freezing temperatures and geographical isolation, are used as a blueprint for human survival in extraterrestrial environments. As well as being mentally and physically prepared for survival in outer space, the astronaut has to be properly clothed. Before man landed on the moon he had to contend with air-travel and the effect of G-force.

Although air-travel is now so commonplace we almost take it for granted, we are more likely to see pilots become redundant before astronauts.

It was predicted that the fighter plane of the 21st century will dispense with its oldest component, the pilot, because the human physique is no longer up to the job. As aircraft become faster and more agile, it seems only a matter of time before pilots will control their aircraft from ground level rather than in the air. Early pilots were given special suits to counter the effect of G-force. The early 'G-suits' applied pressure to the lower limbs in order to force blood back up towards the brain. However, as planes like the new Eurofighter produce forces estimated at up to 9Gs, applied pressure is no longer enough. In response to this, the Royal Air Force have developed a 'positive pressure' system where air is blown into the pilots lungs. This causes the abdominal muscles to contract, holding the blood in the upper body and counteracting the effect of the G-force.

In 1963, a NASA report identified the benefit of cyborg technology for space exploration as 'reducing metabolic demands and the attendant life support systems'. NASA and its European counterpart, the European Space Agency (ESA), have taken two approaches. The first concerns the physical well-being and fitness of the astronaut, of which the AFS-2 programme is one example. The second is the development of the spacesuit which effectively acts as a second skin and enhances breathing, vision and 'walking'. To perform tasks outside the aircraft the astronaut must wear an Extravehicular Mobility Unit (EMU), described as a 'smaller spacecraft' combining a spacesuit with a life-support system. In enabling astronauts to adapt to the atmosphere in space they have created cyborgs.

Physical fitness is given a high priority in preparing the astronaut for travel. The Autogenic Feedback System 2 (AFS-2) is a training suit which helps train astronauts to control their own motion sickness in space. According to NASA: 'Motion sickness is a completely artificial disease which has plagued mankind since we first stepped on to a floating raft or climbed on to an animal's back.' Using a specially developed Autogenic

Feedback Training (AFT), the system focuses on physiological self-regulation, using techniques such as Autogenic Therapy and biofeedback.

Billed by the space industry as the latest thing in astronaut underwear, the AFS-2 is designed to train astronauts to control motion sickness. It does this by making them very ill, then gradually trains them to control this urge. The suit is divided into three subsystems: the garment and cable harness assembly, the Wrist Display Unit (WDU), and the belt assembly. The garment assembly is worn on the upper body and covers the torso and left arm. It consists of the basic garment, cable harness, respiration transducer, accelerometer and ring transducer. The WDU displays real-time physiological data, and it can also indicate malfunction of the system on a custom-designed Liquid Crystal Display (LCD). It is attached with Velcro to the left sleeve of the AFS-2 garment. The system is powered by the belt electronics via the cable harness. The belt assembly is worn around the waist over clothing and contains the electronics, battery pack, TEAC data recorder, belt wrap, TEAC pouch and interface cable. The system has two operational display modes on the WDU: the treatment mode displays the system status, malfunction indicators and monitored physiological data; the control mode displays system status and malfunction indicators only. The importance of this type of development is wider reaching than space travel. It can also have the non-space applications that NASA seeks through its Technology Transfer Program. One of the many possibilities for the AFS in the medical field is as a training device for cancer patients, helping them to suppress the nausea associated with radiation or chemotherapy.

The Extravehicular Mobility Unit, or EMU, has taken over fifty years to develop. In the 1930s the aviation pioneer Wiley Post developed a pressurized suit to help him break altitude and speed records. The pressure suit consisted of an inner gas-bladder layer of neoprene-coated fabric with an outer layer of aluminized nylon. The inner layer retained the oxygen while the outer layer prevented the suit from expanding like a balloon, and directed the oxygen inward on the pilot. These early suits were not very effective; they became rigid when inflated so that the pilot could not operate the controls. Over the following thirty years various improvements were made, but it was not until NASA began its Mercury manned space programme that work got underway in earnest.

The six flights in the Mercury series were followed by ten in the Gemini programme. New suits were developed to serve as pressure backup to the spacecraft cabin. An escape suit was provided in case ejection seats had to be fired. One of the main design innovations was improved joint mobility, using a bladder made from neoprene-coated nylon surrounded by a Teflon-coated nylon netting. The first astronaut to leave the spaceship was Edward White in June 1965. He was connected to the capsule by an oxygen feed hose which also acted as a tether line and communication link, an umbilical line joining man and machine.

Mobility was an even greater issue in the Apollo spacesuits which were designed to allow the astronauts to go on actual spacewalks on the moon surface. Arm flexibility was not enough: the suits also had to allow leg and waist movement so that the astronauts could bend and stoop to pick up samples on the moon. A portable life-support system was also needed. The inner layer of the spacesuit consisted of a garment laced with a network of thin-walled plastic tubing that circulated cooling water around the astronaut to prevent overheating. Next came a three-layer system which formed the pressure garment. The inner garment was a 'comfort layer' of lightweight nylon with fabric ventilation ducts. This was followed by a multilayer outer suit whose inner layer consisted of a neoprene-coated bladder surrounded by a nylon restraint. The improved mobility was achieved by bellows-like joints of formed rubber with built-in restraint cables at each of the joints. Next followed five layers of aluminized Mylar for heat protection, mixed with four spacing layers of Dacron. Outside these were two layers of Kapton and beta marquisette for additional thermal protection. These were covered with a non-flammable and abrasion-protective layer of Teflon-coated beta cloth. The outer layer was white Teflon cloth. Gloves were custom-sized, with moulded silicone rubber fingertips to provide finger sensitivity for handling equipment.

A backpack unit contained the life-support system providing oxygen (for breathing and pressurization), water (for cooling) and radio communications, allowing excursions of up to 8 hours. During the Apollo programme astronauts spent over one 160 hours of EVA on the moon surface.

The Space Shuttle has opened up an entirely new era in space travel. Launched as a rocket, the reusable shuttle operates in space as a spacecraft before returning to Earth as an aeroplane. In the Apollo programme each astronaut had three suits: one for flight, one for training and one for flight backup. Suits for shuttle flights, however, are tailored from a stock of standard size parts and only one suit is needed. Unlike previous flights, where suits had to perform a whole series of functions, the Shuttle designs concentrate on just one function: going EVA.

The Shuttle EMU has a total of nineteen separate items, functioning as an almost complete one-person spacecraft. It provides pressure; thermal and micrometeoroid protection; oxygen; cooling and drinking water; food; waste collection; electrical power and communications. A gas-jet-propelled Manned Manoeuvring Unit (MMU) can be fitted over the life-support system to provide mobility. Without the MMU the suit weighs about 113 kg (249 lbs), but in space it has no weight, only mass that is felt by the astronaut as resistance to change in motion.

On earth the astronaut can put on the Shuttle EMU in about fifteen minutes, but in space it has to be done in stages, and preparation to go EVA takes even longer. Since the suit's atmosphere is pure oxygen, the astronaut has to adapt slowly to avoid 'the bends'. Wearing an oxygen mask for an hour rids the body of nitrogen. A long feeder hose attached to the orbiter's oxygen supply system allows the astronaut to move about during this time.

The first garment that crew members put on is the Urine Collection Device (UCD) for men, and Disposable Absorption and Containment Trunk (DACT) for women made from chemically treated absorbent, nonwoven materials. Both garments are discarded after use. Next comes the Liquid Cooling and Ventilation Garment (LCVG), a full-length undergarment made of a spandex fabric. It removes body heat, contaminant gases and

perspiration by circulating chilled water through the tubes in the garment. The astronaut then prepares the helmet by rubbing antifog compound on the inside. The helmet is a plastic pressure bubble with a neck disconnection ring and ventilation distribution pad.

The upper torso of the suit is made from a hard fibreglass shell. As astronauts put this on they attach a wrist mirror and small spiral-bound checklist to the left arm. A food bar and an In-Suit Drink Bag (filled with water) are placed inside the front of the Hard Upper Torso (HUT). Astronauts do not usually take these snacks while on EVA in an effort to avoid having to use the UCD or DACT. The Communications Carrier Assembly (CCA) is a fabric cap with built-in earphones and microphone for use with the EMU radio. It is also called the 'Snoopy Cap' after the cartoon character. Once these preparations have been completed, the astronaut pulls on the lower torso. This consists of pants with boots. It has joints at the hip, knee and ankle, and a metal body-seal closure for connection to the mating half of the ring mounted on the HUT. Twisting and waist movement is made possible by a large bearing at the waist when the feet are held in workstation foot restraints.

To get into the upper torso, the crew member 'dives' upwards into it with arms raised, aligning the upper and lower body-seal closures before making two connections. The first joins the water-cooling tube and ventilation ducting of the LCVG to the Primary Life Support System (PLSS), while the second connects the biomedical monitoring sensors to the EMU electrical harness which is connected to the PLSS. Then the two body-seal closure rings are locked together.

Last to be put on are the helmet and gloves. Fabric comfort gloves with knitted wristlets are worn under the EVA gloves. One glove has a watch sewn into the outer layer, and both gloves have tethers for restraining small tools and equipment.

The astronauts manually check their suits for leaks by elevating the suit pressure before getting rid of any oxygen/nitrogen atmosphere remaining in the cabin. The airlock is depressurized before the astronauts pull themselves through the outer airlock hatch ready to begin their spacewalk.

DESIGN IN THE CYBORG AGE

As early as the mid-1960s, media guru Marshall McLuhan predicted a 'global village'. His vision was of a world made smaller, more accessible, through the medium of electronic communication. The full title of his 1964 book is *Understanding Media, the Extensions of Man*, reflecting his perception of Information Technology (IT) as an enhancement of man's ability to communicate. Popularization of IT is essential if it is to survive. After all, there is little point in communicating if no one else can receive the information. Today it is uncommon to find a house in the Western hemisphere that does not have some or all of the following tools of communication: telephone; answering machine; television; radio; PC, email and Internet. The move towards electronic miniaturization may soon provide the ultimate human–computer interface by rendering the computer invisible. Many of the new products being developed are external devices which act as a prosthetic enhancement of our senses, with a strong emphasis on devices which are responsive, or 'smart'. The area has been slower to develop than many anticipated at the end of the last century. This can in part be attributed to the issue of power and conductive fabrics. Advances such as lithium batteries and wireless technology are addressing this. Although conductive fabrics are available, they are unlikely to gain widespread use until they prove to be as efficient and easy to use as alternative power supply interfaces.

Fashion designer Hussein Chalayan created a ballerina dress for his 2002 Spring/Summer catwalk show. The intention was that the dress should change shape during the show. To achieve this, 45 metres (148 feet) of shape memory metal (or shape memory alloy, SMA) wires were used. These change shape in response to heat that can be applied using electricity. They are usually made from a nickel and titanium alloy. The wires were inserted into the hem and neckline of the dress in a concertina fashion so that the dress would appear to expand by more than the seven per cent that the SMA was capable of. The designer's intention was to house the power source on the model's person, but the energy needed to achieve a fast result was the size of a car battery. It was placed off-stage and part of the performance saw the dress being plugged into the power supply.

Electronic tagging first hit the headlines when it was introduced as a means of keeping watch over prisoners on remand and those recently released from prison. Civil liberty groups were outraged that such technologies should be used on human beings. Radio Frequency Identification (RFID) tagging is also being used in the retail industry. Consumer groups expressed concern that the tags should be used for stock control only and be decommissioned once the customer had purchased the garment. This was in response to suggestions that the tags would allow the garment and its owner to be traced once they had left the shop. British retailer Marks and Spencer attached the RFID tags to the label rather than inserting them invisibly in the hem or seam. This allowed them to be removed at the same time as the price label at the point of sale and has been given a nod of approval by consumer groups.

The new generation of designers and manufacturers using 'smart' materials and systems that respond to changes in their environment is busy finding ways of making their products more personal. This is being done through various means, through the senses and emotions. The RE:Form! Studio at the Interactive Institute in Sweden have developed a Pillow concept as part of their Play series. This looks at the possibilities of combining IT and textiles. The pillows are designed to be interactive as a means of enhancing the experience of long-distance communication. The system works when the user leans against or hugs a pillow in one location causing the textile pattern to be dynamically altered elsewhere. The technology relies on the Internet for communication between the two locations. The pillows themselves have an electroluminescent wire woven into the fabric that can glow and change pattern when activated. A second concept, Reach, relates to wearable technology. It explores the potential for developing a new vocabulary through interactive clothing. Prototypes developed to date incorporate a range of technologies such as fabrics that are sensitive to ultra-violet light, thermochromic inks and electroluminescent wires. The emphasis is on colour, light and audio changes in the garments.

opposite top
FORD MOTOR COMPANY
Third Age Suit

Mindful of elderly drivers needs, Ford have designed the Third Age suit. The designer wears the suit to experience what it feels like to get in and out of the car with less flexible limbs and to drive without twenty-twenty vision. The suit was used in the design of the Ford Focus.

opposite bottom
CLOTHING +
Cyberia I

Clothing + have developed Cyberia I incorporating wearable technology. Designed to be worn in isolated regions, the garment includes devices for monitoring the wearer's health and a GPS system in case they get lost.

below
W&LT by WALTER VAN BEIRENDONCK
Man in Black
Spring/Summer 1997

Reflecting on the little men from Mars in his Man in Black group from the Welcome Little Stranger collection W&LT by Walter van Beirendonck. The T-shirt is made using synthetic jersey incorporating the sound of an alien and eyes that light up when a button is pressed.

At Sweden's Interactive Institute, the RE:Form! Studio created the prototype Pillows as part of their ongoing investigation of how we might want to interact with products in the future. The intention is to make objects more personal, in this case using it as a means of communication between people. The pillows are designed to be interactive as a means of enhancing the experience of long-distance communication. The system works when the user leans against or hugs a pillow in one location causing the textile pattern to be dynamically altered elsewhere. The technology relies on the Internet for communication between the two locations. The pillows themselves have an electroluminescent wire woven into the fabric that can glow and change pattern when activated.

Dutch designer Hella Jongerius has created an installation titled My Soft Office as an indication of how we might combine our home and office in the future. It was commissioned by MOMA New York as part of their exhibition looking at the office.

THE ARTIST AND THE CYBORG

Artists are becoming technologists and technologists artists in the area of electronics and textiles. From the artist's point of view the move is practical. Benoît Maubrey has been working with electroacoustic clothes since 1983. In order to realize his performance pieces he and his team, Die Audio Gruppe, had to become proficient in audio systems though they also employ the expertise of electronics specialists. Inspired by a PA system in a department store, he decided that instead of painting colours, he could 'speak' them through the air. In *Audio Jackets*, he transformed second-hand jackets into a mobile PA system using old loudspeakers, 10-watt amplifiers, batteries and personal stereos. The recordings were made by friends of the artist; the wearers of the Audio Jackets then strolled around as a mobile sound sculpture. The early work was not tightly choreographed, and movement and sound were left to each performer. There were some technical problems, and the sound was often drowned by traffic and other noise. The group's more sophisticated *Audio Ballerinas* used solar cells instead of 12-volt batteries to provide the energy source. The cells, with speakers, microphone jacks and amplifiers, were all on the surface of the ballerinas' transparent Plexiglas tutus. The new

equipment picked up sounds, and amplified and repeated them in a loop format. This allowed the performers to dispense with the Walkmans and pre-recorded cassettes. It also gave them more control over the sound, as they could change the speed of the loop. The photovoltaic cells mounted on the tutus reacted to sunlight by emitting a high-pitched sound, almost like a Geiger counter responding to radioactive substances.

The performance artist Stelarc presents the body as a pacified, almost anaesthetized recipient of the cyborg state. He has used the term zombie on occasion to refer to the degree to which the human will bends to the will of the mechanical prosthesis used in his work. He works with a range of technical experts that include surgeons, electronics and biotechnology professionals in order to realize his work. In *Ping Body* the physical body is no longer stimulated by its own internal nervous system. Instead it responds to the ebb and flow of data on the Internet. The body is not activated by a single Internet user but by the collective activity of users. By random 'pinging' to Internet domains, spatial distance is mapped transmitting time to body motion and effectively choreographing the performance.

Stelarc's piece entitled *MOVATAR* could be described as an inverse motion capture system. Instead of a body animating

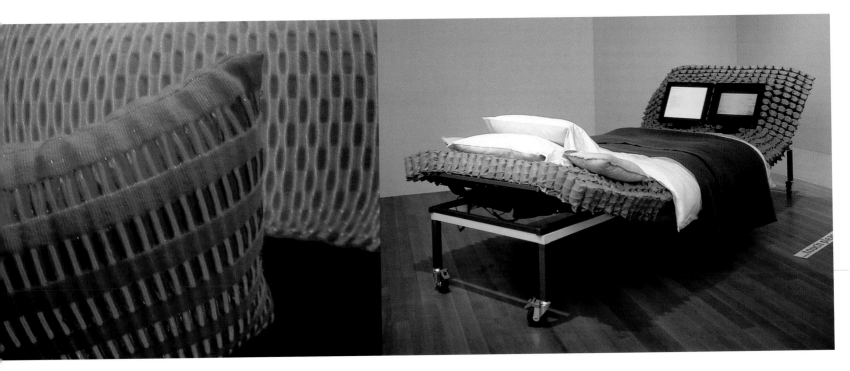

a computer entity, it allows an avatar to perform in the real world by possessing a physical body. This is done by enveloping the upper torso in a prosthesis that controls motion. Restricted to three degrees of freedom for each arm, there are however sixty-four possible combinations. The body is split not left from right but torso from legs. The arms are directed by the avatar, but the legs are free to move as the human host wishes. This in turn can modulate the avatar's behaviour. Stelarc regards the avatar as a viral life form, seeing it as benign and passive as a computer entity, but when it has a body as a host it can affect behaviour. It is

visualized as a doppelgänger human in form and limb movements.

International Fashion Machines (IFM) has been set up by Maggie Orth, a graduate of the wearable technology group at Massachusetts Institute of Technology (MIT) Media Lab. She has migrated from wearable computers to running a company specializing in electronically altering the colour and pattern of textiles. As with several graduates from MIT's Wearable Technology group, she is keen to have the work shown in the context of an artwork. The two main technologies being developed by the company are Electric Plaid (patent pending) and

BENOÎT MAUBREY/DIE AUDIO GRUPPE
Audio Peacock costume

Benoît Maubrey/Die Audio Gruppe have created an Audio Peacock costume using a white polycarbonate plexiglass. This is used as a mobile projection screen during the performance where images are shown on the performer's costume. The performer forms the basis of the narrative as they move and talk over what becomes their own hallucinogenic dream.

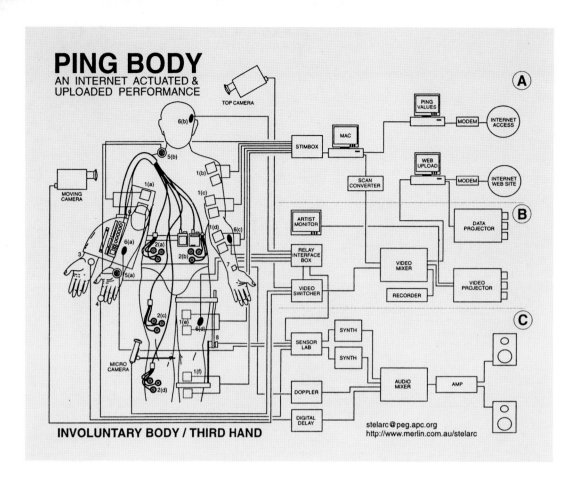

PING BODY
AN INTERNET ACTUATED & UPLOADED PERFORMANCE

INVOLUNTARY BODY / THIRD HAND

stelarc@peg.apc.org
http://www.merlin.com.au/stelarc

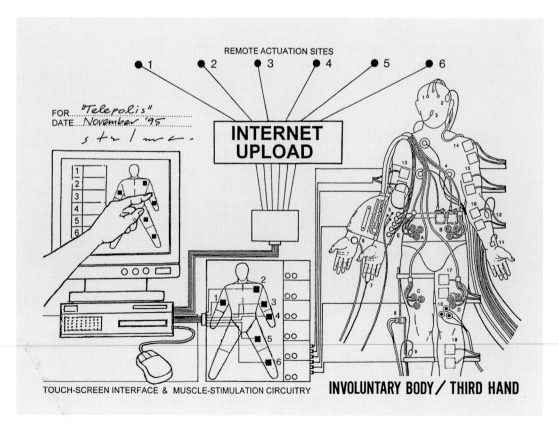

REMOTE ACTUATION SITES

INTERNET UPLOAD

TOUCH-SCREEN INTERFACE & MUSCLE-STIMULATION CIRCUITRY

INVOLUNTARY BODY / THIRD HAND

SwitchSwitch technologies. Electric Plaid combines electronic circuits with thermochromic inks, using the former to heat the inks and thereby change colour. This causes the pattern to change slowly over time. The second technology, SwitchSwitch, refers to textile sensors that can be used in conjunction with Electric Plaid to create an interactive fabric or textile artwork. Though the fabric is essentially a 'smart' material, sensing and responding to its environment, the aim is purely aesthetic.

When the television was first introduced into the home there was a great fear that it would lead to wholesale illiteracy. Half a century on, books have never been more popular. With the advent of the computer as a design tool and potential for wearable electronics there is now a fear that the human element in design will be made redundant. If anything, CAD has encouraged even greater creativity. Designers can experiment with different colourways in a fraction of the time they could manually. The light-based medium with its intensity of colour has also encouraged greater use of strong colours. While wearable technology initially emerged from space and military programmes, now that they have entered the consumer market they have been quick to tackle ergonomic, tactile and general aesthetic issues. The computer and electronics are being treated as they should be, as tools and enablers enhancing good creative design.

opposite
STELARC
Ping Body

In Ping Body the Australian performance artist Stelarc uses collective Internet activity to move the artist's body. Ping values are used to activate a multiple muscle stimulator directing 0–60 volts to the body, thereby choreographing the performance.

right
INTERNATIONAL FASHION MACHINES (IFM)
Dynamic Double Weave I

International Fashion Machines' Dynamic Double Weave I is a textile artwork designed to include Electric Plaid technology. Consisting of eight handwoven panels, each incorporates the technology to allow eight unique colour change areas, effectively creating a 64-pixel display in woven textiles.

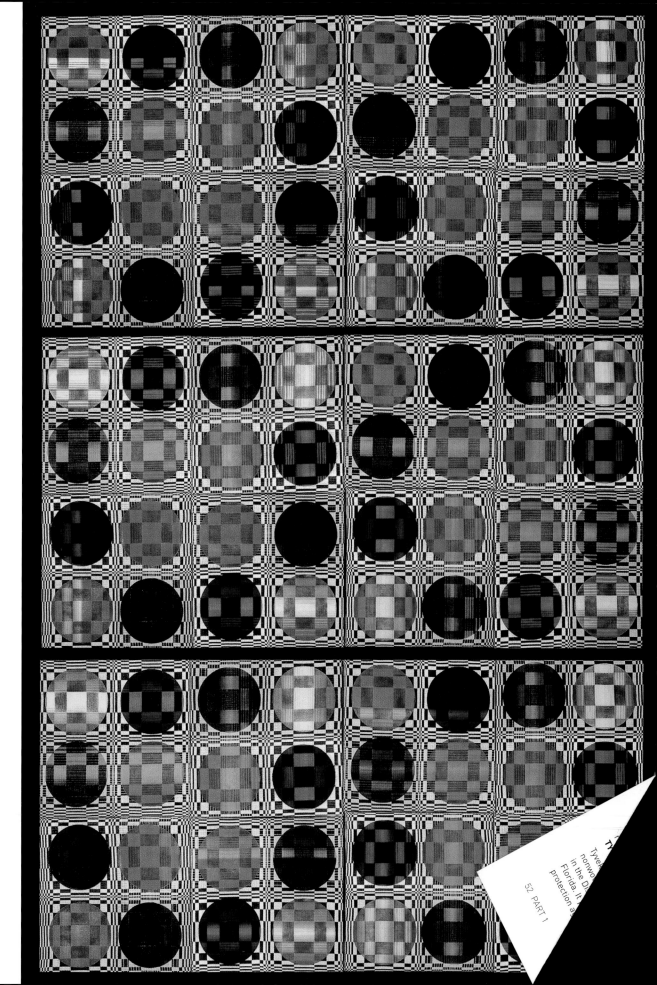

Engineered textiles

Marie O'Mahony

top left
GREEN-TEK
Aluminet

Aluminet is a hortisynthetic fabric designed to protect plants against harsh sunlight with its aluminized coating.

top right
ALPHA
Woven glass fibre

Alpha's woven glass fibre is coated with a synthetic rubber, fully cured then laminated to a Tedlar film. This works as a vapour barrier and is laminated to a corrosion-resistant metallized polyester.

right above
TYVEK

Tyvek used to be difficult to colour and paint onto. DuPont have developed the technology to do this so that decorative surfaces are now becoming commercially available.

right
TYVEK

DuPont's polyolefin
oven, lining walls of a building
ney town of Celebration in
rovides insulation and
ainst rain.

The degree to which it is possible to engineer textiles today is truly astonishing. Development is being driven by industrial applications. There is an increasing need for fabrics that can combine strength and functionality with lightness in weight and competitive costing. In a growing trend, textiles are being considered as alternatives to heavier materials such as metals. New and improved manufacturing processes have played an important role. So also has collaboration between academia and industry. Much of the development is focused in the northern European countries of Germany, Belgium, the UK, the Netherlands and France. Important trade fairs such as TechTextil in Frankfurt and IFAI in the USA act as a showcase and forum for dialogue.

Functionality is the driving force behind engineered fabrics. However, manufacturers are becoming more aware of the design market and the need for an aesthetic element. Nonwovens intended for unseen use below ground are suddenly being used by fashion designers, much to the surprise of

manufacturers. Industrial applications themselves are changing. In the automotive and aerospace industries there is a move to reduce the number of components, and that includes materials. To remain competitive, materials must serve as many functions as possible. That may include strength and rigidity, alongside a soft surface texture and pattern.

Environmental issues have created a whole textile industry of geosynthetics while also making things more difficult for the manufacturer. The life cycle of a fabric now has to be accounted for, from raw material through to its disposal. Fierce competition and increasing market demands are making engineered fabrics one of the most exciting and high-performing areas of the textile industry.

NONWOVENS

There is some debate about what can be correctly termed a nonwoven. The International Organization for Standardization

(ISO) considers it to include manufactured sheet, web or bat consisting of directionally or randomly orientated fibres. These can be bonded by friction, cohesion or adhesion. However, this is a rather narrow definition. Felts, stitch-bonded and paper-like materials are commonly regarded as nonwovens.

The manufacturing process is dictated by the end use of a nonwoven, and this is also the main means of classification. There are a number of standard techniques. The addition of resins, bonding and finishing techniques ensure that the material can be tailored to specific functions. A dry-laid nonwoven can be produced by carding or air-laying to create a web. The card process for staple fibres usually results in a web of parallel fibres, with cross-lapping added for additional strength. Randomly orientated fibres allow a lighter material to be produced. The technique of air-laying is especially suitable for very short staple fibres like fluff pulp. The fibres are fed into an air stream before being deposited on a moving belt or perforated drum to form a softer web structure. Wet-laying is based on the traditional papermaking process. A mixture of fibres and water is deposited on a moving screen before being drained to form a web. The material is then consolidated between rollers and allowed to dry. The technique of spunlaid, or spunbonded, nonwovens combines the fibre laying with the bonding process.

Nonwovens can be further classified by the bonding method used. A common bond is a chemical or adhesion bond. This impregnates the web with a bonding agent such as a polymer resin in solution, powder or foam form. Thermal or cohesion bonding works by applying heat to a web that contains some thermoplastic fibres. Mechanical or friction bonding entangles the fibres and strengthens the web through a system such as needlepunching. Hydro-entanglement, or spun-lacing, uses fine jets of water at high pressure to entangle the fibres. Meltblowing means that the nonwoven is directly formed from a thermoplastic polymer, usually polypropylene.

BFF Nonwovens have developed a patented carbonate process, a method of activated carbon impregnation. By effectively locking the particles into a nonwoven matrix, the dust contamination caused by loose powder or granules can be avoided. Almost any fibre can be chemically bonded in the process, resulting in a very versatile dry-laid fabric. Weight, density and surface finish are tailored to meet individual demands through the addition of chemical impregnates. The material is highly absorbent. Applications could include oil and water removal filters as well as odour prevention in medical dressings. The automotive industry uses substantial quantities of nonwovens. An estimated 15 to 20 square metres (160 to 215 square feet) of textile surface is used in the

below
VERASOL
Print on metal

Verasol's metallic print (left) is an emboss on metal and designed for use in window blinds; its three-dimensional metallic fabric (right) is also designed to provide solar shade.

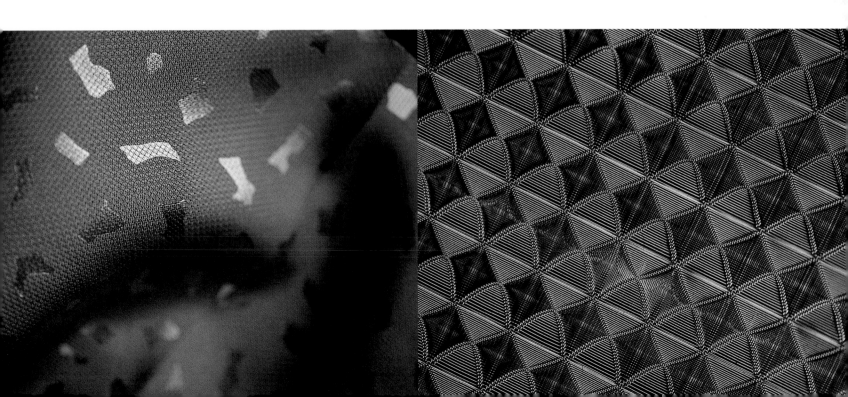

average car (excluding carpet) for sound deadening. Most of this is nonwoven. BFF Nonwovens have produced a mouldable car-bonnet lining face fabric which has a zero burn rate and good sound insulation. This nonwoven uses fibres impregnated with synthetic resin, using a chemical bond process.

Superabsorbent fibres are used in specialized applications such as sanitary products and filtration. The fibres are based on polymers which can absorb many times their own weight of aqueous liquid and retain the fluid under pressure. The polymers were initially available in powder, granular or bead form, and fibres are a relatively recent innovation. Oasis is a superabsorbent fibre produced by Technical Absorbents Ltd. It is based on a cross-linked acrylate copolymer which has been partially neutralized. The fibre is white, odourless and non-flammable. It can be manufactured into a nonwoven through air- or wet-laying techniques.

Although the superabsorbent fibres are more expensive than other forms of the polymer, they do have some advantages. Fibres are easier to incorporate into fabrics, for instance, and they are found to be more stable in a structure. One application identified for the Oasis yarn is as an industrial pipe seal. The yarn is wound into the thread of the pipe, swelling on contact with water and thereby providing an effective seal. Another possible application would be in the seams of waterproof and other protective clothing.

GEOSYNTHETICS

The generic term 'geosynthetics' refers to textile fabrics which are permeable to fluids. It is also applied to related products, such as geogrids, geomeshes, geonets, geomats, and in fact most porous flexible materials which are used in or on soil. Impermeable materials in this context are referred to as geomembranes.

One of the earliest examples of geosynthetics was built around 1400 BC, and still stands. The structure, Ziggurat Aqar Quf, was built close to present-day Baghdad. It originally measured about 45 metres (150 feet) high, and was built using clay blocks which were reinforced with woven reed mats laid horizontally. Our modern geotextiles were first used in the mid 1950s by the Dutch in the Deltaplan, an ambitious project to prevent the sea flooding the southwestern delta region of the Netherlands. They used coarse handwoven fabrics made from extruded nylon tapes to provide mattresses as protection for the seabed of the East Schelde estuary. Nylon bags filled with sand were attached to the mattresses, making them sink.

Reinforcement remains one of the main functions of geosynthetics today, with separation, filtration and drainage. Geomembranes perform a very different function, acting as fluid barriers. All these fabrics have a vital role to play in the protection and redevelopment of urban and rural landscapes.

GEOTEXTILES

The two main types of geotextiles are woven and nonwoven. Occasionally, natural fibres are used in the making of geotextiles, but most use some form of polymeric fibre such as polypropylene, polyamide or polyester. The yarn chosen depends on cost and on the physical properties (thickness per mass), mechanical properties (strength and deformation) and hydraulic properties (permeability).

The range of woven and nonwoven geotextile applications is extensive. One use in temporary road construction is to separate the granular fill material in the road surface from the soft ground beneath. In instances where wear on the ground surface is severe, a geotextile can be used to provide soil separation as well as some physical support. The role of geotextiles is more extensive in permanent road construction. Here, they are used on their own, or combined with geogrids for reinforcement. Individually or combined, these materials can provide sub-structure support, ground drainage and erosion control, and prevent reflective cracking.

The small island of Chek Lap Kok measures just 3 square kilometres (almost 2 square miles). In order to house Hong Kong Airport it has been enlarged to form part of a manmade island measuring 12 square kilometres (7½ square miles). The island has been levelled out at 6 to 7 metres (20 to 23 feet) above sea level, with material being pumped from the bottom of the sea for land reclamation. An estimated 367 million cubic metres (13 billion cubic feet) of stones, sand, gravel and mud had to be moved to the island before construction could begin. A heavy grade of

Fibertex nonwoven geotextile is used to protect 13 kilometres (8 miles) of coastline.

Ground drainage is an important function of geotextiles. By close contact with the soil, the fabric allows the soil to filter itself. The textile can simply wrap the drain, but a more recent development is the fin drain which is a thin, multi-layered, yet two-dimensional sheet, which usually consists of a moulded plastic sheet sandwiched between two geotextile fabric layers. The geotextiles act as a filter for water passing through, with the plastic element bringing the water to the outflow point. The system is being used beside roads and railway tracks as well as for agricultural drainage.

Landfill and waste disposal sites create a number of difficult problems which are now being tackled by the industry. Methane gas is generated by decomposing natural materials, as well as in industrial environments. Gases can also migrate upwards from worked coal seams and even from undisturbed rock formations. The geotextile used in this instance will absorb the hazardous gas, allowing it to continue upwards, selectively releasing it to ground drains which remove the gas rapidly and prevent it from accumulating. An impermeable geomembrane can be fitted below the geotextile if the hazard is waste, or above if the problem is likely to come from below ground.

GEOGRIDS, GEONETS, GEOMESHES AND GEOMATS

The main function of geogrids and related structures is to act as reinforcement. Typical applications include the reinforcement of vertical soil walls, and steep rock or soil slopes. The usual method is an interlocking between the grid and the substance it is reinforcing. The mechanical interlock creates a flexible but stiff platform which can distribute the load evenly. Geonets, geomeshes and geomats all have a similar function, each with its own subtle variations. Polypropylene and polyethylene are the most commonly used materials. However, the main distinction between these different structures lies in their method of production. This is what gives each its unique performance characteristics.

Sheets used in the manufacture of geogrids are extruded before being punched or pierced at regular intervals. The sheet is first drawn in the direction in which the machine is working. The holes in the sheet can be extended to become grid apertures. This induces molecular orientation in the direction of the draw. The result is a uniaxially orientated geogrid. The sheet can then be drawn in the cross-machine direction, widening the apertures and producing a biaxially orientated grid. The resulting structure has a very sophisticated stress-strain distribution under tensile load.

The UK company Netlon produces one of the most comprehensive ranges of geogrids, meshes and mats in their Tensar range. Tensar SS20 is made from high-strength polypropylene which has been orientated in two directions during manufacturing. The squared apertures allow the stone or soil aggregate to be layered on top. A common application for this material is in forest roads and car parks. Tensar ARG has the same grid structure, with the addition of a layer of polyester fabric. Here the fabric element is used to bond the grid to the existing surface using bitumen. The fabric absorbs the bitumen, forming a water-resistant layer, while the grid prevents the asphalt from cracking or rotting. It is often used in the asphalt layers of a road or runway surface. Tensar 80RE is a uniaxial grid, characterized by long slim apertures. The strength is concentrated in the direction of the roll length. Again made from polypropylene, it is used for soil reinforcement in the construction of steep slopes or retaining walls. Tensar Mat is made from high strength polyethylene. The extruded polymer sheets are punched with an array of regularly shaped and spaced apertures. This can then be heated and stretched to provide a high strength grid. The geomat is used for soil erosion control where it can be combined with vegetation. The plants add reinforcement and further help to combat erosion.

GEOMEMBRANES

Geomembranes differ from other forms of geotextiles in that they are impermeable to water. Most geomembranes are manufactured from some form of polymer, such as butyl rubber, chlorinated polyethylene, elasticized polyolefin or polyvinyl chloride. Chemical and petrochemical companies begin the process by producing polymers in the form of solid pellets, flakes or granules.

opposite
NETLON
Tensar geonets and geomeshes

From top to bottom: Tensar SS20 allows stone or soil aggregate to be layered on top; Tensar AG incorporates a water-resistant layer and bonded grid; Tensar 80RE is used for soil reinforcement; and Tensar Mat is combined with vegetation for soil erosion control .

below
UCO TECHNICAL FABRICS
Geosynthetics

Diagram showing some of the ways in which geosynthetics can be used to strengthen roads.

following pages 56–57
Photomicrographs of typical geosynthetic fabric structures

(top row, l to r) woven extruded flat tape; needlepunched continuous filament nonwoven; underside of warp-knitted geotextile; woven fibrillated slit-film tape
(middle row, l to r) woven fibrillated tape yarn; woven multifilament-on-monofilament; excelsior geomat; woven multifilament
(bottom row, l to r) woven coir yarn geomesh; topside of warp-knitted geotextile; woven extruded tape-on-monofilament; fleeced extruded tape-on-tape.

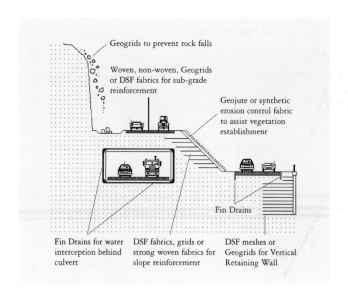

top
CELEBRATION, FLORIDA
Hortisynthetic

This hortisynthetic in Celebration town is used to stop bugs and wildlife entering the garden. Despite the lush vegetation in the Florida town it can be eerily quiet. Legend has it that the town is sprayed twice a year to destroy insects.

above
GREEN-TEK
Shade-Rite

Shade-Rite from Green-Tek is a hortisynthetic used to protect seedlings from excessive heat or from being eaten by wildlife.

opposite top
DOROTHEA REESE-HEIM
Tetralogie Metrik im Raum

The German artist Dorothea Reese-Heim uses composite technologies such as glass fibre reinforced with resin as well as copper in this sculpture.

opposite bottom
ALPHA
Glass fibre

This glass fibre from Alpha has been laminated to an aluminium foil and is awaiting further processing.

These are then heated to melting point before being extruded, or drawn, through a cooling process to form yarn or flat sheets. Geomembranes are used in the construction of lagoons, waste-disposal liners, wherever there is a need for water containment.

It is rare to find geomembranes used in isolation. They are more usually combined with other geotextiles. In this way each brings its own benefit to what eventually becomes a composite structure. A typical waste-disposal liner system might start with a cushion textile above the soil. This protects the geomembrane which is laid on top. Above the membrane there may be a layer of clay, protecting the membrane from direct contact with any chemicals or from physical damage by the waste. A slightly more sophisticated system could include a further geotextile laid over the membrane. This might have an embedded wire mesh to protect against rodents. Drainage and leak detection systems could also be added to help maintain and monitor the site.

The Belgian company UCO Performance Fabrics have produced a system which can detect and locate leaks beneath waste-disposal sites. This is achieved electronically, using an Electric Leak Detection Geotextile (ELDEG). INOX wires are woven into the warp direction of a polypropylene geotextile. The steel wire is strong and inert with high conductivity. Two layers of ELDEG are placed in the ground at right angles to each other, with another geotextile sandwiched between to separate them. Each wire is connected to a centralized computer system, which allows the system to be monitored as a grid. Any leaks would cause an alteration in the system's electric current and thus be detected and located immediately.

As concern for the environment continues to grow, so does the importance of the geo-synthetics industry. The layering of materials in many applications implies that there is an increasing demand for multiple functions. Today's geosynthetics do not simply reinforce what is there. They perform other vital functions, such as continued safety monitoring. With growing disquiet over contaminated land, there is an urgent need for a geosynthetic that will render chemicals and waste harmless. At the present rate of progress, it seems only a matter of time before this is possible.

HORTIFABRICS

The term hortifabrics refers to textiles, nets and membranes used for horticultural applications above ground level. The function is generally protective: keeping excessive heat, birds or insects away from seedlings and small plants, for instance. The majority of manufacturers and users are located in North America.

Aluminized thermal screens are one of the most common hortisynthetics and are produced by a number of American companies such as Plaspack USA Inc. and Green-Tek. Green-Tek produce Aluminet and Shade-Rite, two variations on solar protection for plants.

Aluminet is an aluminized thermal screen that acts like a mirror, reflecting excessive sunlight during summer and conserving heat during the winter. The net-like fabric is knitted using a mono-orientated aluminized high density polypropylene (HDPE).

Shade Rite also uses HDPE and comes in black, white or green and is also knitted but using a lockstitch construction giving the net a triangular pattern. This effectively creates thousands of small air vents, putting less wind stress on the structure while providing ventilation at the same time. The ultra-violet (UV) protection varies from 30 to 90 per cent depending on how close the knit is. The higher the density the better thermal insulation provided.

The company also manufacture protective insect screens, some with holes of only 150 microns. These are woven using a polyethylene monofilament with a high tensile strength. The transparent structure is UV-stabilized with an expected lifespan of three to five years.

HYBRID MATERIALS

Industries are increasingly replacing heavier materials with part textile (flexible), part non-textile (glass, carbon, metal and ceramic) hybrids. These offer high performance but with reduced weight, an important consideration in many industries, including construction, aerospace and automobile industries. The availability of these materials is bringing some innovative design solutions to many problems. Carbon-impregnated fabrics improve the resistance of concrete structures to seismic shock. Chimneys and other large structures can be wrapped by simply coiling the fabric. In the automobile industry, E-glass roving is being used in silencers, as a replacement for basalt wool. This sound-deadening material remains intact under the stresses of heat, vapours and condensation. E-glass allows designers to use flatten silencers, which creates more space in the boot of the car. In the sports industry, one of the most dramatic design changes has already occurred in tennis. When carbon fibre-based materials were first used to manufacture tennis rackets the design altered substantially. Carbon fibre behaves in a very different way from wood and all the other materials that it and other hybrids are now replacing.

GLASS

There are three basic types of glass fibre: E-glass is the most common and least expensive; S-glass is stronger and is used where strength is at a premium; C-glass exhibits a high degree of chemical stability and is used for corrosion resistance. The fibres are made by drawing heated glass through small holes in electrically heated bushings (made of platinum, rhodium or other precious metal alloys) to form filaments. The diameter is determined by the size of hole through which it is drawn, as well as the temperature (about 1260°C or 2300°F).

The viscosity of the melt and the rate of cooling are also important factors. Once drawn, the fibres are water- and air-cooled before being coated with a chemical binder. This coating protects the delicate filament during subsequent handling. The sizing can be removed at a later stage and replaced by a finish and coupling agent. The purpose of the chemical finish is to enhance the compatibility of the fibre with the polymer matrix, while a coupling agent creates a bond between the silane structure of the glass and the polymer resin. Finishes, such as antistatic agents and lubricants, can be added depending on the manufacturing process to follow, and the intended use.

Microlith is a glass fibre manufactured by Schuller. The fibre is made by being drawn through platinum spinning nozzles at a temperature of about 1200°C (2190°F)

before being spun into a yarn. Continuing improvements in weaving looms are making it much easier to weave with glass fibres. Because there is less damage to the loom, the cost of these fabrics is slowly coming down.

Companies such as Schuller and P-D Interglas Technologies Ltd are producing glass fibre wall coverings mainly for use in offices and public buildings. The fabric can be woven in a traditional diamond or herringbone weave, before being painted with a latex paint. Unsurprisingly, this is more expensive than conventional wall coverings, but it does offer additional benefits. The build-up of static electricity is very low, for instance, which is an important consideration in computer-rich office environments. The use of natural minerals – quartz sand, soda, lime and dolomite – in the fibre structure ensures that the material is free of toxic components, making it a healthy environment to live and work in.

Once woven, glass fibres can be given a range of coatings to suit individual applications. Alpha is a British division of P-D Interglas Technologies Ltd. As the name suggests, the company specialize in coatings and laminates for industrial fabrics. They produce a wide range of woven fibreglass with various finishes, including silicone rubber, Neoprene and Teflon.

Alpha Martinex 8403-2-5W is a heavy duty satin weave fabric which has been coated with a specially formulated silicone rubber on both sides. The glass fibre makes it fire-retardant, while the finish allows it to be steam-cleaned. The fabric is used for roofing membranes. Alpha Martinex 'Teflon' is coated with Teflon to give protection against chemicals. This fabric can withstand temperatures ranging from -35°C (-31°F) to 260°C (500°F). Alpha Sil 90-2220 was developed to replace asbestos fabrics where protection against extreme heat is needed. It uses pre-shrunk silica fibre and is particularly effective in providing protection against splashes of molten metal. A Neoprene coating is used in the Alpha Alaflex 1032-2-BN to provide resistance to abrasion, grease and oil absorption. Like all these fabrics, it is intended for industrial applications, such as flexible ducts and tarpaulins.

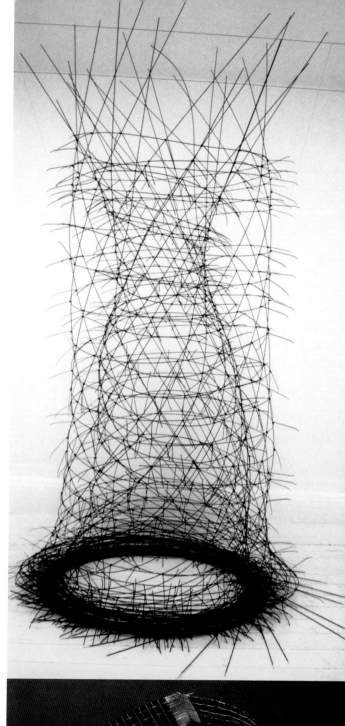

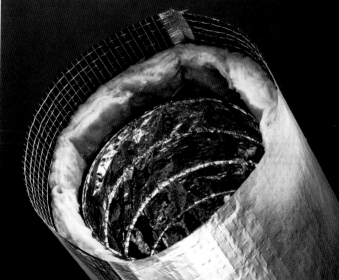

METAL

Today's workplaces have a high concentration of electronic equipment, which can cause problems. High-frequency transmitters used in communication and micro-processing equipment can cause interference with the equipment itself. The problem is widespread from offices to hospitals, and it can go undetected for some time. The traditional way to install a shielded room system has been to use zinc-plated mild steel plates or a heavy steel. Recent developments in metal fibres and finishes have prompted a number of companies to develop solutions which have the combined benefit of being lightweight and easy to install. The Belgian company NV Schlegel are producing Isowave, a copper-plated nonwoven material. The basic fabric is made from nylon fibres. These are covered with metal particles which bond with the cell structure of the fibre. The result is a smooth, uniform finish, with the nonwoven retaining its dimensional stability, and its resistance to corrosion and tearing. The fabric is applied in a similar way to wallpaper and can be covered with carpet or wallpaper. DLMI produce a knitted fabric for similar applications. The company specializes in knitted fabrics which combine fibre with a range of metals, including copper, silvered copper and copper alloys. The fabric is self-adhesive with a removable peel-away card backing.

Bekintex produce Bekitex, a stainless-steel fibre which can be knitted, woven or braided. Bekitex is a brand name for textile yarn which includes a percentage of Bekinox, and it is usually used where the latter cannot be applied directly to a material such as polypropylene tape. The main use of Bekitex is in static control in a variety of products from carpets to bulk containers, where spark discharges might cause an explosion. Bekinox is used in a continuous filament form in the manufacture of anti-static brushes for fax machines and photocopiers, where it helps to prevent malfunction due to the build-up of static electricity. Bekitherm is knitted, woven or needlepunched either in 100 per cent metal or in a blend of metal and manmade or natural fibres. It has been found to be particularly useful in the manufacture of complex glass and metal forms where it acts as a separator between the material and the mould, cushioning against optic defects. Applications include car windows, television tubes and stainless-steel cooking saucepans.

The speciality knit company Tec-Knit have recently launched a low current heating system made of integrated metal fabrics. Copper and nickel alloys are used with textile filament reinforcement to form a mesh system. The material can be manufactured in large sheets or three-dimensional shapes, which makes it very flexible. BMW have developed a heatable car steering wheel, but

above and top
SOPHIE ROET
Metallized fabrics

As part of the Hitec-Lotec project (see Chapter 6, pp. 137–38), textile designer Sophie Roet worked with Alpha to realize metallized fabrics suitable for fashion and interiors. Silks and other lightweight fabrics were combined with the metal foils to create a range of textiles that can be formed by hand to create three-dimensional shapes. The fabrics can be smoothed by hand to regain their original shape.

right
DLMI
Metallized fabrics

This selection of knitted metal and metal coated fabrics from French manufacturer DLMI can be used to line the walls of offices to protect workers from electromagnetic radiation.

BEKINTEX
Stainless steel fibre

Bekintex stainless steel fibres and yarns have the gloss and drape of silk but carry the weight of a metal.

NV SCHLEGEL
Isowave

NV Schlegel produce Isowave to protect against electromagnetic interference. Though a fabric, it can be installed like wallpaper and painted over.

DLMI
Metallized fabrics

Metallized fabrics can be produced as weave, knit, and nonwoven fabrics as well as tape. Applications range from conventional linings for walls to shirts and underwear.

the material could also be used for car seats, truck tarpaulins (to thaw snow) and even to transport molten chocolate where a constant temperature has to be maintained.

Metallic finishes are increasingly being used to provide a protective coating for many fabrics. Alpha produce several of these fabrics, mainly for industrial uses such as duct or pipe insulation. Alpha Alaflex 4315 MA is a flat tube of aluminized polyester film, coated with a black elastomeric compound, then laminated to a fibreglass scrim. The Alpha Martinex 84215/ 9480/AA1S is a heavier fabric designed to act as a car heat shield. It also provides protection against radiant heat for fuel lines. The fabric is a lamination of glass fibre and aluminium foil, with a high temperature resin backwash to protect the exposed fabric surface from fraying. Alpha Temp VRP-3 is a lightweight three-ply laminate. A white vinyl facing backed with a metallized polyester film is bonded to a fibreglass scrim with a high-performance flame-retardant adhesive. It is used as a facing on metal-clad building insulators or ceiling boards where it acts as a vapour barrier.

CARBON

Carbon fibres are now being produced in many forms. These include yarns, woven, nonwoven and composite structures. The aeronautics and leisure industries value carbon fibre's qualities of strength, odour absorption, fatigue resistance, vibration absorption and electrical conductivity. Deprived of oxygen, natural carbon becomes an inorganic insulator which is resistant to high temperatures.

Protective and, in particular, cleanroom clothing has found a number of applications for textiles containing conductive yarns, such as those utilizing carbon. Cleanrooms were first developed in the United States in the early 1960s around the time of the first manned space programme. The term is now used to refer to a wide range of industrial manufacturing processes that are carried out in contamination-controlled environments, such as the production and assembly of semiconductors. Klopman International are one of the companies specializing in fabrics suitable for cleanroom clothing, using conductive yarns in the Superbandmaster fabrics, for instance. These lightweight

above
MITSUBISHI RAYON CO. LTD
Solar-powered car

Mitsubishi Rayon Co. Ltd have designed and manufactured a solar powered car. The main body of the car uses Pyrofil carbon fibre to ensure that it is as lightweight as possible and uses low energy.

right
MITSUBISHI RAYON CO. LTD
Pyrofil

Mitsubishi Rayon's Pyrofil carbon fibre is manufactured by carbonizing polyacrylonitrile (PAN) fibres at a high temperature.

opposite
LINDA WORBIN
Prototype for fabric with interactive pattern

Carbon fibre being used for its conductive properties in this prototype by Swedish designer Linda Worbin. The fibre is woven into the fabric (top) and when a voltage is applied (middle), the heat activates a thermochromic ink and the fabric changes colour in a pre-selected pattern (bottom).

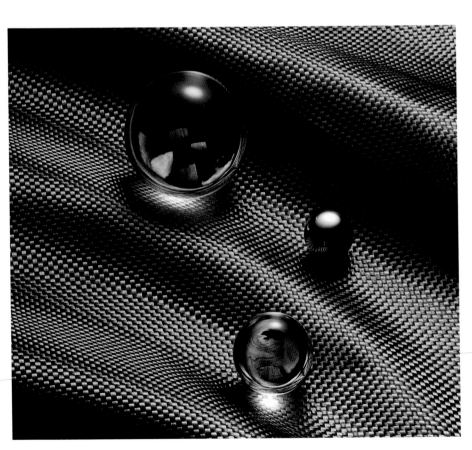

fabrics are made of a blend of polyester and cotton, and are designed to withstand repeated washings. They are used in healthcare, food manufacturing, and the hotel and catering industries. The conductive yarns provide the fabric with anti-static characteristics and are woven into the fabric in a grid format.

Cleantec was a brand name used by Multifabs for their fabrics for cleanroom clothing. The polyester fabric used less than one per cent carbon fibre. The weft fibre was Pontella, a microfibre with moisture-wicking properties – this ensured that the fabric remained soft and comfortable to wear. The emphasis in all these garments was light weight, comfort and performance.

The aeroplane cockpit is an electronics-rich environment which needs to be protected from electrostatic discharge from the human body. Unchecked, there is a real danger of static discharge which could ignite flammable atmospheres such as aviation fuel vapours. This effect is usually counteracted by making the aircrew's clothing conductive, using anti-static chemicals, but, because the chemicals rely on moisture, their effectiveness is reduced in low humidity. A consortium led by ML Lifeguard Equipment Ltd have developed a solution to this problem. P140 is a carbon-loaded core surrounded by carbon fibre. The fibre is protected by a polymer skin which is then inserted in a Nomex Delta anti-static fabric. The carbon concentrates the electric field of static charge which builds up in the fabric. Once the charge has reached a high level, a discharge will occur by ionizing the air. This reduces the charge in the fabric and prevents further build-up. The fibre has been used in anti-static clothing designed for the aircrew of the Eurofighter 2000 combat aircraft.

The combination of strength and lightness in weight means that carbon fibres are increasingly being used to replace metals. DIALEAD and Pyrofil are two of Mitsubishi Rayon's carbon fibre materials. DIALEAD is made from an ultra-high modulus carbon which is pitch-based. Pyrofil is supplied to manufacturers either as pellets for moulding or as woven fabric. Pyrofil's high rigidity and X-ray permeability make it ideal for use in hospital X-ray beds. Its strength and light weight have proved an asset in many sports and automotive applications.

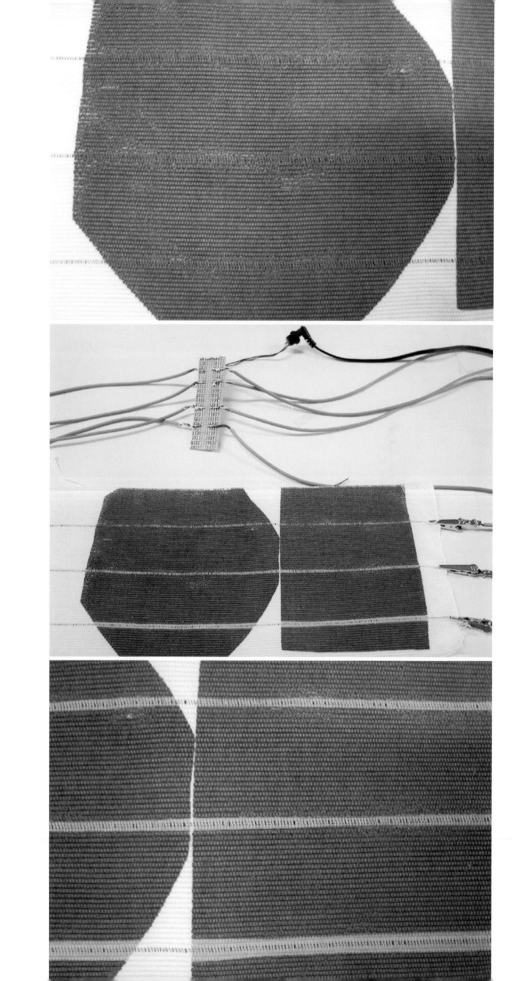

below left
RIVAL
Children's swimsuit

With a growing awareness of the danger of ultra-violet light many sportswear companies are producing UV-protective swimwear. Both the overall design and choice of fabric is designed to safeguard the wearer. Australian designers Rival have produced this children's swimsuit. It covers a large portion of the arms, legs and neck using a UV-protective and chlorine-resistant fabric.

below right
SHANGHAI-FU KNITTING CO.
UV-protective fabric

The Shanghai Fu Knitting Co. Ltd have produced a range of UV-protective fabric for swimwear. Coming in blue and brown colourways, these stripy fabrics use ceramic to provide the UV-protective element.

opposite left
FAIREY INDUSTRIAL CERAMICS
Ceramic foam

Fairey Industrial Ceramics produce this porous ceramic as an open-cell structure to produce a sponge-like material. The foam is impregnated with oxides before being fired. The high temperature during the firing process burns away the foam substrate leaving behind a ceramic foam. It is used to filter molten metal.

opposite right
MARCEL WANDERS/DROOG
DESIGN/ROSENTHAL
Sponge Vase

In designing this ceramic vase Marcel Wanders has applied the same principle as is used in the production of industrial ceramic foam. He has used a natural sponge and the result is a fine porcelain vase. The project was part of a commission from Rosenthal to Droog Design.

CERAMIC

One of the most outstanding characteristics of ceramic fibres is their ability to withstand very high temperatures without deformation or loss of tensile strength. The reason for this resistance to thermal shock is the ability of the fibres to move in relation to one another, thereby relieving any thermo-mechanical stress. 3M's Nextel ceramic fibres are made from continuous polycrystalline metal oxide fibres. The ceramic fibres can be used to manufacture textiles in a conventional weaving and braiding process, without the need for metal inserts or another fibre. Besides low thermal conductivity, the fibres offer good insulation and chemical resistance. Nextel is used for energy control in furnace curtains, for instance, and as thermal protection for gaskets and seals. A new product has been developed for diesel particle filtration. The cartridge filters are made by winding Nextel fibre around a perforated metal tube. One end of the tube is blocked, forcing the exhaust gas through the ceramic fibre where the soot particles are retained. The filter can regenerate itself by burning the soot to clean the filter.

Japanese companies are producing a range of ceramic-based fabrics designed to protect the wearer against the sun's harmful rays. The Kuraray Co. Ltd have introduced Esmo, a staple fibre where powdered ceramics are mixed with the polyester fibre. Ceramic and polyester are also combined in Sunfit fabric, which again shields the wearer from the heat while absorbing and neutralizing ultra-violet rays. Unitika have developed an Aqualine filament yarn based on a ceramic core which is capable of converting solar energy to heat energy. In swimwear, the manufacturers claim that the yarns prevent the body temperature from cooling too rapidly when the wearer gets out of the water.

Porcelain in its pre-fired state is now being produced in sheet form by Kerafol GmbH. By supplying the material in a textile form it prompts the industrial designer or crafts-person to work with it in an unconventional way. In sheet or foil form the porcelain can be cut, stamped, calendered, embossed, laminated, deep-drawn or moulded. Once formed, it can be hardened and rendered semi-transparent in the sintering process. It is the shape, weight and transparency of the material in this state that sets it apart from conventional porcelain.

PALMHIVE
Bobble camouflage

This three-dimensional warp-knit
from British manufacturer
Palmhive is designed for use as
military camouflage. Because of its
ability to stretch it is sold by height
rather than by length.

THREE-DIMENSIONAL TEXTILES AND PREFORMS

Given the range of three-dimensional textile products on the market, it is difficult to believe that less than a decade ago there were few commercially available outside the composite industry. Three-dimensional textiles as prepegs for use in the composite industry are still a dominant market. Other areas that have grown in importance include sports footwear that uses substantial quantities of three-dimensional knitted fabric, also known as spacer fabric. Weaves can be used to provide I-beam profile fabrics for the construction industry. Structured embroidery is a niche market with few producers, but one that is finding uses in the medical and automotive industries. Three-dimensional nonwovens are among the most commonly available products, finding markets in the automotive and construction industries where they are often used to provide acoustic insulation. The innovation in foam is not that it can be produced in three dimensions, rather that the materials being used – ceramic, metal and wood – can all be manufactured in this form. Applications vary from automotive to product design.

GRIFFIN
Camouflage jacket

Fashion designer Jeff Griffin has created a non-military camouflage in this blade cut camouflage jacket.

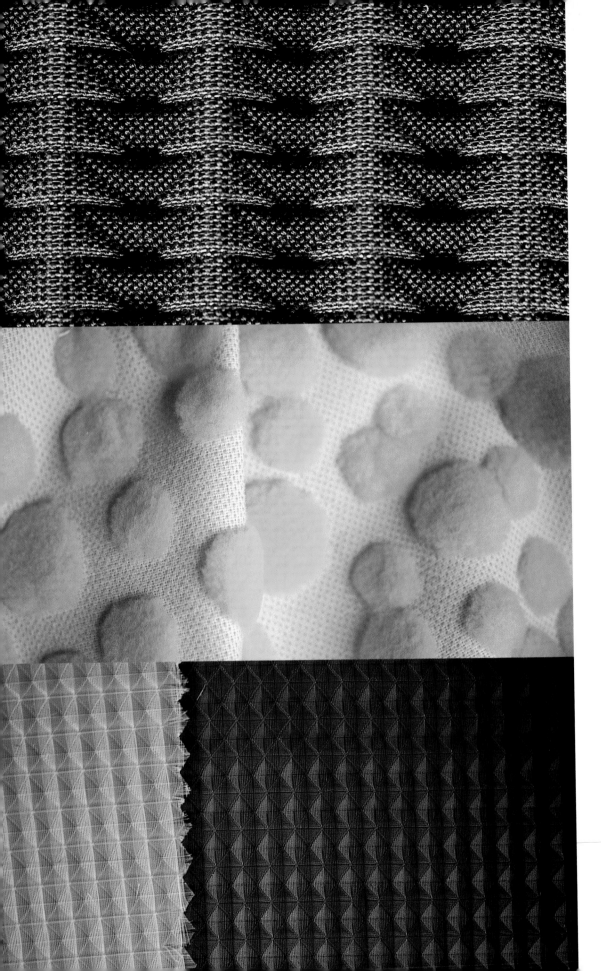

THREE-DIMENSIONAL WEAVE

Much of the research into three-dimensional textiles began in academic institutions, quite often in collaboration with industry. Universities in Belgium and Germany are particularly advanced. At the Department of Textile Technology in the Institut für Textiltechnik in Aachen (ITA), Germany, special narrow fabrics are woven on a loom manufactured by the Swiss company Jacob Müller Forschung AG. The textile is first woven as a flat fabric, before being cut open at both sides to produce an I-beam profile fabric. The fabric can then be used as stiffening beams in light construction.

Buckminster Fuller (1895–1983), US-born technologist and polymath, once noted that a three-axis, or triangular weave would be far superior to a conventional two-way or two-axis weave. The difference, he predicted, would be in the strength it would provide and resistance to tear. Triaxial weaving, originally developed in its modern form by NASA, is now being used in such applications as hosiery, snowboards and tennis racket strings, where it provides better friction, power and shock dispersion.

Exhibition curator Matilda McQuaid cites an early example of triaxial weaving in her book *Structure and Surface* which accompanied the MOMA exhibition of the same title (1998–99). She has found an example of the process dating back to 710–94 AD. Referred to as a 'ra', the triaxial weaving has been preserved in the Shosoin Temple at Nara in Japan. Sakase Adtech Co. Ltd produce a triaxial weave using carbon fibre. Nitto Boseki Co. Ltd manufacture a quadraxial weave in glass fibre.

Multi-axial fabrics, as the name suggests, comprise one or more layers of fibres with different orientation that are stitched together, usually with a lighter thread. ITA have produced some examples using glass fibre on its own and combined with carbon fibre. They are usually used in the production of high performance laminates. Although these fabrics do not look like traditional plain or satin weave, to be defined as a weave a fabric simply has to show at least two sets of interlacing perpendicular threads.

opposite top
HYBRIDS + FUSION
Galaxy

Dutch designer Hybrids and
Fusion have produced a range of
three dimensional fabrics. Galaxy
is a woven fabric incorporating
copper yarn.

opposite middle
PHARENTA

This 3-D tufted effect has been
used to create a range of fabrics for
use in paint rollers to provide
pattern when applying paint.

opposite bottom
SCHOELLER
3-D fabric

Three-dimensional fabric from
Swiss manufacturers Schoeller
utilizing the thermoplastic qualities
of polyester.

right top
INSTITUT FÜR TEXTIL, AACHEN
'I' beam fabric

The Institut für Textil have been
developing three dimensional
fabrics for a number of years. This
'I' profile fabric uses glass and
polyester hybrid fibres that have
been friction spun. It is designed for
use in the construction industry.

right bottom
INSTITUT FÜR TEXTIL, AACHEN
Cured multi-axial
warp-knitted fabric

Cured multiaxial warp-knitted
fabric from the Institut für Textil.
Glass fibre is used to provide
additional strength. The material
is designed to be used as
a reinforcement for concrete
in buildings.

THREE-DIMENSIONAL KNIT

Three-dimensional knitted fabrics are most commonly produced as seamless forms for medical supports, lingerie or whole garments. The most famous example of the latter is Issey Miyake's A-POC series (see Chapter 5, p. 125) which revolutionized the way in which designers and consumers think about clothes. In our high-technology age, stitched seams appear laughably old fashioned, yet it remains the main method for joining fabric together. Another approach to three-dimensional knits can be seen in the spacer fabrics. These are predominantly used in the sports and medical industries where they provide cushioning and support. The knit can be open, like a mesh or net, or appear as a close knit on the front and back. In either case the fabric is springy, giving under pressure then regaining its form once pressure is released. Resins or other coatings can be added to provide additional performance characteristics such as rigidity.

THREE-DIMENSIONAL EMBROIDERY

Embroidery, even as an industrial process, is very much a niche area and is almost exclusively used for decorative purposes. England's Ellis Developments specialize in industrial embroidery where a form is embroidered onto a fabric substrate that is later removed. This forms a prepeg, the basis for a three-dimensional form. Examples range from wheel hubs for cars to medical prosthesis. Ellis have collaborated with medical product manufacturer Anson Medical Ltd to develop a vascular prosthesis for use in the repair of abdominal aortic aneurysms. Here the embroidery is used to create the tube form of the stent that is stitched onto a polyester fabric. Shape Memory Alloy (SMA) wire is incorporated into the form on both sides by the embroidery where the metal is used to stop kinking and prevent leakage.

THREE-DIMENSIONAL NONWOVEN

Volume plays an important role in many applications for nonwovens providing sound or thermal insulation in the walls of buildings or under the bonnet of the car. Volz Luftfilter specialize in nonwoven fabrics for filtration, including some three-dimensional examples.

Densities vary dramatically from the loose, net-like structures to heavier more compact examples that resemble felt. The former are often used in air filtration and the latter for acoustic insulation. Combinations of the two are common and a needlepunched layer can provide stability on the outer layers for handling. Aspen Aerogels Inc. produce a product called Aerogel. Developed for use in the military and space industries, it has remarkable thermal properties relative to its weight and density. Not strictly speaking a nonwoven, it is included here because the finished form most resembles a nonwoven. It is generally made from silica, although other materials including polymers can also be used. Aerogel is produced by extracting liquid from a micro-structured gel, then a variety of doping and reinforcing agents can be added to modify and stabilize the structure. Although it has been around for a number of years it is only relatively recently that technologists have worked out a way of handling it. Blankets have been produced using the material using fibres for reinforcement. Spaceloft provides nanoporous insulation in blankets designed for use in temperatures ranging from cryogenic to 200°C (390°F). Pyrogel blankets go up to 650°C (1200°F).

THREE-DIMENSIONAL FOAM

Since the development of CFC-free foam, there has been a rush of further environmentally friendly products in this area. Metzeler Schaum GmbH have produced a foam made from sunflower seed oil. Using a cold-foaming process, alcohol, oil and water are combined by a process of poly-addition. Carbon dioxide and heat result, so that the mass foams. Not only is the process CFC-free, but no additional heat or energy is needed. It can be produced to different weights and densities and is currently used in mattresses. In the USA, the International Cellulose Corporation in Texas produce a range of asbestos-free foams for acoustic insulation in buildings. Sonaspray is one of their products. It is cellulose-based and designed to be applied by spraying.

A very different process is used by Fairey Industrial Ceramics Ltd to produce porous ceramics. Puremet is formed as a reticulated irregular three-dimensional open-cell

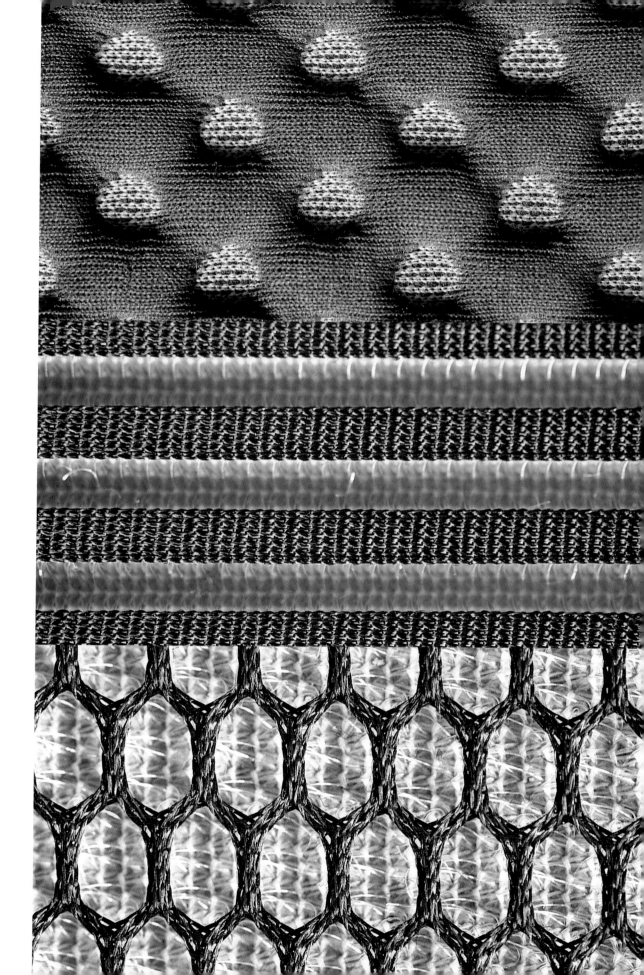

HYBRIDS + FUSION
Spacer fabrics

3-D knit (top) and spacer fabrics
(middle and bottom), while
designed primarily for use in
sports applications, are now
attracting the interest of other
product and furniture designers.

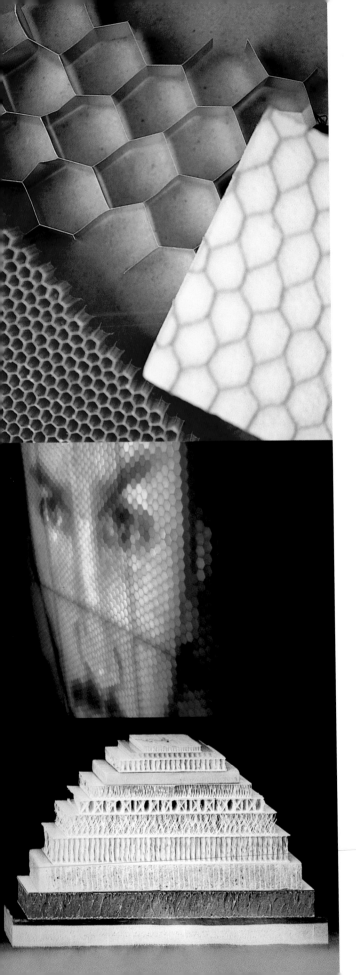

structure to make a sponge-like material. Open-cell foam is impregnated with various oxides before being fired. The high temperature firing burns away the foam, leaving the ceramic 'foam' with a pore size which can be as small as one micron. The main application is in the foundry industry for filtering molten metal. However the material has a unique tactile quality and a similar foam is used by the American designer Harry Allen to make his lighting fixtures. He uses Selee A ceramic foam, which contains aluminium oxide, to produce a series of geometric lights which resemble building blocks of sugar cubes.

Metal foams have also become available for use in filtration, automotive and aerospace industries. Weight, density and costs vary dramatically. In Germany the Fraunhofer Institut (IFAM) have been developing closed-pore metal foams. The process is similar to the production of ceramic foam. Metal powder is first mixed with a foaming agent, then put into a mould. The foaming agent disappears during the subsequent firing process, leaving behind the metal foam. The speed of heating and cooling the foam determines the size of the pores to a great extent. Low in density, the foam is capable of absorbing high impacts, so aluminium foam is sometimes used in cars as a safety feature.

COMPOSITES

The term composite is used where two or more materials, differing in form or composition, are combined to make a new material with enhanced performance characteristics. Composite materials contain a base reinforcement material, such as a glass fibre prepeg, along with a resin for further reinforcement, filler to improve dimensional stability, and additives for additional functionality such as flame retardancy. The use of resins to harden the structure has been problematic for environmental reasons. However there are now organic resins available that are less harmful to the environment. There are around a dozen main processes used in composite manufacturing. Factors such as end-use, size and cost determine the manufacturer's choice of technique.

Composites can be created in as few as three production stages. The first step is to produce a sheet-like structure, impregnated at a second stage with resins to produce a semi-finished product which can be stored until required. This is what is commonly referred to as a prepeg. The third stage is to mould the prepeg by thermoforming it in a heated mould. The resin cures while the shaping process is carried out. This can take from fifteen seconds to three minutes, depending on the temperature and the type of resin. The moulds are usually of a fairly simple design. To produce a conical shape, a perforated plate and counter-plate are fitted with cylindrical pins. The mould is made from an unalloyed steel which is anti-adhesive and hard-chromed to protect it against wear. A prepeg can be drawn from a flat textile sheet to provide an increase in mesh width with a light structure. Alternatively, the textile can be moulded first, then thermoset or applied with a plastic resin for stabilization.

Hand lay-up is one of the most basic moulding processes used in composites. A reinforcement such as polyester or glass fibre is placed by hand on to the surface of an open mould along with a liquid resin. It is also possible to use biopolymers extracted from sugar beet, potatoes, maize, plant oils or cellulose produced from waste paper. Natural fibre fleeces such as flax, hemp or ramie fibre can also be used. Reinforcements from these renewable resources are relatively new and less common, with strength an issue. The spray-up technique is very similar, but here the resin and reinforcement are sprayed on the mould. Both techniques are used to produce large parts where strength is needed, such as boat hulls. For hand lay-up, fibres are used in a mat form. In spray-up, a spray gun chops continuous fibres (such as glass fibres) into the required lengths and mixes a catalyst into the sprayed resin. The resin, normally polyester, serves as a matrix for reinforcing the fibres. Additives may be mixed with the resin to ensure that the composite cures at room temperature. Brushes or rollers are used to remove any trapped air. The parts are often stiffened with the addition of a structural core such as honeycomb, cardboard, plywood or a closed-cell plastic foam.

While much of the composites industry is focusing on mass production, there are still some sectors where customization is vital. A US company, Springlite, produces thousands of prosthetic lower limbs every year. Their main prosthetic, Springlite II, is still made by hand lay-up techniques to fit the customer's specific requirements, but the company favours compression moulding for their new semi-custom product. The new prosthetic is light in weight, can simulate natural bending and eliminates the need for stiff joints. Design and weight improvements meant that amputees could walk or run greater distances with less fatigue and discomfort.

When high volume is required, a compression-moulding process is often used. There are four main methods: sheet-moulding compound; bulk-moulding compound (including transfer moulding); wet system compression-moulding and reinforced thermoplastic sheet compression-moulding. The composite in each case is compressed under hydraulic pressure in matched metal dies. These hold the reinforcement in the desired shape until the resin has cured. One benefit of the sheet-moulding compound technique is that several parts can be incorporated into a single moulding. Bulk-moulding compound is mainly used as a replacement for cast metal in power tools and computer equipment components. Two disadvantages of the wet compression-moulding system are that it is labour intensive and produces considerable process waste. It was the first compression-moulding process used, dating back to the 1940s, and it is still employed in a number of appliance and equipment markets. The system of thermoplastic sheet compression-moulding has the benefit of high productivity and low labour, and is used for helmets and car bumper beams.

Resin transfer-moulding is a closed-mould process whose applications include storage tanks and sports car bodies. Pre-cut or preformed fibre reinforcements are clamped together in matching male and female moulds. Resin is pumped in through injection ports which hold the resin under pressure. Many woven and nonwoven glass fibre products have been developed specially for this process, although carbon fibre and aramids are also used.

The pultrusion process uses reinforcements which are continuously pulled through a thermosetting resin bath before being held in shape and allowed to cure and harden. Continuous or chopped strand mats, woven tapes and continuous glass fibre rovings are commonly chosen for reinforcement, with polyester the principal resin. One advantage

of the process is that a high degree of reinforcement orientation is possible, making it ideal for electrical strain and oil well sucker rods. It is also used in products to provide corrosion resistance. This is the fastest growing area of the pultrusion market.

Weight is an important issue in freight transportation, with solutions to the problem being developed by companies on both sides of the Atlantic. Stoughton Composites Inc. of the USA have designed an airtight composite freight container which is about 450 kg (1000 lbs) lighter than a comparable metal container. Glass fibres and nonwovens account for more than half its weight. Eleven basic pultruded profiles are used, with beams and hollow sections insulated with polyurethane foam. The advantage of pultrusion is that fibre orientation and weight can be altered for different structural loads, reinforcing where there is likely to be most stress.

Filament winding means that complex shapes can be produced. With a cylinder as the basic shape, reinforcing fibres and resins are applied to a rotating mould surface. The process allows additional fibre to be placed in areas of high stress, optimizing fibre use and making the composite more economical. Reinforcing fibres can be used in different forms, including woven and unidirectional tapes. A resin, such as polyester or epoxy, is applied by passing the reinforcement through an impregnation bath. Applications include fuel and water storage tanks.

Perhaps the most popular method of producing complex shapes is injection moulding. Granular thermoplastic resin is fed from a supply hopper into one end of a heated metal cylinder. A screw, or auger, inside the cylinder rotates, bringing the resin into the hot cylinder. The resin becomes semi-fluid when heated, and is ready for injection into the mould. As well as rotating, the injection-moulding machine screw can move backwards and forwards along the cylinder axis. The mould may contain more than one cavity in the shape of the parts to be made. The resin is cooled in the mould, and solidifies. The reinforcement mainly used is chopped glass fibre with a urethane or polyester resin.

DuPont have developed an infusion moulding process in an effort to produce large composite parts in an environmentally

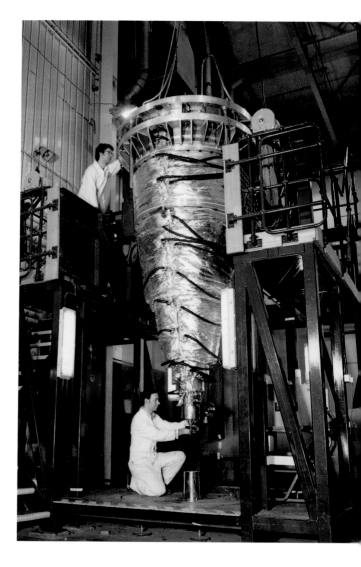

Nigel Marshall is concerned about the environmental impact of composites. He examines ways of adding the finished aesthetic at composite stage rather than as an additional layer of finish or cladding.

American designer Critz Campbell uses a resin reinforced glass fibre illuminated from within to make his Eudora chair series.

The collection is inspired by the softness of the beetle's body contrasting with its hard wingcase. The garments are all made from the inner tubes of car tyres that have been cleaned and polished with a silicone spray. The sculptural shapes have been formed by following the natural drape of the material on the body.

clean system. Glass or carbon fabrics are pre-cut along with the foam inserts required. This process creates an internal reinforcement once the resin is cured. A release liner is placed over the dry preform and plastic hoses are attached to the distribution medium. The entire structure is then sealed in a vacuum bag and full vacuum applied. Once all entrapped air has been evacuated, the resin is allowed to flow into the distribution medium. The distribution medium and fabric form a network of 'fluid resistors'. The resin, following the path of least resistance, flows through the medium and ultimately through the dry preform. The resin fills all available space and is allowed to cure. Large parts which are already manufactured using this process include 3.5 metre (12 feet) long bridge decks and boat hulls.

Honeycomb structures have been found to add significant strength without noticeable weight gain to many sandwich structures. Nomex honeycomb is strong and lightweight as well as heat and chemical resistant. Nomex itself is a meta-aramid produced by DuPont in many different forms, including staple fibres and filament yarn. The fibre form has a very wide range of applications from electrical insulation to protective clothing. In order to make paper, short Nomex fibres are combined with fibrils (a fibre/film hybrid). An adhesive is then carefully placed in parallel lines on the flat paper sheets using a gravure printing process. The sheets are placed on top of each other before being cured at a high temperature. The adhesive-free areas can then be expanded, opening to form the familiar hexagonal cells. The expanded block is repeatedly dipped into a liquid phenolic resin, followed by oven curing, until the required density is reached. The block sheets are then cut into the thicknesses needed and form the basis for honeycomb composite and sandwich structures.

Hexel Composites produce a large number of metallic (aluminium) and non-metallic (Nomex paper) honeycomb composites. The smallest cell size Nomex (0.013 mm) has been used to produce a CFC-free air-conditioning system which operates with a desiccant wheel. Designed for domestic and industrial use, it has no compressor and does not use ozone-destroying CFCs, but copies the human body's system for keeping cool – transpiration. Besides strength and weight performance,

Nomex-based honeycombs can provide cushioning which helps to filter out vibration and improve manoeuvrability. Used in commercial aircraft, such as the Airbus A320, the honeycombs were found to give a 20 to 25 per cent weight saving over metallic components. This had a substantial effect on the operating costs of the aircraft. Hexel Composites produce Fibrelam, which uses unidirectional cross-plied glass fibre skins. These are bonded to an aramid honeycomb core to form structural sandwich panels used for aircraft flooring. Their Aeroweb aluminium honeycomb possesses very good kinetic energy absorbing properties, and has similar applications.

Westwind Composites Inc. of the USA produce a range of foam-filled honeycomb cells, Weskor. These have the advantage of thermal insulation and sound-deadening properties. Kraft paper is used to form the honeycomb structure, which is filled with a polyurethane foam and then sandwiched between a fine laminate of granite, marble, wood or an aluminium skin. A Swiss company, Tubus Bauer AG, have developed honeycomb-based sandwich panels for air filter, safety and sports applications, employing a thermoplastic, such as polypropylene or polycarbonate, fusion or adhesive bonded to a nonwoven or to glass fibre for stronger reinforcement.

There are very few industrial sectors that have not been affected by the development of engineered textiles. The most immediate benefit is usually in weight, strength or safety, yet the most lasting gain is only starting to emerge. In embracing these new materials, the design industry is re-evaluating much of its thinking about aerodynamics, form, process and, of course, materials themselves.

Textiles have ceased to be regarded as a flexible, permeable, decorative material, best suited to clothing and soft furnishing. The change in attitude is apparent in industry trade fairs such as TechTextil in Frankfurt and Industrial Fabrics Association International (IFAI) Expo in North America. In the past few years there has been a tremendous growth in diverse applications for the new fibres and fabrics shown at these fairs. It seems that no area of design activity has been unaffected, from the automotive industry to medicine, architecture, sport, product design, aerospace and fashion.

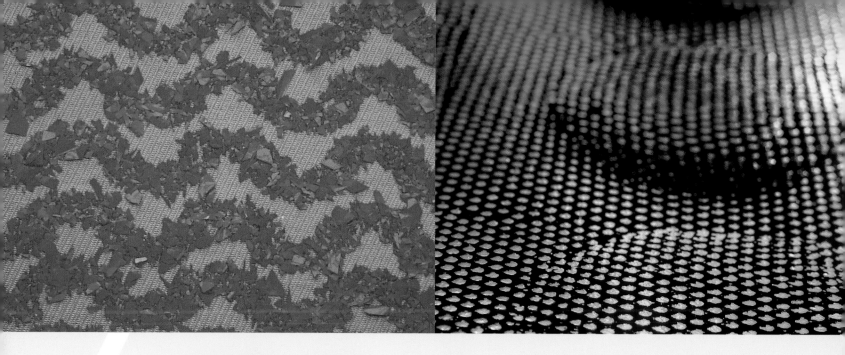

Textile finishes

Sarah E. Braddock Clarke

above left
EUGÈNE VAN VELDHOVEN
Textile finish. 2002

This polyamide textile has been printed with polyester fluorescent flakes. A very textured effect is created. The textile is intended for interior application.

above right
HELEN ARCHER
3Ds. 1995

Holographic foil has been laminated to a textile substrate and then hand screen-printed. An illusion of a relief surface is created. This fabric has been developed with Astor Universal Ltd and is intended for flooring.

right
SOPHIE ROET
Oyster Shell. 1999

This textile has a silk organza warp and a weft of high-twist viscose and polyamide. When the resulting textile is immersed in hot water the highly twisted viscose yarn tries to expand and move but cannot, in doing so irregular movement in the cloth is created. This textile was purchased by Eskandar, a fashion designer based in London.

The finishing treatment of a textile is increasingly important, and fibre and fabric manufacturers are investing in research and development in this area. A textile can be host to diverse looks, textures and performances; finishes are extremely versatile and can take place at various stages of textile manufacture. Some treatments are very subtle, while others can alter the original state to be almost unrecognizable. Visual effects include surfaces that are ultra-smooth, high-gloss, lacquered, fluorescent, phosphorescent, holographic foiled and ones that reflect light.

Coating and laminating can convey high glamour and a futuristic aesthetic, while patinating and even burning can give an attractive aged appearance. This often works best with natural materials. A great deal of research is also being undertaken into the feel of a fabric, for example to create extremely soft surfaces by sanding and brushing. Abrading a surface which has been dyed and/or printed can achieve a desirable, distressed look; while brushing

a fabric on its 'wrong' side (next to the skin) gives increased performance by trapping air to insulate the wearer. Waxing, oiling, coating and laminating can provide a fabric with technical properties and fundamentally alter its appearance and texture. They can be made crease-, moth- and stain-resistant, crush- and wrinkle-proof, non-iron, easy-care, permanently pressed, stretchable, windproof, waterproof and breathable. Like advanced synthetics, many of today's textile finishes were originally designed for high-performance wear, and are now also widely used in fashion.

The processes vary widely from high-tech versions of existing treatments, such as coatings and laminates, to printing, embossing, moulding and sculpting the latest thermoplastic ultra-microfibres to create high-relief surfaces or three-dimensional structures. Understanding a fibre's inherent properties is important, and contrasting different textiles, such as a synthetic with a natural before subjection to a finish, can create interesting coloured effects and

NUNO CORPORATION
REIKO SUDO (design)
Burner Dye. 2000

Stainless steel top, cotton base.
To enable ultra-fine stainless steel
fibre to be woven without damaging
the looms, Nuno coated the metal
in water-soluble fibres to create
smooth, resilient warp threads.

After weaving, the surface fibres
are dissolved to reveal the metallic
surface. The fabric is then treated
by hand-burning using gas jets
to achieve this wonderful iridescent
look. A dye technique is achieved
by literally burning the fabric.
Included in the collection of the
Metropolitan Museum of Art, 2000.

left top
EUGÈNE VAN VELDHOVEN
Textile finish. 2003

A metallic foil transfer print on
a cotton Jacquard weave with effect
yarn in long floats. The untrapped
yarns appear to float on a liquid
metal surface. The weave design
is by Hélène Dashorst. The textile
is intended for interior application.

left below
EUGENE VAN VELDHOVEN
Textile finish. 2002

A mohair weave is fused with
a metallic transfer print by means
of needlepunching. A new and
contemporary looking fabric
emerges. The textile is intended
for interior application.

opposite
INOUE PLEATS INC.
Transcriptions Pleats (top) and
pleated scarves (bottom)

Polyester fabric can be permanently
pleated due to its thermoplastic
property. The Tokyo-based company,
Inoue Pleats Inc. explore different
patterns for fashion fabrics and
accessories such as scarves. Their
range of designs and colours
ensures many visual possibilities.

textures. Some might absorb dye readily; some might shrink dramatically. Even the simplest finishes can create great changes – for example, hot-washing a fabric constructed from mixed fibres can make each component yarn react in its own characteristic way. Stone or enzyme washing can emphasize texture; over-dyeing can create complex colouring; bleaching in an irregular pattern can create a contemporary and innovative look. Mechanical processes, such as calendering, or chemical methods, such as mercerization, can be used to give a lustrous, smooth appearance to a cotton fabric. These treatments have now become so advanced that some actually alter the molecular structure of the fibre, and take place in the laboratory.

Many of the leading textile designers and manufacturers determine look, texture and performance through advanced finishing techniques. Also, fashion designers are frequently alert to the latest treatments as they can transform a traditional textile, updating it for a contemporary look to ensure a wide appeal. Many textile practitioners creating fabrics for fashion are interested in finishing techniques and sometimes work closely with specialist laboratories using water, heat and chemicals to create wonderful textures. Dutch designer Eugène van Veldhoven combines various textile finishes with print for decorated yet functional cloth. He employs both naturals and synthetics as his substrates and experiments freely with many advanced techniques. Eugène van Veldhoven has supplied fashion designers with wonderful printed textiles and is now working with the textile industry and for interior applications.

There are many ways of interpreting advanced textile finishing treatments and shown here is the work of innovative designers using them to create beautiful, new materials.

THERMOPLASTICS

Thermoplastic means a material can be transformed through heat into new configurations which on cooling are completely stable. Most synthetics are inherently thermoplastic, while wool also has this property. Being thermoplastic enables a fabric to be permanently wrinkled, crushed,

embossed, pleated or moulded into a totally three-dimensional form.

Pleating is one of the most ancient techniques of finishing a fabric, dating back to the Ancient Greeks and Egyptians, but it is only since the invention of synthetics after World War II that permanent pleating as a finish has been possible. A fabric used for permanent pleating should be either a pure synthetic or a blend containing at least 65 per cent synthetic. A technique called Siroset is used for permanently pleating wool. Pleating by hand can create great variety in relief surfaces and forms, but it is time-consuming and therefore expensive; the fabric is placed between two sheets of thick paper which is then folded into patterns and steamed. Machine pleats are formed by passing the fabric over edged rollers and heating, a quicker and cheaper process but one which allows for less variety. All-over crinkled surfaces can be produced by scrunching the textile into a tube which is then heated. Woven, nonwoven and knitted textiles can be pleated and will create different effects. It is especially interesting when a printed design is then pleated as it will reveal only part of the image or motif when relaxed and the full design when expanded. This gives much scope for creative experimentation.

Inoue Pleats Inc. was the first pleats-processing business in Japan, and create beautiful pleated materials, most of which are polyester. Their showroom in Tokyo displays a range of hand- and machine-pleated textiles for fashion and interior applications. Issey Miyake Inc. is one of the many leading fashion companies supplied by Inoue Pleats Inc. With his forward-thinking fashion designs, Issey Miyake has really pioneered the use of new pleating methods, using this classic technique with finely knitted polyester. In his Pleats Please line Issey Miyake manipulates the cloth in imaginative ways, bringing together hand-craft with its evidence of process and the slickness of recent technology.

Nuno Corporation's innovative textiles often take the rich traditions of Japan and give them a new lease of life by using them with sophisticated synthetics and advanced finishing treatments. Reiko Sudo investigates many different materials and techniques, delighting in the aesthetics achieved through a combination of the traditional and the state-of-the-art. Exploiting the thermoplastic

left top
**NUNO CORPORATION
REIKO SUDO (design)
Delphi. 1996**

Pleated polyester organdy. Different
colours in the warp and weft create
an iridescent quality which is
further enhanced by the pleating.
Due to its thermoplastic property,
the polyester keeps the pleats
permanently. Included in the
collection of the Israel Museum
1996, Jerusalem and the Baltimore
Museum of Art, 2002.

left bottom
**NUNO CORPORATION
REIKO SUDO (design)
Kumo-Shibori. 1996**

A sheer polyester organza fabric
maintains its shibori textures due
to the thermoplastic property of
synthetics. The entire design is
hand bound and then heat-set
in pleats.

opposite
**JAKOB SCHLAEPFER
Lola (top) and Kirie (bottom)**

Laser cut textiles from the Décor
collection for Création Baumann.
A wonderful moiré effect is created
in Lola when the laser cut circles
are allowed to fall onto the cloth
beneath. A theme of nature is used
for intricate cutting in Kirie.

qualities of synthetics using heat-moulding techniques on a plain woven cloth, she creates both surface and structural interest. Working with industrial techniques and frequently collaborating with manufacturers from different disciplines, she interprets her sources (photographs, drawings, paintings and collages) in a direct and creative way.

Using the property of a thermoplastic material to become liquid when subjected to heat, laser or ultrasound treatments can etch or cut a material. Diverse patterning can result where the laser tool is used with varying pressure and duration of time. Much scope for creativity is possible with these processes. In a multi-layered cloth, laser cutting can remove a face fabric to reveal another underneath, burn and cut through a single cloth completely or burn through its many layers quite easily. Ultrasound is generally used if a design is complex as more control is possible than with a laser.

PRINTING

Printed textiles have gone beyond decoration to be extremely bold and striking, and may often be the main reason to buy a product. New methods are being explored by textile designers and artists and the opportunity for innovation is enormous since there is a vast range of finishing techniques particular to the printing process. Contoured relief printing using synthetic rubbers can create appealing aesthetics and textures, while metallic powders combined with various resins can produce spectacular optical effects. Chemicals transform fabrics to reveal layers and to distort the basic textile into unique surfaces and forms. Developments in pigment printing allow exciting new looks, matt surfaces on shiny fabrics and glossy, glazed or translucent features on matt, crêpe textiles. Sophisticated printing inks, such as thermochromic inks, can change colour according to temperature change; hydrochromic textiles will respond to water; and piezochromic responds to pressure. Different types of printing are examined here to show that some of the more traditional techniques have been updated using the latest technologies to provide us with methods that are creative and ecologically sound.

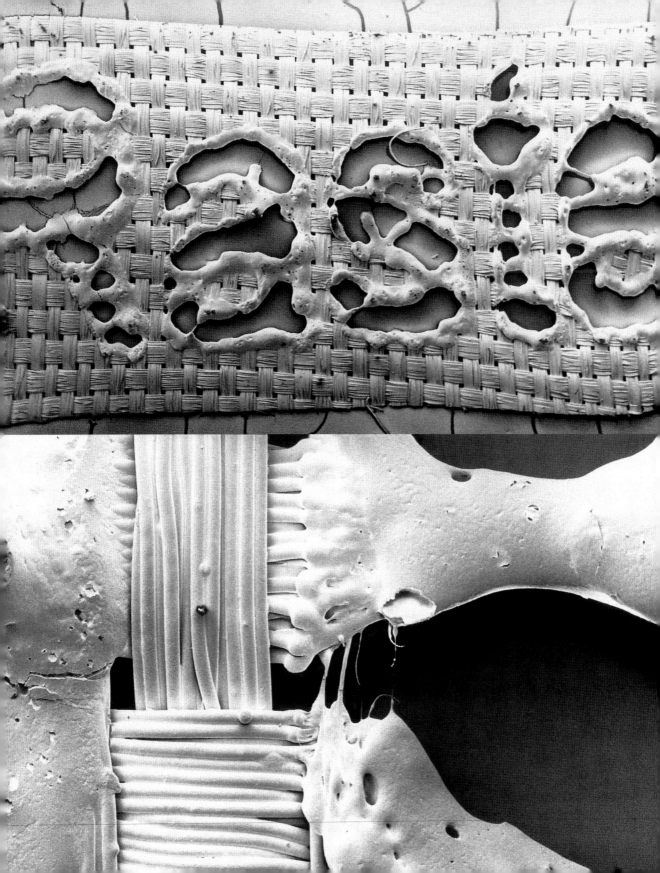

left
SAVITHRI BARTLETT
Laser-treated Polyamide 6.6. 2004

These two images are taken using a Scanning Electron Microscope. This enables the effect to be seen when the extreme heat from a laser is applied. The change is visible at polymer level. The top image shows the fabric laser-marked with text (it spells part of the word 'raster' – the pattern of lines followed by an electron beam) and the warp and weft are clearly apparent. The bottom image shows the fabric decomposing due to heightened temperatures and poor heat conduction by the polymer fibres.

right top
EUGÈNE VAN VELDHOVEN
Textile finish. 2000

A sharp geometric design is cut out using a laser on an acetate fabric. The textile is intended for interior application.

right bottom
EUGÈNE VAN VELDHOVEN
Textile finish. 2002

Polyester fabric is embossed using ultrasonic welding. The ultrasound melts the thermoplastic synthetic to create a new and interesting surface. The textile is intended for interior application.

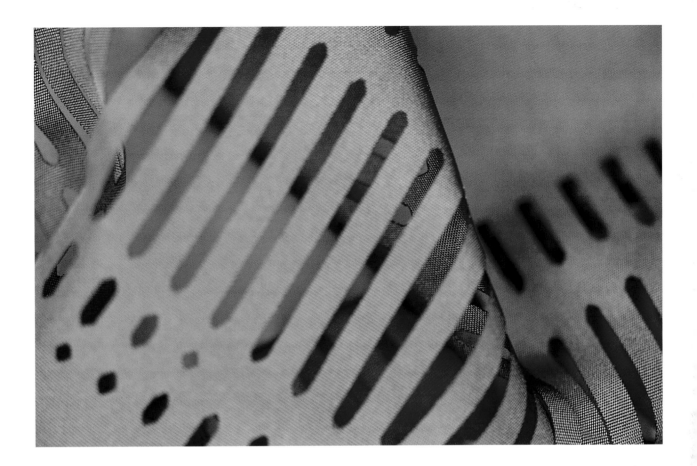

right
ISABEL DODD
Rubber printed polyester velvet.
2004

Liquid synthetic rubber creates
a contrasting surface when printed
on a sumptuous light-reflecting
velvet. The wonderful undulating
relief is demonstrated with this
large shawl.

below
NORMA STARSZAKOWNA
Wood. 2003

Silk organza is given a beautiful
texture by employing various
finishing techniques including
mixed media printing and a glazing
process. This textile was conceived
as an experimental fabric for use
either in fashion or interior
applications.

HEAT-TRANSFER

Heat-transfer printing was developed by the pharmaceutical company Ciba Geigy and first introduced in the 1960s. By painting varnishes on paper, sandwiching fabric in between two sheets of this paper and passing through rollers, a reproduction technique is achieved. The method of heat-transfer has been greatly improved by advanced technology. It is a favoured technique as it does not require screens, enabling the designer to be very experimental. The print is made on to a special release paper and disperse dyes used, which are then transferred using heat and pressure to a synthetic fabric using a sublimation process. In this case pre-treatment of the textile is not necessary. Many colours can be transferred simultaneously, allowing complex prints which use hand-generated photographic and digital imagery.

Investment in heat-transfer printing technology continues and special inks and dyes have been developed which can be used on a variety of surfaces, from naturals to the latest ultra-microfibre fabrics. In fact, heat-transfer printing works particularly well with the compact, smooth surface of a microfibre fabric.

It is a finishing process which the 'textile planner' Jun'ichi Arai uses to maximum effect in his textile art pieces. Often creatively subverting equipment and employing it in ways for which it was never intended, he takes the heat-transfer press and permanently wrinkles and pleats synthetic fabrics while also adding colour. In his experiments to create new surfaces and structures, Jun'ichi Arai often relies on the thermoplastic qualities of synthetic textiles, transforming them into fully dimensional forms. Starting with a machine-perfect cloth, such as a polyamide or a polyester, he introduces a hand-finished, irregular look and texture by using traditional techniques such as tie-dyeing and pleating to give the finished fabric a unique identity.

RELIEF

Relief is a popular method of creating pattern and texture in printed textiles. Embossing can give delicate and subtle effects or obvious surface interest with high relief. Beautiful visual and tactile qualities can be achieved by using various dyeing and printing techniques.

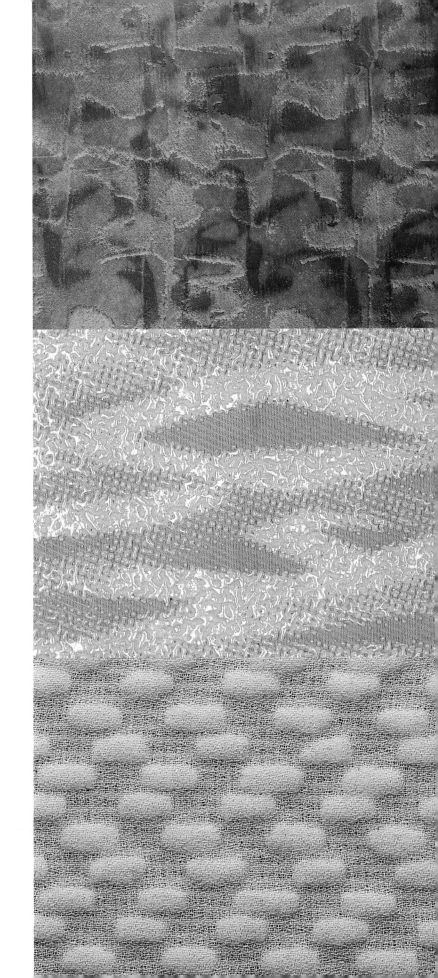

NIGEL ATKINSON
Embroidered Chrysanthemum.
1986 (original motif) and 2001
(this interpretation)

Raised surface printing onto
viscose acetate velvet creates the
look of an embroidery using the
different technique of hand
printing. Interior application.

opposite
NIGEL ATKINSON
Florentine Leaves. 1989 (original
motif) and 2004 (this
interpretation)

The 18th century Florentine design
is reinvented and transformed here
by Nigel Atkinson. He uses heat-
reactive ink encrusted with gold
leaf on cotton velvet. Two separate
fabrics are shown here providing
a striking contrast of colour. The
beautiful raised and textured heat-
reactive surface has a thin layer of
gold leaf applied to it before being
heat pressed to fix the gold to the
printed areas. Interior application.

A pioneer of one technique of obtaining a
contoured surface is British textile designer
Nigel Atkinson. He selects heat-reactive inks,
and prints fabric to create wonderful relief
surfaces. Those who use his textiles often
work with both sides, contrasting the bold
effects against the more subtle. His fabrics
have a distinctive look which is nostalgic and
romantic while also being contemporary and
sophisticated. Choice of colour and pattern is
often informed by his travels: frequent visits
to India have inspired rich and bold colour for
dyeing and printing. Nigel Atkinson's textiles
make reference to traditional cloth, employing
labour-intensive techniques, such as hand-
finishing the fabrics, in his belief that it is
important to handle the cloth directly. He
manipulates fabric into many forms, using its
particular properties to achieve results which
can be transparent, opaque, textured and
smooth but always fluid and beautiful.
Nigel Atkinson's work demonstrates superb
craftsmanship with his keen eye for detail.
He has supplied fashion designers, interior
architects, theatre, film and individual clients
with his own range of fashion accessories.
He is now concentrating on textiles for
interiors which he sees as an expanding
market as well as creating one-off works.
Nigel Atkinson's textiles are heirlooms
of the future, to be passed on to the next
generation.

Silicone can also be used to achieve a relief
surface and it typically gives a high-gloss
appearance. Used in many decorative ways,
it can be printed on a range of fabrics, woven,
nonwoven and knitted, to create an unusual
relief surface. Applications for silicone
include interiors, fashion and sportswear for
strong, waterproof, flexible and breathable
materials.

Another technique of creating a relief
surface is flocking, where minute textile
particles are made to adhere to the fabric's
surface either by static electricity or with
adhesives. New interpretations of this
technique have dramatically changed its very
traditional image.

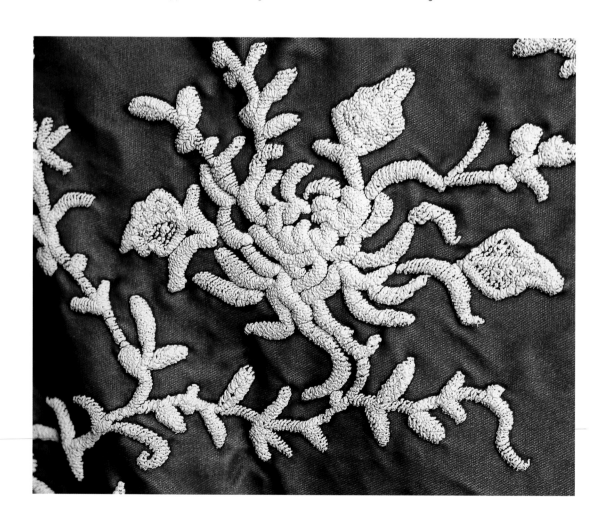

left (full view) and opposite (detail)
NIGEL ATKINSON
Fire 1. 2004
300 (height) x 120 (width) cm

Japanese kimono silk is hand
painted with various printing inks
including heat-reactives. A relief
effect is achieved with the surface
printing technique which Nigel
Atkinson has developed and a
certain tension exists between the
areas of silk that have been worked
and the areas left plain. The piece
is a one-off work created directly
onto the printing table by Nigel
Atkinson while he was in Japan.
It is the first of a series.

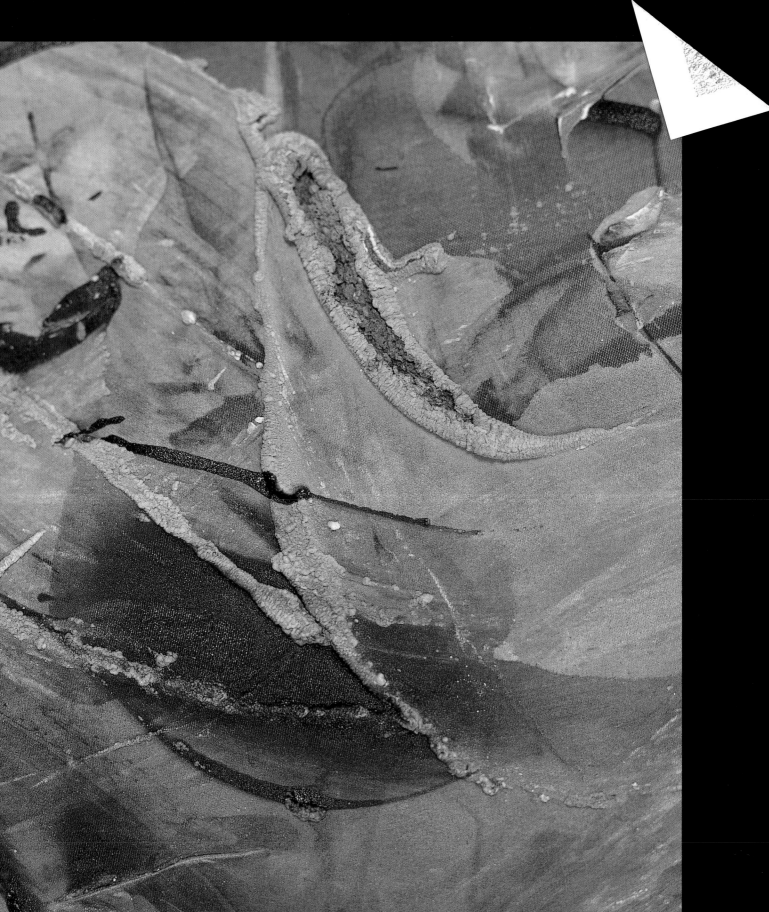

EUGÈNE VAN VELDHOVEN
Textile finish. 2002

Black silicone rubber is coated on to a blend of cotton and viscose woven in a bouclé design. The sleekness of the silicone works as a foil to the textural surface of the bouclé weave underneath (a bouclé weave is a fabric which uses a looped or curled yarn). The textile is intended for interior application.

left below
EUGÈNE VAN VELDHOVEN
Textile finish. 2003

This textile has a transparent acrylate coating with bicolour pigment combined with a flock print on acetate. Flocking is interpreted in a new and contemporary way. The textile is intended for interior application. It is in the collection of the Dutch Textile Museum.

opposite
JAKOB SCHLAEPFER
Wassily

Ink-jet printed textiles from the Décor collection for Création Baumann. With its reference to the 20th century fine artist Wassily Kandinsky, colour is explored with the latest digital printing techniques. Intended for exquisite curtains or free-hanging panels as room dividers for contemporary living.

INK-JET

This is an area which has grown considerably in recent years and digital printing is definitely changing the way people conceive their imagery and the design process.

No screens are necessary and large expanses of cloth are capable of being printed at one time. An infinite number of colours can be utilized and with digital technology the size of repeat imagery is no longer a constraint. Also, the designer or artist can easily work on a much larger scale. The speed of digital printing is increasing due to advances in technology and in the future both the art and design worlds will see digital prints becoming more significant.

Ink-jet digital printing can be carried out on most types of fabric but they need to be prepared beforehand. A chemical coating makes them receptive to the dye. The ink-jets fire the dye (the chemical coating cannot be incorporated into the dye as it would block the fine ink-jets). After printing the textile is steamed to fix the print and washed to remove the coating and excess dye – the result is a permanently printed cloth.

Different types of dyes are used for various fabrics, just as in traditional screen-printed textiles. For digital printing on to natural substrates such as cotton, reactive dyes work well and for silk and wool, acid dyes can be used. At present pigment inks cannot be used for digital printing as the jet heads are too fine for them to pass through. Pigment inks work well on most textiles, they are much easier to work with and their colour fastness is very good. Technology in this area is moving on rapidly to allow pigments and when they do they are bound to be very popular.

Sophisticated computer hardware and software mean the textile designer and the creator of gallery textiles have a wealth of techniques with which to realize their imagery. The potential for generating and manipulating imagery is enormous: original drawings, collages, photographs and even three-dimensional objects can be scanned, further manipulated if desired and then printed as one-off art work, all-over designs, or complex repeat patterns. Through the computer, layers of imagery can be created, an illusion of depth achieved, scale experimented with, patterns morphed into other forms and various Photoshop effects incorporated.

JAKOB SCHLAEPFER
Sonja

This textile intended for interior application pays homage to the 20th century artist Sonia Delaunay who explored colour not only in her paintings but also in her applied fabrics. The cloth is ink-jet printed with circular motifs for the Décor collection for Création Baumann.

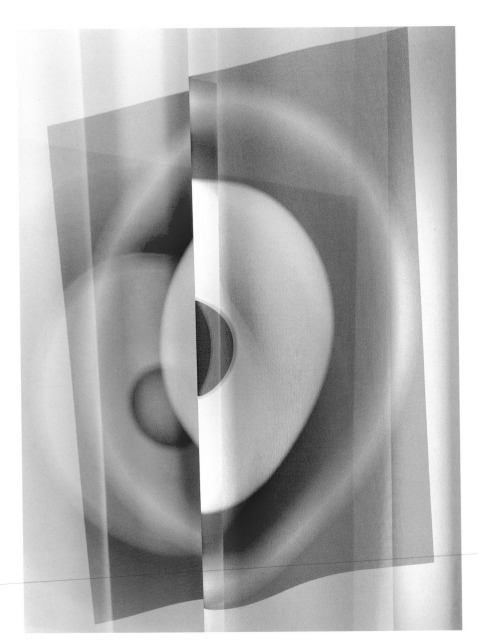

When digital printing, the textile practitioner can design on the computer screen and take this work directly into fabric rather than starting on paper. Popular printers are the Stork ink-jet printer from the Netherlands and the Mimaki textile digital printer from Japan. These printers are becoming more widely used in industry but are also available to textile students in many educational institutions. Artists and designers are now working with digital printing techniques, and the potential of this area is far-reaching with much to be explored. Experimental use of this technology does not end at the digital printing stage; instead this could be the first layer of a multi-media process. The textiles could be further worked by hand or by traditional screen-printing techniques, such as dévoré or discharge printing for a highly creative approach.

EMBELLISHMENT

In addition to dyeing and printing a textile there are many other methods of embellishing it. Decorating a fabric includes embroidery and fabric manipulation and there has been renewed interest in craft couture hand skills. Often old and present-day techniques are combined to create a new aesthetic. If something has been made by hand it generally feels more special, luxurious and individual. Using technology such as multi-head embroidery, a handmade look can be created in the factory. Embroidery puts the price of clothing up, sometimes significantly, as work is hard to copy. However, due to technical advances these often labour-intensive techniques are no longer being kept solely for the world of haute couture. In fact there is a new wave of textile designers operating on a level in between haute couture and prêt-à-porter, combining craft with the high-tech.

Many textile designers invent their own techniques and also combine textile and non-textile materials. Overlaying print with embroidery can offer another dimension. Subtle all-over textures, such as print with bold embroidery or print simulating stitch evolving into actual stitch, can create a visual play using these techniques. Manipulating an existing fabric includes structural decoration such as folding, wrapping, wrinkling, twisting, knotting, gathering, ruching, tucking,

pleating, bonding, pressing and their various combinations. Heat-treating thermoplastic synthetics has made many of these techniques permanent, and combined with dyeing and printing effects the scope for creativity is almost limitless.

There remains a strong tradition across the world for embellished cloth which spans centuries and techniques are passed down from generation to generation. Those pursuing research and development in advanced textile technology can learn from looking back at certain techniques, adopting an international perspective while also looking ahead. Considered by many to be the future of fashion, surface decoration of a textile often involves both artisanal and industrial techniques. Using recent advances in technology, traditional methods can be renewed and updated while craft and manufacture can come together to create something unique and precious. Textile designers and artists are rethinking traditional stitched textiles. The result is a vast range of surfaces and structures, for example a hand-stitched microfibre fabric instead of the traditional linen, to set embroidery in a different context.

A plain base cloth such as a polyamide or polyester can be made much more interesting by using a variety of techniques. In the world of fashion, with its often refined and understated silhouettes, embellishment is given real emphasis. The powerful form of visually decorating a textile can give a look and personality which is strongly individual and evident in both womenswear and menswear collections. Not only specific pattern or imagery but in texture with its subtle nuances – embossed, contoured effects are achieved using raised embroidery in the same colours as the underlying textile.

LAMINATES

A laminate incorporates several layers of fabric, with fine-membrane laminates often utilizing microtechnology. Used with many types of fabric, a main advantage of laminates is that they adapt a textile to give it a new technical property. For example, a membrane can be used in conjunction with a textile base or several substrates together. Previously, laminates and coatings tended to cause uncomfortable condensation from

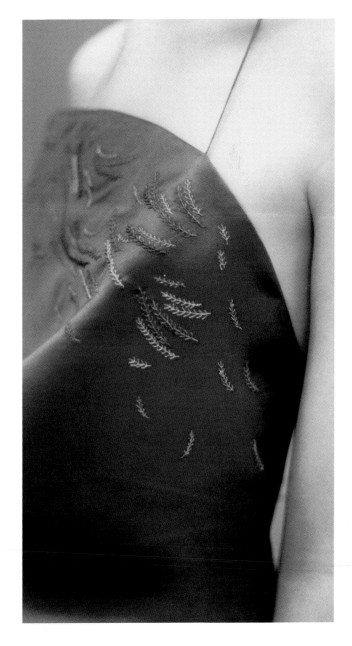

KAREN SPURGIN
Textile design for Dosa. 2002

Embroidery on grey duchess satin using Scotchlite™ reflective thread together with a spun steel thread. The pure steel thread was developed by Christina Kim (the name behind the L.A. label Dosa) with Jun'ichi Arai in Japan.

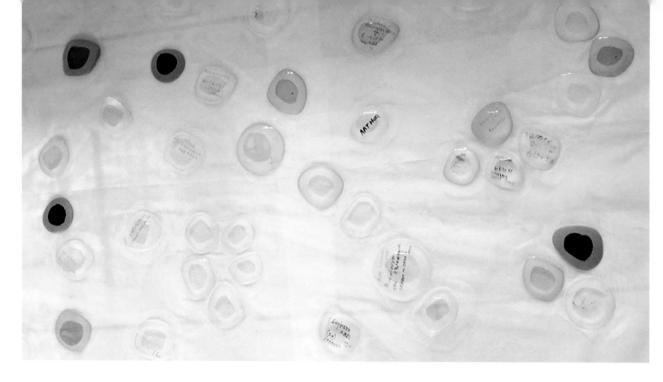

right
KAREN NICOL
Arthur. 2002

Textile design for a fashion fabric with unusual embellishment techniques. Karen Nicol took an assortment of optician's lenses which varied from sunglasses to thick lenses and set them between two layers of silk organza. The back layer of silk was cut away and the top layer cut just at the centre to reveal each lens. The optician's writing can be seen on some prescriptions – numbers and the name, Arthur.

right bottom
NIGEL ATKINSON
Mirror Work. 2000

Cashmere is hand-woven in Scotland and hand-embroidered in India with a contemporary take on the traditional application of mirrors or reflective surfaces found in Moroccan and Indian textiles. Nigel Atkinson has applied the mirrors densely in bands running through the fabric as if they were part of the woven structure. The embroidery creates different tensions – contrasting the embroidered and plain areas of the fabric. For interior and fashion applications.

opposite
ISABEL DODD
Silk satin and polyester velvet machine-embroidered for scarves. 2004

Textile designer Isabel Dodd creates richly textured surfaces by embroidering the silk and polyester together and then passing them through a caustic soda solution which distorts the fabric.

**SCHOELLER TEXTIL AG
3XDRY**

This advanced textile treatment (which has both hydrophobic and hydrophilic properties) can be applied to various fabrics and have many applications. It can keep the wearer dry on the inside by transporting moisture rapidly away to the outside where it can evaporate. As it repels water, clothing made with 3XDRY can keep the wearer dry from the outside. It also dries very quickly when wet and on washing. The 3XDRY technology is used for extreme and active sports and also for fashion.

perspiration on the inside of a garment. Advanced technology means that fabrics can now be waterproof, windproof, lightweight, durable and totally breathable – all the qualities demanded for functional textiles.

Both laminates and coatings can be made breathable by using either a microporous or a hydrophilic membrane. A microporous membrane has ultra-fine holes which allow the passage of water vapour but prevent the passage of rain or wind. A hydrophilic super-fine membrane attracts water and allows the warm water vapour in the form of perspiration to pass through to the generally cooler environment outside the garment. The only place where the hydrophilic property will not work is in very humid conditions where the temperature is higher outside the garment (the passage of water vapour is always from a high to a low temperature). Both microporous and hydrophilic membranes work with most fabrics and are used for a range of applications from extreme sportswear to fashion.

VISIBLE LAMINATES

The finished textile can be laminated with a visible polymer membrane or invisibly on an interior surface. These techniques are used in many different ways – as a means of expression in textile art, to create new aesthetic effects for innovative fashion fabrics, for practical easy-care interior textiles and in

functional high-performance outerwear. Jun'ichi Arai has explored lamination techniques in the creation of his textile art pieces. An example being the lamination of a very thin layer of metal such as titanium, platinum or aluminium to a synthetic base. A vacuum sealer ensures an extremely fine layer of metal is deposited and the result is a fluid, metallic textile.

There is a great demand today for fabrics which refract light or are reflective; holographic laminates can create three-dimensional illusions. Such textiles can be used in clothing for personal safety and in the world of fashion. Textile designer Helen Archer is very interested in the play of light, and has collaborated with Astor Universal Ltd, the largest UK manufacturer of hot stamping foil, to create laminated textiles which feature bold optical effects. Holographic foil is laminated to the reverse of her chosen fabrics which gives a different effect from bonding on to the right side of the textile. Potential applications of her textiles include interior surfaces but they would also be very striking as fashion fabrics.

INVISIBLE LAMINATES

High-performance invisible laminates are an important area for research and development for many textile companies worldwide. Covered here in detail are examples of invisible laminates using the different

methods already described – either the microporous or the hydrophilic system. They are selected for many levels of sport from leisure activities to dangerous sports in hostile conditions.

Gore-Tex was originally designed for space travel by W. L. Gore in the USA in 1958, and was the first laminate to use a breathable membrane. It is unique to W. L. Gore, and its development has prompted much research in this area. Gore-Tex came on to the general market in the late 1970s but is constantly being improved in its handle, strength, durability and performance. The membrane is made from polytetrafluoroethylene (PTFE) which is similar in chemical composition to Teflon and is punctuated with microscopic holes. These perforations are much smaller (approximately 20,000 times) than a drop of water and yet larger (approximately 700 times) than molecules of water vapour, allowing perspiration to escape. These micro characteristics make a fabric with Gore-Tex rain- and windproof while also being breathable. The skin of Gore-Tex is invisible, being sandwiched between fabrics. It can be bonded to almost any fabric, and W. L. Gore manufactures a range of different layers suitable for many users, from a family walking in mild rain to an Arctic exploration team.

Companies who manufacture Gore-Tex clothing work under strict guidelines from W. L. Gore who stipulate that outdoor clothing be designed and made to exacting standards. W. L. Gore have researched and developed special seam-sealing tapes which are durable under washing and dry cleaning, and these must be used with a hot-melt adhesive for securing the seams of a garment made from Gore-Tex. W. L. Gore undertake their own tests with the Gore Rain Simulator, with electronic sensors to pinpoint any water leakage. Since NASA took it up, Gore-Tex has been at the forefront of protective clothing and performance sportswear. It is widely used for military and police uniforms, and, since the breathable membrane prevents the entry of bacteria, is also used for surgeons' clothing. Gore-Tex has been used extensively in jackets and trousers for active walking and for hiking and trekking footwear and many fashion designers have used it and combined the highly functional properties with their own creative look.

The Italian company Raumer Spa have collaborated with Gore Italia, the Italian branch of W. L. Gore, to create a fabric using the membrane Windstopper with pure new wool. Like Gore-Tex, Windstopper is made from PTFE, and is patented by W. L. Gore and Associates. It allows perspiration out, yet prevents wind from penetrating.

Tetratex, another microporous laminate which uses PTFE, is made by Toray Textiles Europe, part of the established Japanese group. They concentrate part of their research on textile finishes and have developed a film

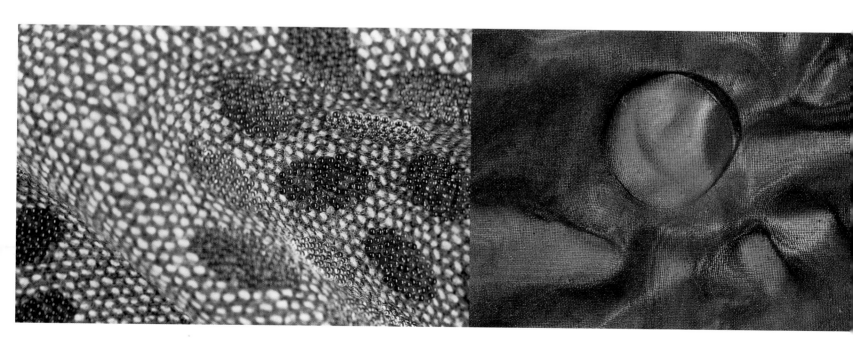

with ultra-fine pores. Tetratex has a three-dimensional structure and is lightweight, protective, breathable and capable of being laminated to a range of substrates.

Sympatex, manufactured by Akzo Nobel, is the trade name for an extremely thin hydrophilic polyester/polyether membrane. This is used by sandwiching it between fabrics. As with many of the new developments in textile technology, research began initially for high-performance sportswear. Lightweight, comfortable fabrics were needed that were completely weatherproof yet breathable and allowed total freedom of movement. Sympatex answers these demands by allowing perspiration molecules to pass through the membrane by bonding with its hydrophilic zones, but does not allow even the smallest drop of water through. It is so dense that the wearer will not feel the slightest chill from a high wind. Being a lightweight, breathable, elastic, durable membrane there are no pores to become blocked with dirt. Its elasticity means it can be laminated to a range of fabrics as when stretched performance is not lessened and it is comfortable to wear while engaged in sporting activities.

There are various ways of using the Sympatex membrane which all give slightly different performances. An advanced adhesive enables the membrane to be laminated to a lining which would then have a separate face fabric. This provides excellent breathability, as generally the nearer the membrane is to body perspiration the faster the water vapour can pass through. Alternatively, the membrane can be laminated to an insert fabric, typically a nonwoven or a fine gauge jersey, that lies between the lining and outer fabric, which is given a waterproof coating. This method allows more scope for creativity and would be a good choice for functional fashion. Finally, the membrane can be laminated directly to the outer fabric, again with a lining, and it is this combination which ensures maximum protection from the elements. In footwear, Sympatex is laminated to a textile upper and then lined; an injection-moulded sole completes the shoe or boot. The result will be lightweight and comfortable and no water will be allowed to penetrate, even in severe conditions.

As with Gore-Tex, seams are a potential area of weakness. Akzo Nobel only approve seam-sealing with their specifically designed tape. The garment manufacturer heat-seals the tape, and this process, like the garment, undergoes rigorous testing. There are no toxic products from the manufacture of this comfort membrane and the company are working towards the laminate being totally recyclable.

COATING

Coating is a textile finish which has been used a great deal in recent years to change the appearance of an underlying textile. Technical coatings can be applied to most textiles: some coat the surface of the fabric, while others coat the actual fibres. They range from ultra-fine films to thick, heavy coatings. Reflective, neon, holographic, lacquered or plasticized (and in a myriad of colours, both subtle and vivid) they can transform the look of a fabric. Three-dimensional relief effects are possible together with illusory or optical features. They can also give a fabric texture by making it granular, contoured and velvety-soft or papery to the touch. Fluorescent and phosphorescent textiles are often in bright, vivid colours and will emit light and glow.

Fishermen's and farmers' sweaters are traditionally knitted from wool with its natural oils left in, giving protection from the elements. Working on a similar principle, fabrics with wax or oil coatings for outerwear have been manufactured for many years. Based on this technique, modern coating technology is now so sophisticated that it can make super-thin films (usually polyurethane) adhere to a fibre's or a fabric's surface.

There are several factors that can influence the success of a finished textile: the type and thickness of the coating, the kind of substrate and the method of application. Extremely thin coatings can create a barrier to the elements but also retain the original look, texture and even the drape of a fabric. A thicker coating is sometimes necessary on a heavy fabric or one with a raised surface, reducing breathability. Fragile-looking but at the same time strong and durable fabrics can be made by applying coatings, particularly transparent ones, to lightweight synthetics. Fabrics for high-performance wear can be coated with a fine film of liquid polyurethane which is either microporous or hydrophilic. Applied to the back of a fabric, it has no visible effect;

SCHOELLER TEXTIL AG
Variations of soft-shell
(trademark) textiles with WB-400
formula

Innovative bonded soft-shell stretch
textiles have been given a WB-400
finish. A triple-layered fabric, it has
a synthetic on the outside,
a functional coating in the middle
and the inner side can be various
linings. Its main characteristics
are that it offers high weather
protection with good breathability.
In addition, a soft-shell textile
provides stretch for freedom of
movement. This technical textile
is used for many outdoor sporting
activities.

left below
EUGÈNE VAN VELDHOVEN
Textile finish. 2002

This fabric uses a white acrylate
coating as a finishing treatment to
transform the underlying textile.
The substrate is a linen/cotton/wool
weave with an overspun effect yarn.
The textile is intended for interior
application.

**NUNO CORPORATION
REIKO SUDO (design)
Otterskin. 1995**

This nonwoven polyester has a beautiful soft handle and is made from recycled plastic bottles using a needlepunch technique. The surface is then coated with polyurethane resin. This textile is ideal for padding as it is warm and breathable while also being wind- and waterproof.

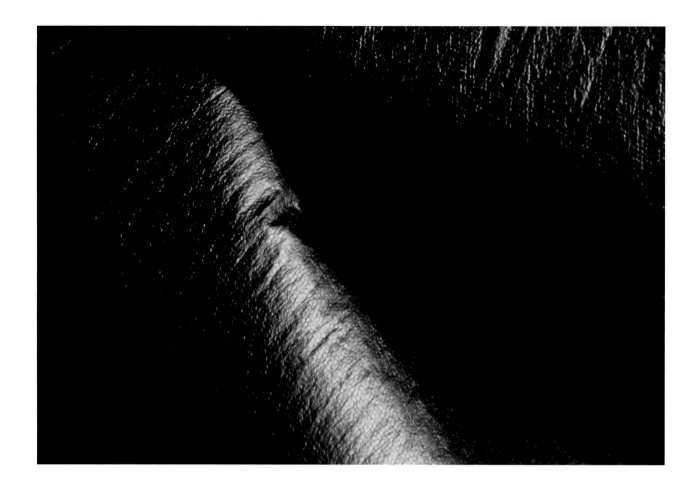

applied to the face it can create a deliberate resinous look and texture.

Working with high-tech coatings, fashion designers have created futuristic looks by contrasting them with natural materials. These finished textiles have good performance properties while also retaining the advantages of a natural fabric. For instance, cotton with a fine resin layer can be beautiful and practical – extending the appeal of a garment and accessories such as bags and shoes. The surface of such a coated natural fabric can be wiped clean, and the latest in technological advances also makes them scratchproof. Fashion designers often create imaginative ways of working with sophisticated coatings which will in turn inspire new technical finishes.

Silicone as a coating material gives a waterproof, breathable fabric. Used as a finishing treatment to soften and improve the texture of a fabric, it imparts elasticity, ensuring that the textile will keep its shape after repeated washing. On a wool fabric this finish provides non-shrink and anti-pill

qualities. A very dilute solution as a fine film on either a natural or a synthetic fabric results in a flexible cloth which is easy-care. Silicone-treated fabrics have many uses: for interiors, outdoor garments, sportswear and fashion. They are also popular for industrial textiles and protective clothing as they can be radiation- and heat-resistant, flame-retardant, durable and will be flexible even in extreme conditions.

Teflon (tradename for polytetrafluoro-ethylene or PTFE) coatings are water-repellent and durable, and often used for outerwear as an invisible, robust barrier for wind, rain and snow. The finish is also stain-resistant, making the fabric easy to care for. To create an even more effective shield against extreme conditions, an additional coating of polyurethane can be given to the inside surface of the textile. Teflon treatments on very fine yarns can combine high-performance properties with a delicate appearance. Toray Textiles Europe, part of the established Japanese group, produce Teflon treatments on ultra-fine yarns.

Coatings such as resin and polyurethane can have many uses. In Nuno's metal fabrics using copper, the wire is given a very fine polyurethane layer to prevent the copper from oxidizing and turning green and brittle. It therefore keeps its warm colour and stays flexible. Reiko Sudo gives various substrates such as silk, wool and polyester ultra-gloss looks and relief textures by layering aluminium, acrylic or urethane resin foils on to a cloth using pressure. The outcome is very rich and beautiful textiles.

Likewise, fascinated with metallics, Jun'ichi Arai has experimented with advanced finishes such as coating metal textiles. The metal layer can be further enhanced by giving it an ultra-thin film of polyamide resin which allows the take-up of dye for a range of shimmering colours. He has used this technology to dye aluminium-coated polyester and further experiments to remove the coating either partially or entirely can result in a textile with a fascinating metallic, crystalline appearance. Jun'ichi Arai continues to investigate textile finishes and unusual treatments at the Japanese Textile Research Centre in Kiryú.

Japanese manufacturers Komatsu Seiren and Itoi Textile both use a silk protein powder (ground waste silk from kimono production) combined with a polyurethane resin. Komatsu Seiren's high-performance textiles coated with silk protein powder are called ProteinTex fabrics; properties are an attractive ultra-soft handle, water and wind resistance and breathability. Itoi Textile's Silky Powder is a similar coating applied to fine wool and the end result is very smooth wool which has the sheen of silk.

Many of the latest coatings are also environmentally friendly. Originally developed for markets such as extreme sportswear, they are now offering new aesthetics for everyday clothing. The customer can only benefit from this fusion of function and fashion.

SPATTERING

The technique of spattering or spatter-plating involves metal powder being dissolved into

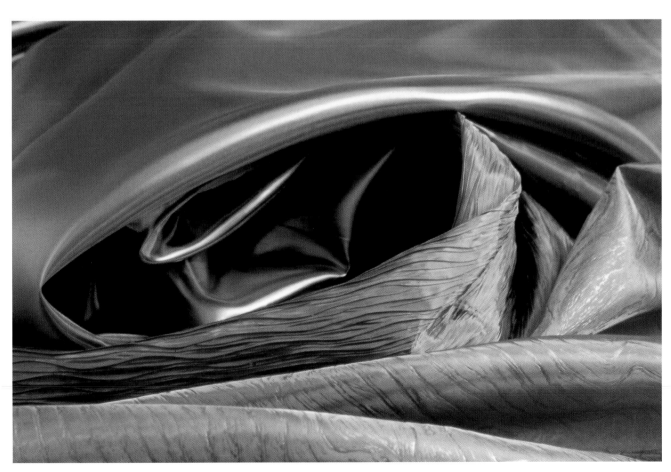

**NUNO CORPORATION
REIKO SUDO (design)
Stainless series. 1990**

Plain woven polyester is given an ultra-fine 'spatter-plating' of stainless steel, a technique borrowed from the Japanese automobile industry for applying metallic trim to car parts. The technique is altered for a textile and the result is a cloth which is fluid, sensual, light-reflective and very desirable. The spattering is repeated three times, once for each of the three powdered metals, chrome, nickel and iron which make up the alloy, stainless steel. The powder is dissolved into a solution and then sprayed on to the fabric base using a vacuum coating technique. Different finishing effects can be achieved to vary the lustrous look and surface texture. The top fabric is Stainless Steel Gloss where the plain woven polyester is polished smooth before being spatter-plated. The middle fabric is Stainless Steel Pleats and the bottom fabric is Stainless Steel Emboss.

above
HELEN ARCHER
Cactus. 1995

Spray-enhanced polyester/cotton
and holofoil. A dévoré fabric works
with a holographic foil and
transforms into an amazing
surface with light-reflecting
properties. The fabric has been
developed with Astor Universal Ltd.

opposite
NIGEL ATKINSON
**King Lear Leaf. 1989 (motif) and
2004 (this interpretation)**

This Florentine design uses
a polyester velvet with a cotton
back and a burn-out dévoré
process. A wonderful contrast
is created between the shiny
synthetic velvet pile and the
threadbare open areas where the
yarn has been removed. Interior
application.

a solution and then very finely sprayed on to
a base fabric using a vacuum method of
coating. It is a permanent finish and is both
eye-catching and intriguing. The technique
tends to work best on a synthetic textile,
and woven polyester in particular, and the
resulting fabric can be washed by hand or
machine or be dry-cleaned. Modern
technology has allowed the use of much
safer metallic chemicals; previously, many
were harmful if the minute particles of
metallic dust were breathed in.

Spattering was created in Japan by
Masayuki Suzuki for the company Suzutora,
who hold many patents. This technique is
now used by many textile and fashion
designers and artists who combine the
aesthetic and physical qualities to create
new ideas. There has been a great deal of

research into metallic fibres and fine coatings
in recent years.

A variety of beautiful effects can be
achieved including matt, high-gloss, relief
and three-dimensional opticals. Reiko Sudo
looked to the Japanese car industry where
a protective finish of stainless steel is very
finely spatter-plated on to door handles or
other car parts. The technique was modified
so that fabrics could be coated in this way –
chrome, nickel and iron powders in solution
are finely sprayed on to a substrate. Nuno
have experimented with the spattering
technique on woven polyester to create
different looks and textures. As well as
being very seductive in appearance and
handle, a metallic coating on a textile can
give performance benefits. A stainless-steel
spattered cloth is resistant to many weather

conditions, and fine copper coating with polyurethane resin gives an anti-bacterial and deodorant fabric. Metallized textiles can also be anti-static and reduce radiation emitted from televisions and computers.

CHEMICAL TREATMENTS

Nuno Corporation often focus on woven structures, designing complex Jacquard patterns to achieve a wonderful variety of textures. The finishing treatments they employ are often just as important as the construction in creating the final look, handle and performance. The combination of a variety of yarns and finishing processes can cause certain yarns to react, producing new and interesting surfaces. Using advanced technologies based on traditional crafts, Reiko Sudo has used chemicals to etch into or sometimes completely dissolve layers of cloth, creating exquisite textiles.

Silk Road Corporation, a Korean company, has developed chemically crushed and pleated silks that are permanent finishes. This was previously not possible with this natural material.

Tencel Limited have created a crushed finish using chemicals. Called Scrunch, it is a permanently creased fabric with a soft drape and inherent stretch.

Dévoré (burn-out) textiles have enjoyed huge popularity and continue to do so. A special fabric is usually necessary with a cellulosic yarn and a non-cellulosic in both the warp and the weft. A chemical is printed on to the woven fabric which eats into the cellulose areas to create a wonderful new cloth that contrasts the dense with the sheer. Alternatively, a resist paste can be applied which will protect areas from the chemicals applied. Dévoré velvets are particularly sumptuous. Combining such techniques with laminates, foils and coatings for example, produces imagery with added relief surface interest.

As well as chemical treatments to alter the aesthetic and texture, performance is an area of much research and development. The Japanese company Kanebo Ltd manufacture highly functional textiles, including a chemically treated synthetic to control the growth of certain bacteria and thereby reduce odour and the deterioration of the textile. This finish has many applications, including clothing for sportswear, fashion, lingerie and bed linen. Other chemical fabric finishes can protect the wearer from harmful ultra-violet rays or maintain the skin's natural pH balance in any environment. These and even more futuristic-sounding finishing treatments are being developed to create textiles with exacting performance qualities.

The special finishes available and under research are increasingly important at a time when customers are demanding high quality in terms of aesthetics (both visual and physical) and the behaviour of a textile. Finishing is, of course, the last process in textile production, and at this point unusual and innovative fabrics can often be created. The latest finishing technologies can produce fabrics that answer very specific needs in performance – flexibility, durability, the ability to retain their shape and shield against a variety of damaging or uncomfortable external factors while also being environmentally sound. Considered by many to be an important part in the future of textiles, much imaginative thinking and experimentation is being devoted to this final stage.

opposite
NUNO CORPORATION
REIKO SUDO (design)
Paper Roll. 2003

This polyamide lace with a delicate and intricate pattern is made by lining up the polyamide tape and basting it down to a water-soluble fabric. The design is machine-embroidered in place and then the backing is dissolved using a chemical lace technique. It is inspired by rolled up papers viewed in cross-section.

right
EUGÈNE VAN VELDHOVEN
Textile finish. 2003

A dévoré or burn-out print transforms a cotton textile and the result is intentionally placed holes which vary in size and shape. The textile is intended for interior application.

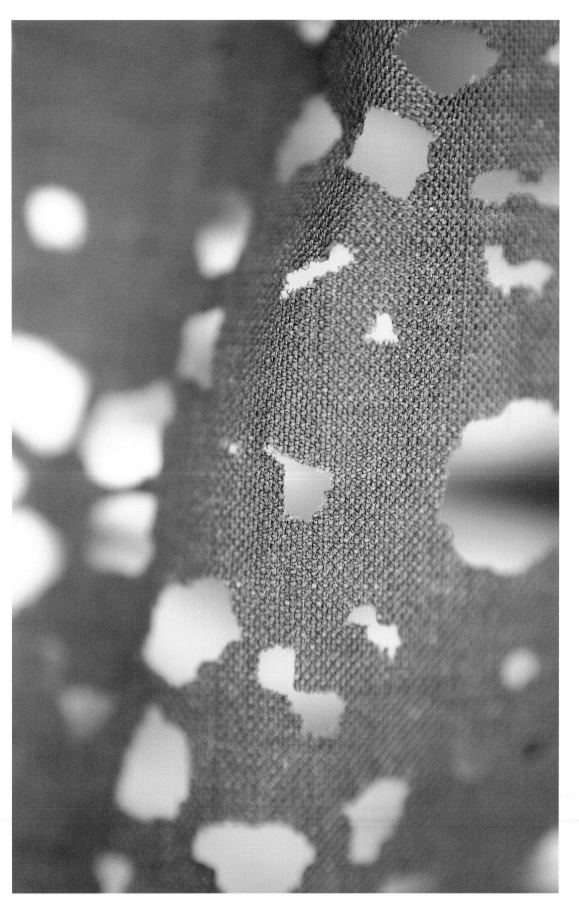

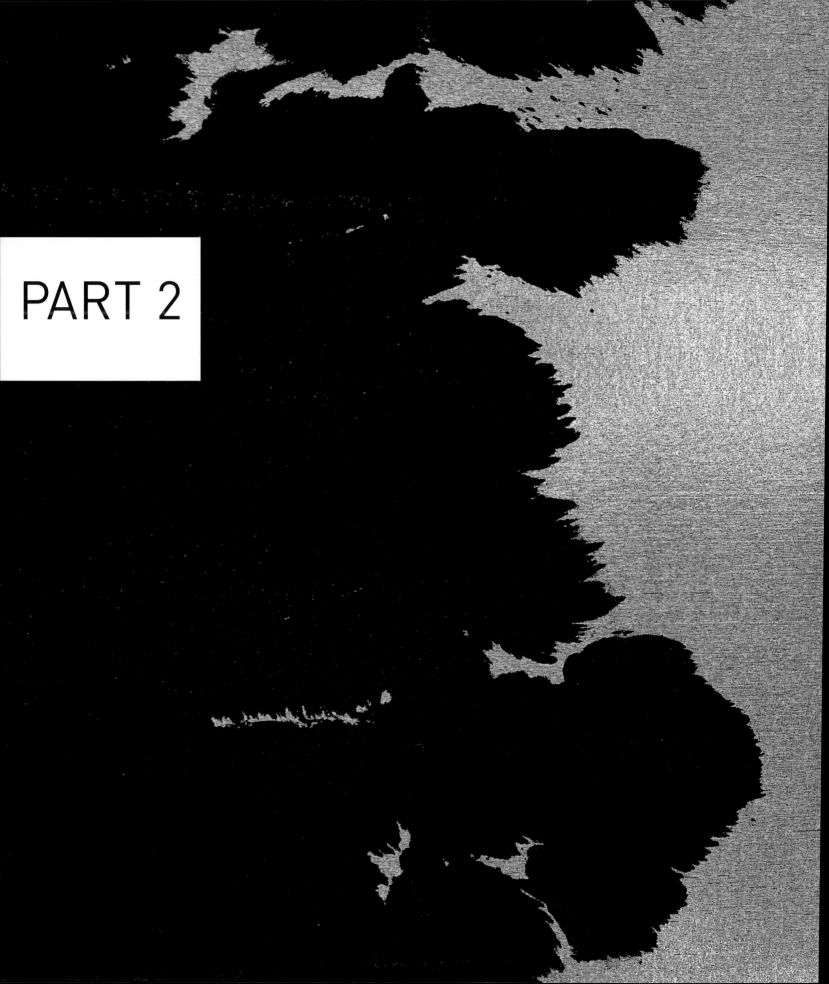

PART 2

APPLICATIONS

Fashion

Sarah E. Braddock Clarke

Design

Marie O'Mahony

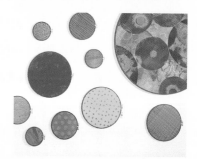

Architecture

Marie O'Mahony

Art

Sarah E. Braddock Clarke

Fashion

Sarah E. Braddock Clarke

above
**NORMA STARSZAKOWNA
Scarves and Rust-Stripe –
accessories and textile for fashion
designer Shirin Guild
Spring/Summer 2003**

Silk scarves, pleated, metal-rusted
and printed with white pigment to
provide added texture and contrast
(left) and Rust-Stripe, metal-rusted
silk (right). A metal rusting technique
is achieved by applying iron filings,
rusted wire or metal shapes to
salted, wet silk prior to wrapping it
in polythene and leaving or burying
for a few days. The end results are
wash-fast and suitable for fashion.
Printed by Jamison Print.

right
**MICHIKO KOSHINO
Autumn/Winter 2004/05**

Thick protective sports fabrics are
padded to create this dramatic look
for a jacket in acid green with
contrasting blue lining. The collection
is inspired by 1960s Alpine skiwear;
the harness belt detailing makes
reference to function.

In the fashion world new technological
textiles have made a huge impact with
their unique look, handle and performance.
In the last two decades momentous advances
in textile technology have provided all areas
of fashion with futuristic fabrics that are
totally functional as well as beautiful.

Important experimentation is taking place
into the development of new materials and
many consider fabric to be the future of
fashion, with the latest innovative textiles
being applied to both prêt-à-porter and
haute couture. Haute couture fashion often
expresses the designer's vision in its purest
form and is seen by many to be equal in
status to the fine arts. Attention can be given
to a fabric by using clean, uninterrupted
garment lines and the latest ultra-stretch
textiles enable a close fit without the need
for intricate tailoring.

What we wear often conveys a message
through our choices. Designers are aware of
this and understand that if we select techno
textiles we are demonstrating to society our
appreciation of the contemporary world.

Technology applied to fashion helps us to
adapt to multiple and ever-changing lifestyles,
and comfort, freedom, versatility and
functionality are key. The latest synthetics and
finishing treatments answer our needs with
their eye-catching appeal, desirable touch
and high performance. We are incorporating
these new advances into our clothing, often
combining them with traditional materials to
create an interesting balance.

In terms of textile technology many of
the most important developments have
been made in technical materials originally
designed for extreme sports and the streamlined aesthetic owes a great deal to the
influence of functional clothing. International
fashion designers incorporate such textiles
in their diffusion or sportswear lines and
mainline collections, and even for evening and
occasion wear. Neoprene, a material used
primarily for wetsuits, can be combined with
materials such as silk chiffon to create a
unique textile. Fashion designers choose the
new textiles largely for their progressive
appearance and sometimes regardless of

their supreme performance properties. Instead, they enjoy the distinctive appeal of technical textiles which are rarely designed for beauty, finding them intriguing to work with and seeing that they offer something a bit different. They use them in unusual ways for clothes that are very much part of the twenty-first century. It is the customer who takes on the often extraordinary capabilities of the materials and now expects more from their wardrobes.

In the 1960s many fashion designers experimented with a space-age aesthetic and looked to the future with their use of high-tech materials and new methods of constructing garments. For example, Pierre Cardin used vacuum-formed and moulded fabrics, André Courrèges used bonded jerseys and synthetics and Paco Rabanne made metal-linked and chain-mail and even paper garments. These three continue to inspire many of today's fashion designers.

Helmut Lang is well known for his interest in technology, as demonstrated by his predominant use of highly sophisticated synthetics and finishing treatments. He was the first fashion designer to show collections on the Internet. Helmut Lang designs for both sexes and the often androgynous look of his collections, with their clean-cut and contemporary shapes, are mainly inspired by the urban street. Sleek silhouettes give full attention to the textiles and his trademark is the use of ultra-lightweight synthetics and techno materials such as latex rubbers, metallics and reflectives. His hard-edged

style for womenswear can also be sensual depending on the fabrics he chooses. Each season's collections relate to the last; he does not jump from one idea to another for the sake of it. Instead, his simple cutting, which reveals perfect, basic and classic shapes, is refined with details of cut. There is never anything superfluous as he pares his ideas down to achieve a minimalist yet expressive style. Helmut Lang inspires many fashion designers with his contemporary aesthetic and he has achieved a cult following.

New York-based fashion designer Donna Karan believes that 'technology is the future of fashion'. She has a deep interest in the new synthetics and sophisticated textile finishes which often provide the starting point for her collections. She works closely with textile designers who create unique fashion fabrics for her. Donna Karan's aim is to create clothes that look good and which function well – the latest materials available frequently answer her need for comfortable and elegant dressing.

The future for textiles is very exciting as the large textile companies continue to invest in research and development. Already on the market are fabrics which look attractive, feel good, protect the wearer from the elements and are beneficial to health and well-being. The possibilities are infinite, including hybrids of textures and volumes. Together textile and fashion designers are creating a new vision and sensory, tactile experience – proving that twenty-first century clothing contains a myriad of ideas and expressions.

Previous pages:
page 106
GRETHE WITTROCK
Obsidian (detail). 2003 – see p. 175

p. 107
Chapter 5
(left) **ELEY KISHIMOTO** – see p. 121
(right) **NORMA STARSZAKOWNA**
Black Crush for Shirin Guild. 2003

Chapter 6
(left) **LE CHARLEROI**
Geomesh – see p. 139
(right) **JULIE RYDER** – see p. 145

Chapter 7
(left) **KOCH, Hostaflon** – see p. 153
(right) **LANG AND BAUMANN**
Breathing Pillows – see p. 157

Chapter 8
(left) **ISSEY MIYAKE** – see p. 172
(right) **SONJA WEBER** – see p. 9

right top and bottom
HELMUT LANG
Spring/Summer 2004

This collection was inspired by delicate dragonfly wings and uses iridescent colours contrasted with neutral skin tones. Simple vest shapes with cut-outs (top) give attention to the fabrics for a look which is striking and intensely modern. The eye-catching silver fabric used for these trousers (bottom) expresses a futuristic look that is a statement on its own. Helmut Lang is known for his use of technological fabrics and creates both menswear and womenswear. Pared down silhouettes are the basis for his design approach.

PACO RABANNE
Autumn/Winter 2004/05

Paco Rabanne is an innovative fashion designer who became famous in the 1960s for his use of new materials and ways of constructing garments. He worked with metals, plastics and papers and the collections still demonstrate the use of non-traditional materials. Here, a very open silver mesh is worn over a simple black dress to create his signature look.

DIESELSTYLELAB
Spring/Summer 2004

DieselStyleLab are inventive with their choice of materials and cutting and styling. This dress owes much to a sportswear aesthetic with its drawstring and functional pockets. White imparts a clean, fresh look, ideal for summer, and gives attention to the utilitarian detailing.

DONNA KARAN
Autumn/Winter 2004/05

Known for comfortable and flattering dressing using the latest materials with traditional naturals, Donna Karan creates effortless glamour. She often uses stretch fabrics and here contrasts body-conscious cutting with fluid draping around the body and embellishment feature. An asymmetric neckline gives a contemporary edge to a feminine silhouette.

PRADA WOMAN
Spring/Summer 2003

This short tunic is made of precious brocade fabric, reinvented with a technical trim inspired by wetsuits. Reference to the era of the 1960s is made with its fluorescent colour cut into short, sharp shapes. It is accessorized with a dramatic yellow plastic stone necklace and silver pointed flat shoes.

PRADA WOMAN
Spring/Summer 2003

This collection's focus is reminiscent of the 1960s and suggests an atmosphere that looks to the future with its minimal silhouettes with linear shaping and applied decoration. Here, a cotton jersey dress in futuristic white is studded with white and coloured plastic stones.

PRADA WOMAN
Spring/Summer 2003

Silk jersey dress with beaded necklace – the jewelry is part of the clothing and decorates the neckline of this garment. Miuccia Prada makes reference to the 1960s where garments had sewn-in gem and paste necklaces, but she does so in a contemporary way, without nostalgia.

DESIGNERS OF FASHION TEXTILES

The textile designer, always important to the fashion designer, is especially so now that there are so many inventive new materials around. Some textile designers work very closely with a single fashion designer and some with several at one time. They can work more as a collaboration/partnership and sometimes over several seasons or even years. Establishing a definite rapport, each will understand and respect the others' approach. Ideas, themes, colours and silhouettes will be discussed beforehand to create a basis for the textile designer to then explore and come up with a range of exciting fashion fabrics. Some fashion designers employ a team of textile designers to create cloth specifically for them. Other textile designers prefer to not be linked long term to an individual and create designs which they sell as one-off pieces to the fashion designer or company, sometimes through an agency or at one of the many international trade fairs for fashion fabrics. Some designers create specialist show textiles for the catwalks; for printed textiles, sometimes these are engineered, where the print is not in a repeat but follows the garment silhouette. The design is very carefully placed so the image does not cross the seams achieved by masking off certain areas of the design. Others produce definite repeat patterns put into metrage for production. Whichever way

they wish to work it is evident that the worlds of textiles and fashion have become increasingly close in the last two decades.

The end focus can even be on the fabric itself, its look, texture, performance, the way it is manipulated or embellished. The choice of textile can significantly influence the eventual silhouette and the entire message of a collection. Many fashion designers use polyester (microfibre or ultra-microfibre fabrics, in particular) as it is such a versatile fabric and can be treated for a range of different effects. Stretch textiles are extremely important in contemporary fashion and are used by many designers. The use of DuPont's Lycra in percentages to either create a comfortable, relaxed fit or to be like a second skin is almost commonplace in the international collections. Blended with natural textiles or the latest synthetics, the incorporation of Lycra creates stretch textiles which ensure a modern look, both flattering and functional.

Experimentation through handling the materials directly is still a very important part of the design process. It is very difficult to design a textile solely on the computer as the inherent physical properties must be carefully considered. The combination of a strong craft production and use of technology has informed the international fashion scene – much in evidence in Japan during the 1990s and now highly visible worldwide.

above and right
BOUDICCA
Leave
Spring/Summer 1998

Fashion designers: Zowie Broach and Brian Kirkby of Boudicca. Mould maker: Keese van der Graaf. Textile designer: Savithri Bartlett. The fabric is the result of MPhil research carried out at the Royal College of Art by Savithri Bartlett. She worked with nonwoven fibres using a bicomponent thermoplastic polyester fibre called Wellbond manufactured by Wellman International. This fibre combines a low melting temperature with high fibre strength. Boudicca created a seamless, moulded bodice that reflected the silhouette of the contemporary woman. They collaborated with a Harley Street plastic surgeon and his client in taking a cast of her silicone breast implants.

(above) The white and blue bodice on the catwalk gives a futuristic, even space-age look. (right) This image shows two of the bodices dyed with indigo blue using CIBA dyes and chemicals.

Digital technology has greatly changed the look of textiles. Computer-linked Jacquard and knitting machines allow for extremely fine and intricate patterning which can faithfully reproduce a hand-drawn, photographic or scanned image. Using the computer can allow for layers of imagery to be built up for rich effect. Complex weave structures with varying textures and surfaces such as double, quadruple and even multilayer cloths are more easily possible. Digitally printed textiles eliminate the need for traditional screens and enable a more economic and ecologically sound process. Previously, different colourways were done by hand, whereas now they can be performed by computer at great speed In the textile and fashion industries there are only a few companies that will do short print runs. The latest digital textile printers can even print on a stretch Lycra blend textile, once considered a very difficult substrate to print on.

Applicable to both constructed and printed textiles, the use of computer-aided design and computer-aided manufacture (CAD/CAM)

allows for different scales to be achieved for one-off designs or art works; variety of repeat size (large repeats are more viable), layering of imagery and for much greater flexibility. At its best, the computer not only speeds up production, but acts as a facilitator, giving the user the freedom to conceive new ideas.

Collaborating for many years with the famous Japanese fashion designer Issey Miyake, textile designer Makiko Minagawa has worked with leading and specialist textile manufacturers to develop innovative fabrics. Makiko Minagawa is acutely aware of the physical and sensual properties of textiles and explores their inherent characteristics. She reinvents and rejuvenates traditional textile techniques by experimenting with natural and synthetic fibres, different fabric constructions and textile finishes. Makiko Minagawa has always been interested in creating fabrics using techniques that may not have been thought possible to apply to a textile. Some of these may be found in the traditions of handcrafts, others from breakthroughs in technology.

above left
SAVITHRI BARTLETT, DEBORAH MILNER & KAREN SPURGIN
Dress using layers of laser-cut fabrics

This garment was made for the exhibition *Great Expectations* in New York, 2001 hosted by the Design Council. Layered fabrics of different weights and opacities were laser-cut to create eye-catching moiré effects. Opaque habotai silk and translucent resin-coated paper nylon were used. The textile design is by Savithri Bartlett, the garment by haute couture designer Deborah Milner and the embellishment by Karen Spurgin. Savithri Bartlett has been involved with many collaborative projects, combining her scientific knowledge of lasers with an interest in fashion. Her current research as a PhD student at Loughborough University explores both natural and synthetic textiles and the range of aesthetics possible using laser technology.

above right
SAVITHRI BARTLETT & KAREN SPURGIN
Detail of fabrics

Textile design by Savithri Bartlett and embellishment by Karen Spurgin. Layers of cloth (opaque habotai silk and translucent resin-coated paper nylon) have been subjected to the beam of a laser to cut a pattern of holes. A wonderful optical effect is created by choice of colour and fabric superimposition. The surface has opaque and translucent sequins sewn on the different fabrics to enhance the layered effect.

above
BOUDICCA
Autumn/Winter 2003/04

Fashion designers: Zowie Broach and Brian Kirkby of Boudicca. Textile designer: Savithri Bartlett. Laser-cut textiles are superimposed to make an optical effect. The top two layers in black and flesh tone are acrylic and lighter in weight than the third layer of Indian pink Polyamide 6.6. The polyamide is left uncut to act as a backdrop for the top layers. By combining different weights of fabric, colour and design, the illusion of volume is created which really comes alive when worn.

right
B. EARLEY
Zip Print Boots
A collaborative research project with Paul Thomas. 2000

Rebecca Earley commissioned these boots, which were made by Paul Thomas, as a prototype. The vegetable tanned calfskin has been Heat Photogram printed and embossed with a metal zip. This process can transfer detailed impressions of objects to the textile, often with such wonderful trompe l'oeil effects. The zip was stitched into a mirror image template of the boot pattern, and then painted with disperse dyes, before being baked and heat pressed. The illusion of a zip on the side of the ankle boot achieves this surreal result.

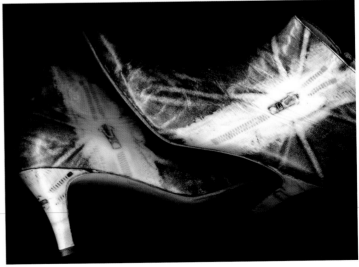

B. EARLEY
**Heat Photogram Exhaust Printed
Samples. 2002**

Rebecca Earley has been developing her signature Heat Photogram technique since her MA fashion studies at Central St Martins. In 1998 she started to consider ways of being more environmentally friendly and was inspired by the Chelsea College Project, Textiles Environment Design. Exhaust dyeing is where the same dye vat is used over and over until the fabric or yarn absorbs all the dye and the water runs clear. B. Earley applied the same principle to printing and uses a sequential heat photogram print on Alcantara Suede, a polyester microfibre. She uses disperse dye, brown craft paper and fern leaves as stencils and prints with them over and over again until all the dye is used up. A gradual fading is noticed which ends with an attractive ghostly effect. This print came from working in Cornwall on the Eden Project, 2002.

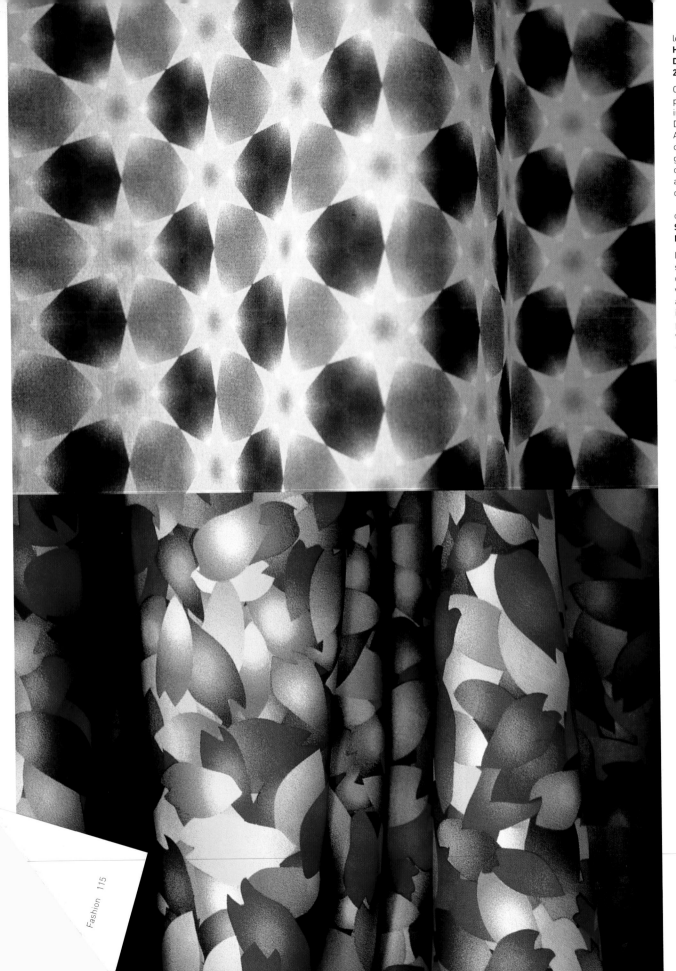

left and left below
HELLE ABILD
Digitally printed fabrics for fashion.
2000

Cotton printed with an ink-jet Stork printer (left) and silk printed with an ink-jet DuPont printer (left below). Danish textile practitioner Helle Abild builds up colour and form to create patterned fabrics. Rich gradation of colours and complex overlapping of motifs can be achieved more easily using the digital textile printer.

opposite
SUE GUNDY
Red Ripples. 2004

Digitally printed silk chiffon for scarves and shawls. Sue Gundy is often inspired by the endless variations of colour, texture, pattern and form found in nature. The inspiration for this design came from photographs of the sun reflecting off water and rippling over smooth granite at Georgian Bay, part of Lake Huron, Ontario, Canada. Red flowers are contrasted against the blue water and green foliage. She uses Photoshop to create the design, its layer management allows her to combine different images in a seamless style. Here, three layers, a background of water ripples, the colour gradation in water and red flowers are brought together.

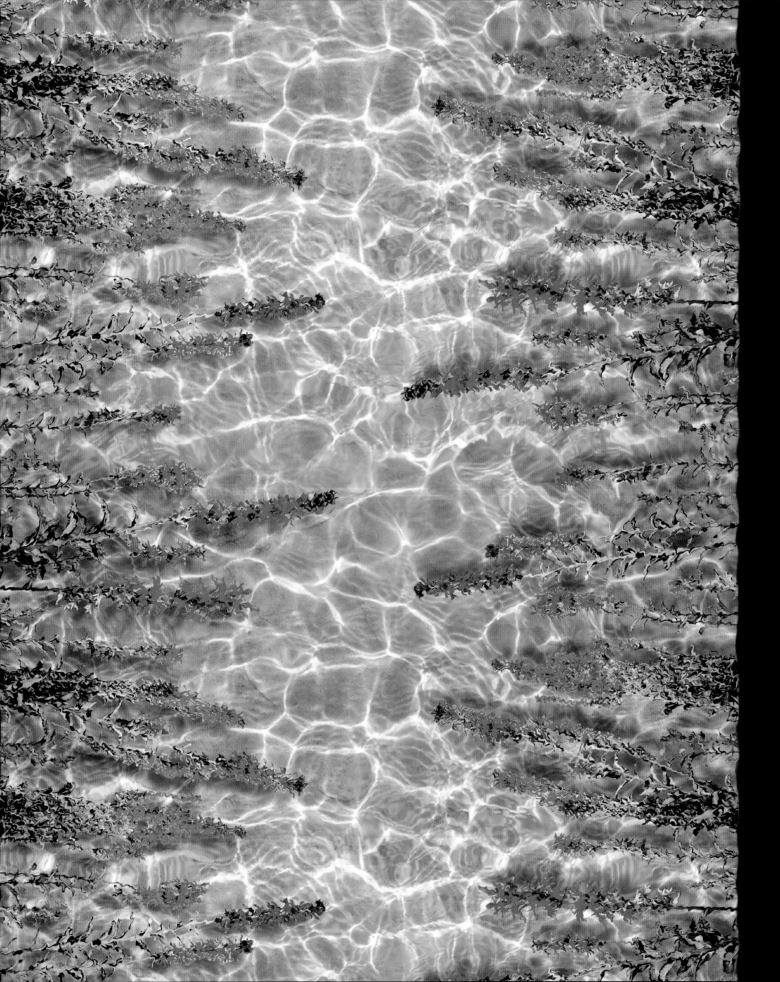

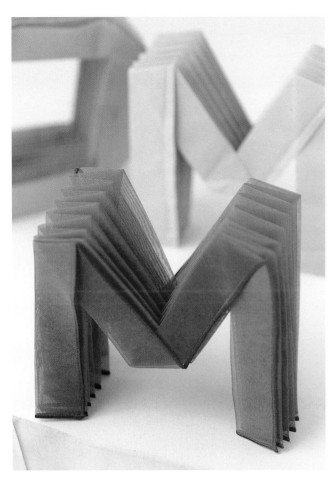

above and right
NUNO CORPORATION
Origami Bag and Origami Pleats
Reiko Sudo and Mizue Okada
(design). Origami Bag and Origami
Pleats. 1997 & 2002

Polyester fabric is hand folded
repeatedly in sharp, crisp angles as
in origami and then dyed in two
separate colours. The fabric is then
permanently pressed in a special
pleating process which is patent-
pending. The resulting textile with
its abstract structure can be used
for fashion accessories such as
scarves and bags. The textile is
included in the Design Collection of
the Museum of Modern Art, New
York 1998, the Collection of the
National Museum of Modern Art,
Tokyo, 2001 and the Baltimore
Museum of Art, 2002.

Where she has looked at ancient Japanese textile traditions or those of other cultures for inspiration, she has developed them further using sophisticated and modern techniques. Some of Makiko Minagawa's discoveries have been the development of ways of creating the look of traditional textiles using more practical and less labour-intensive and time-consuming methods. In this way ancient craft techniques, such as resist-dyeing, sashiko and shibori, are kept alive. The textiles acquire a particular aesthetic which makes reference to the past while being contemporary. Makiko Minagawa's textiles make important individual statements and have played an essential part in the final look of Issey Miyake's clothing. Makiko Minagawa produces the HaaT collection, still under the Issey Miyake umbrella. It is a collaboration with manufacturers in India and includes many craft techniques such as hand/machine embroidery, stitching, quilting and mirror-work decoration.

Nuno Corporation are known for their exceptionally inventive textiles and have supplied many fashion designers. From 1970, the original founders of Nuno, Jun'ichi Arai and Reiko Sudo, were creating textiles for the fashion world, even before Nuno was founded in 1982. Making clothes from Nuno fabrics demands skill as the garment should not compete with the fabric. Simple silhouettes and designs draped around the body, rather than cut to fit, display the fabric to the full. In Nuno's main Tokyo shop there is a small selection of garments and accessories.

Jürgen Lehl designs many things, including textiles and fashion. Born in Poland of German nationality, he is now based in Tokyo and has over forty-three shops throughout Japan and is well known there. He makes reference to both Eastern and Western cultures in his work. Jürgen Lehl is passionate about fabric and this is where his true creativity lies. His designs are all exquisitely made with great attention to detail and a significant emphasis placed on texture with subtle colouring. High twist yarns are often used and he is interested in revealing the fibres' inherent properties, contrasting the characteristics of, for example, silk and cotton in a single fabric. For many years he has only used natural materials and works with eco-friendly materials which will totally biodegrade. In contrast to this, Jürgen Lehl's

textiles can be technologically complex using computer-controlled knitting machines with a Jacquard inlay to create highly sophisticated patterning. Irregular surfaces and random effects are introduced and he enjoys the look of a hand-produced textile. Many use handspun yarns and natural dyes. Ancient craft techniques, natural materials and the latest production methods are brought together to create a modern aesthetic. Jürgen Lehl's clothes give the fabric prominence by being cut in an understated and elegant way and they are comfortable – allowing movement from the wearer. Fusing tradition and innovation, he is considered by many to be one of the world's most important contemporary textile designers.

Sophie Roet is a freelance textile designer who creates fabrics mainly for fashion. She takes great care in sourcing her yarns and works with specialized textiles, enjoying the play of synthetics and non-textiles against naturals and the more traditional. She is always striving to get away from the strict horizontals and verticals so typical of the weaving process. Inspired by traditional Japanese water cloth, she often manipulates her fabrics once woven to create an irregular and gentle movement. Sophie Roet also enjoys exploring various finishing processes from the simplest to those which utilize the most sophisticated technological developments in treating a cloth. Interested in the transformation of a fabric, she is especially drawn to Japanese textiles, liking their sensitivity to a fibre and their honest approach to working with cloth. She respects the Japanese textile designer's understanding of a fibre's inherent properties, pushing their capabilities to achieve very creative results.

Textile design duo Mark Eley and Wakako Kishimoto of Eley Kishimoto are well known for their bold, innovative textiles. They typically use various printing technologies and frequently invent their own processes. Preferring to work directly with cloth rather than making designs on paper, they experiment freely with the particular characters of their chosen fabrics. Eley Kishimoto have worked to commission for top international fashion designers, intuitively interpreting the theme given. A very creative process, their input as textile designers for fashion has often been significant with their eye-catching, unforgettable designs. Eley

above left
JÜRGEN LEHL
Spring 2004

This top uses silk and cotton yarns and is a double structured Jacquard fabric made on a computer-controlled knitting machine. Two thin layers of single jersey are interlocked to show either in the front or back.

above right
JÜRGEN LEHL
Autumn 2004

The textile for this dress is created by using high-twist cotton with an intarsia technique. The design of the knit together with the direction of the highly twisted yarn makes the wavy pattern. It is knitted on a computer-controlled machine which allows for such sophisticated construction.

left
JÜRGEN LEHL
Spring 2002

For this fabric length cotton is tuck-knitted on a computer-controlled machine. The high-twist cotton yarn creates an uneven pattern and gives added surface texture.

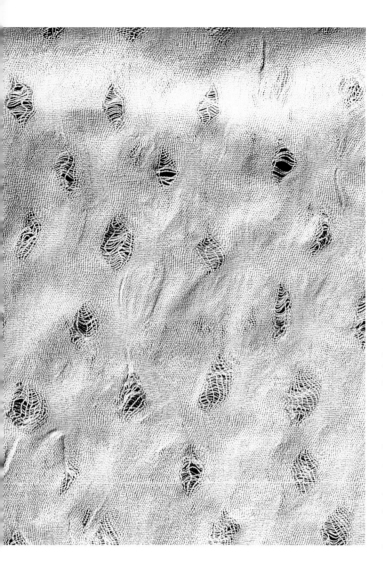

above
SOPHIE ROET
Cobweb. 2001

The warp is linen and the weft is a blend of silk/steel and metallized polyester. The steel is extremely fine and twisted with the silk and the stainless steel gives a sculptural quality. The textile has been hand woven and manipulated to create the open spacing. Placed stripes of metallized polyester have been woven into the cloth, creating subtle shine when reflecting the light. This textile was designed for shawls and produced for the fashion designer Eskandar.

opposite left
ELEY KISHIMOTO
Flash
Spring/Summer 2001

Optical effect print using just red and white. Eley Kishimoto often limit their colour palette to allow them to control their end result better. This is a one-colour dye paste print on cotton poplin. They have created prints on a variety of media from textiles to wallpaper and even ceramics.

opposite right
ELEY KISHIMOTO
Turbulence
Spring/Summer 2004

Two-colour dye paste print on pre-dyed stretch cotton. The linear patterning of this design works with the curvilinear cutting of the garment silhouette enhanced by the use of a stretch textile. The garment looks as if it is swirling around the wearer.

Kishimoto have worked with a diverse range of materials and techniques, from natural fibres to the latest functional textiles such as stretch microfibres and coated materials, and from hand-painting to manipulating imagery on the computer. Since 1995 Eley Kishimoto have offered their own label which gives them more room for experimentation. They design both the textiles and the garment/accessory collections themselves, each season having a title and theme. In their London studio they experiment, design, print, cut and sample, following through the process from beginning to end. Constantly experimenting with new applications and end products for their designs, they may also offer something additional to clothing – umbrellas, bags, shoes/boots, socks, sunglasses, wallpaper and even ceramics. By having their own label they see their designs (both textile and fashion ideas) on the catwalk under their own name, whereas when they designed textiles for fashion designers the name Eley Kishimoto tended to be in the background. Examples of their textiles include new interpretations of florals, bold geometrics, trompe l'oeil effects and hand-drawn checks – their imagery is often fun and witty. Printing methods they have used include chemical treatments such as bleach and dévoré and ways of achieving an antiqued look. Eley Kishimoto have an eye for colour, often using a small range (to allow them to control it better) and are not afraid of imagery on a large scale which is kept simple and fresh for maximum impact. The silhouettes of their label are frequently inspired by Wakako Kishimoto's own childhood dresses and have an appeal to all ages.

FASHION DESIGNERS

Primarily concerned with aesthetics, today's fashion designer has a myriad of fabrics and finishing treatments from which to select. Not only the look but also the feel and the performance are deeply influencing fashion designers. Many create pared down silhouettes to give attention to an unusual material they have sourced or worked on themselves with a textile designer or company.

During the 1990s many of the new developments came from Japan and Japanese fashion still often typifies creative use of the latest synthetics, chemical treatments and sophisticated technology. However, in the past decade many textile companies outside Japan have been putting large financial investment into research and development and also offer new textiles for the world of fashion.

Japanese fashion designer Issey Miyake has a real passion for textiles and clothing. He is supremely creative and has used numerous advanced technologies to make garments and accessories. Exploring the various properties of both natural and synthetic fibres, he enjoys their contrasts and inherent properties. His past collections show the subjection of fabric to various finishes including moulding garments, permanent pleating using heat processes and laser cutting for complex detailing. His clothes look to the future while never abandoning the rich traditions of a global cultural past of fashion and textiles.

Issey Miyake is fascinated by the transformation of a two-dimensional, flat and inanimate fabric to the moving sculptural form it becomes when worn. Simple shapes give emphasis to the interesting textures and technical finishes of his chosen textiles. The way the fabric is cut and slit around the body often makes reference to the kimono and its underlying principles of construction. Western clothing is cut and tailored, shaping the cloth by seaming and darting, whereas in Japan the shape is often directed by minimally cut cloth.

Issey Miyake trained in Paris and New York and has striven to unite Eastern and Western cultures while still retaining the essence of each. The kimono has had an influence on his creations, but it is only a part of his understanding of the way in which fabric relates to the body; his work is truly international. He has travelled a great deal, inspired by textiles and clothing from many countries, including traditional Japanese workwear with its indigo-dyed fabrics to the most sophisticated high-performance clothing. He also celebrates nature – the colours and forms of the earth.

Pleats Please Issey Miyake embodies his design philosophy. First shown in 1993, pleats have been offered each season in new colours and prints and are still immensely popular. The designs use thermoplastic polyester jersey to create permanent heat-set pleats for inherently flexible and beautiful clothing and accessories. His aim was to create universal

above and opposite left
PLEATS PLEASE ISSEY MIYAKE

Issey Miyake selects 100 per cent polyester jersey for its ability to be heat-treated, its easy-care characteristics and for the particular aesthetic. He has explored the thermoplastic property of polyester to create permanent pleats. Photographed by F. Giacobetti with dancers wearing the clothes; the movement of the textile and the interaction of body and garment are beautifully demonstrated.

opposite right
ISSEY MIYAKE A-POC
Yellow Baguette Roll

A-POC ('a piece of cloth') is experimental in its approach to a form of democratic dressing. The customer completes the idea by cutting out the clothes and makes design decisions – for example, whether to have short or long sleeves.

wear that could be dressed up or down and look good while also being practical. Polyester jersey is the ideal choice as it is a very fluid, lightweight and versatile material – it does not crease, washes easily and dries quickly. The garments roll up into the smallest of spaces, making them ideal for travel.

Pleating has a long history, back to early Egyptian times, and these collections fuse this ancient technique with a look and wearability for the future. Polyester can be shaped when heated to give permanent new forms, and Issey Miyake explores this by pleating horizontally, vertically and diagonally. This fabric takes dye well and a wide range of colours can be achieved.

Normally a designer makes the garment from fabric that has already been pleated. With Issey Miyake's patented garment-pleating process, the garments are first cut and sewn into an oversized two-dimensional shape, then sandwiched between two layers of paper, which is reduced to a normal size by machine-pleating, and set using the intense heat of an industrial oven. Texture and form

are created simultaneously using this process which reacts with the memory of the fabric, resulting in permanently pleated garments. As a further exploration of this thermoplastic material, he has used laser and ultrasound cutting techniques to create detailed patterning, used, for example at hem and cuffs as features. Being synthetic the edges fuse and do not need overlocking. Additional techniques include printing stripes of contrasting colour which appear different when the pleats are expanded or relaxed.

The shapes he uses are distilled to their purest form and generally need no fastenings although zippers might be used on thicker versions of the fabric as a feature. Graphic when displayed flat, they become sensual forms when worn. Issey Miyake builds up layers of clothing and colour by combining sleeveless garments over clothes with long sleeves and under a jacket, with a pleated rucksack to complete this contemporary look. The layering makes references to the kimono and the junihitoe (a decorative Japanese garment, made up of twelve kimonos in layers, the different colours and patterns

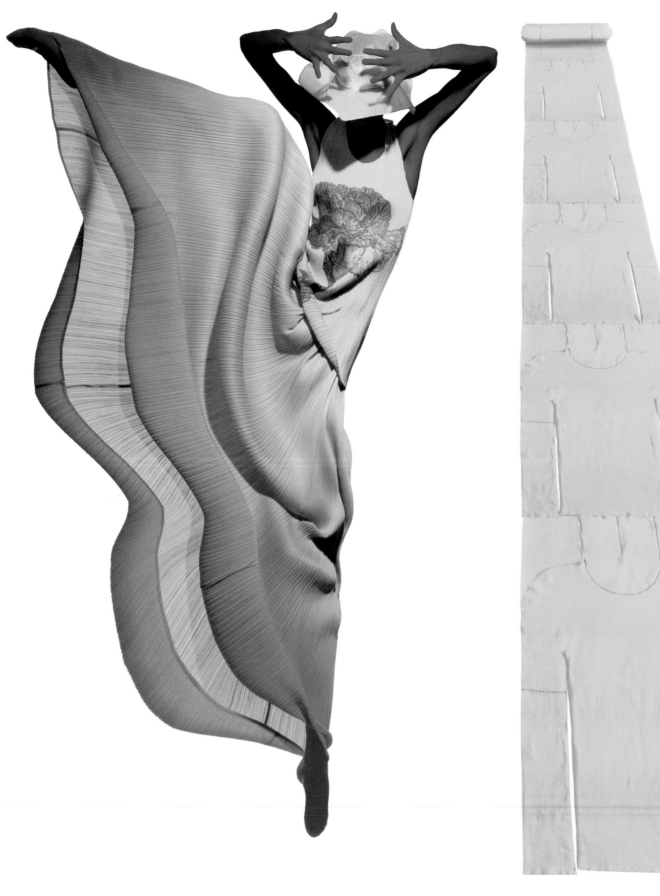

being visible at the edges, the neck, cuffs and hem). However, his clothes are not meant to be quite so formal or serious. Integral to his approach in all his designs is an element of fun and that clothing should bring happiness. Previous collections have included inflatables and holographic textiles for futuristic clothing which is at once child-like and sci-fi.

The Japanese fashion designer Naoki Takizawa now creates the mainline collections under the name 'Issey Miyake by Naoki Takizawa', with Issey Miyake as creative director. Naoki Takizawa's debut collection was Spring/Summer 2000; he previously worked for Issey Miyake Men. He has become known for his distinctive use of unexpected materials employing both the traditional and the very high-tech. Industrial techniques he has used include ultrasound cutting and heat-taping for garment construction. Freed from his main collection, Issey Miyake has time to concentrate on Pleats Please Issey Miyake and A-POC ('a piece of cloth').

A-POC is a customized line designed with textile engineer Dai Fujiwara and was first produced for Spring/Summer 1999. Then they connected an old German knitting machine to a computer and today continue this approach by combining traditional industrial machines with the very latest computer software. Knitted tubes are made with special cutting lines built in and the wearer completes the design by cutting on these lines of demarcation. The textile keeps its shape and edge and does not unravel or ladder. In this way the consumer is directly involved in the creative process. A range of possibilities is therefore open to the wearer – dresses, skirts, shirts. A top, for example, can have full or three-quarter or short length sleeves, or none at all, and hem lengths can be cut to suit. Accompanying accessories such as socks and bags can also be cut free. A-POC offers an organic and democratic approach, adaptable and flexible for a contemporary lifestyle. It demonstrates how clothes and even a capsule wardrobe can be made from a single piece of cloth. Both Pleats Please and A-POC work with timeless silhouettes and the latest technological textile design and manufacturing processes. Ever the inventor, Dai Fujiwara has worked with an engineer of Illinois Institute of Technology and created new construction materials for buildings or bridges. A traditional technique of braiding in

opposite left
ISSEY MIYAKE BY NAOKI TAKIZAWA
Spring/Summer 2004

Use of metallic-looking textiles creates a bold look – one which is simultaneously looking to the past and the future. The top is made of polyester and accessories of polyvinyl chloride.

opposite right
ISSEY MIYAKE BY NAOKI TAKIZAWA
Spring/Summer 2004

This collection was based around the body and considered skin as a form of clothing. Here, polyester is used for the garments with asymmetric and short silhouettes. The unusual accessories are made of polyethylene, a resin-like material that feels good next to the skin.

right
ISSEY MIYAKE BY NAOKI TAKIZAWA
Autumn/Winter 2004/05

This collection was inspired by 'A Journey to the Moon'. Naoki Takizawa, like Issey Miyake enjoys experimenting with various materials. Here, the sculptural form of this jacket uses polyester and the trousers are made of a polyamide and polyester mix. The result is a contemporary and distinctive look.

Y-3
Spring/Summer 2004

Japanese designer, Yohji Yamamoto
teamed up with adidas to create Y-3
which demonstrates the huge
influence that sport has made
on today's clothing. He began by
designing womenswear and later
introduced menswear which here
balances a street-wear aesthetic
with sportswear. The 'Y' stands
for Yohji Yamamoto and the '3'
represents the trademark three
stripes of the adidas logo.

opposite
COMME DES GARÇONS
Spring/Summer 2004

A dramatic ensemble accessorized
with an eye-catching hat. Rei
Kawakubo for the label Comme des
Garçons constantly challenges the
way we define beauty. The sheer,
ultra-lightweight top is hardly
there, while the draped skirt works
around the body influencing the
space between the fabric and the
wearer. Her collections frequently
make reference to both Japanese
and European sensiblities. Rei
Kawakubo is known for her
conceptual collections.

a tube form is used where carbon fibre is woven and then finished with a plastic resin treatment to create a strong shape.

Yohji Yamamoto is a Japanese fashion designer who works with fabric as a sculptor would, first handling it to see how it moves and drapes, and then folding, cutting and shaping his material until he arrives at the end result. Yohji Yamamoto's main interests are material and form and their symbiotic relationship. He believes that the sense of touch is of paramount importance and the direct physicality of his chosen material is often the first inspiration for his collections, where the cloth might suggest a certain shape. Yohji Yamamoto has worked with many different fabrics, from naturals to the most sophisticated synthetics. Previous collections include heat-treated synthetics and fabrics given advanced treatments such as holographic and lacquered effects. He has collaborated with adidas for a fashion/ sportswear look, and created Y-3 which promotes a functional appeal for both womenswear and menswear. Often selecting lightweight, fluid textiles which move around the wearer in a sensual way, he balances sheer with dense fabrics, exploring their inherent characteristics. His work constantly fuses ideas from both oriental and occidental cultures; many of his designs are asymmetrical, for which there is a tradition in Japan, and he is also an excellent tailor, as in the Western tradition. Black has been a favoured colour for many of his clothes as it emphasizes texture and form. Shapes are sculptural, and his collections frequently demonstrate dark volumes of cloth which work with the human body. Evidence of the hand with irregular textures and random effects is important to him: he wishes to demonstrate his belief that human beings are unable to make something that is totally perfect. Yohji Yamamoto is passionately interested in creating expressive clothes which are all about the present rather than the future – where we are now as human beings in the twenty-first century. The German film maker Wim Wenders made a film called *Notebook on Cities and Clothes* which documents Yohji Yamamoto searching for the essence of a garment. Wim Wenders demonstrates the intimacies and intricacies of working with the fluid medium of textiles. The future is discussed together with the potential use of digital imagery. Made in 1989, it is still valid many years on.

Rei Kawakubo, the name behind Comme des Garçons, is a leading Japanese fashion designer whose clothes maintain a balance between femininity and masculinity (as the company name suggests), tradition and technology and Eastern and Western cultures. Well known for her avant-garde and conceptual approach, she did not train as a fashion designer, and it is without preconceptions that she clothes the human form. Her early collections, with their minimalist purity, featured many shades of black, giving emphasis to texture and volume and her clothes, like those of Yohji Yamamoto, have a leaning towards asymmetry. Every fashion designer has their own distinctive language, signature and way of working. Rei Kawakubo has been known to describe her ideas verbally with a certain word, or show a photograph of a building, for example, to her team of expert pattern-cutters, who then interpret her ideas into two-dimensional plans. Rei Kawakubo believes that architecture has much in common with the structure of clothes and in particular cites Le Corbusier as inspiration. Interested in new textiles, Rei Kawakubo often juxtaposes ancient craft techniques with modern fabrics to result in highly contemporary clothing. Textile designers create fabrics to her particular specification and inspiration for her collections frequently begins with the textile. She has used the latest synthetics and advanced finishing treatments and worked in close collaboration with the leading specialists. Heat-treated polyester, pleated and formed into complex shibori and origami-like relief surfaces, were used for one collection; another featured polyamide and polyurethane mixes and synthetic foam. Rei Kawakubo has a playful approach to textile machinery and has been known to tamper with computer-controlled looms to create 'flaws' to escape from monotonous, soulless textiles and the uniformity of production. She uses sophisticated computer programmes, with their random effects and self-generating patterns, to help her create wonderful textures and irregular surfaces, both traditional in Japanese clothing. Her deconstructivist approach has attracted a cult following and inspired many international fashion designers.

Japanese fashion designer Junya Watanabe presents collections under the Comme des Garçons umbrella. He is fond of creating futuristic fashion with the latest materials such as ultra-fine polyamide jerseys, neoprene, glass fibre and industrial fibres usually used for insulating computers or for chemical filters. Advanced finishes he has used include lacquered and iridescent cellophane coatings, polyurethane laminated synthetics and stainless steel-spattered polyester. One collection even had a rainstorm on the catwalk to show his effective use of high-performance water-resistant materials. He frequently juxtaposes the traditional with the new, for example printing a floral design on to a fabric developed from computer film (this fine anti-static material is normally used on the inside of computers to protect the machinery) and using natural-coloured linen with a silver-foiled finish. Sometimes he balances the high-tech with fabric manipulation such as padding to create lightweight volumes. His work begins with the textiles and the form, with his unusual cutting and tailoring techniques, follows afterwards. Minimalist shapes have cyber-like cutting (robotic armour with slit vents for ease of movement) and complex contour seaming. Junya Watanabe has become internationally prominent for his distinctive and provocative collections.

Japanese fashion designer Michiko Koshino enjoys using innovative textiles and is deeply influenced by new textile technologies. She loves to shock with her catwalk clothes, and her designs celebrate youth and street culture, particularly that of London, where she has a base. Her clothes, which are fun and comfortable, are very popular with the young and trendy. The fabrics she chooses each season often determine her look and she has used fluorescent, glow-in-the-dark fabrics (created from light-reflective plastics, a material which has filtered down from space technology), high-performance sportswear fabrics, bonded textiles, inflatable materials, fake fur, synthetic rubbers, industrial plastics and advanced finishes such as reflective and metallized surfaces. Sources of inspiration include traditional Japanese dragons, the flickering of TV interference, futuristic Tokyo cityscapes and holidays in tropical Hawaii. Her printed and embroidered textiles convey such imagery in powerful and eye-catching designs.

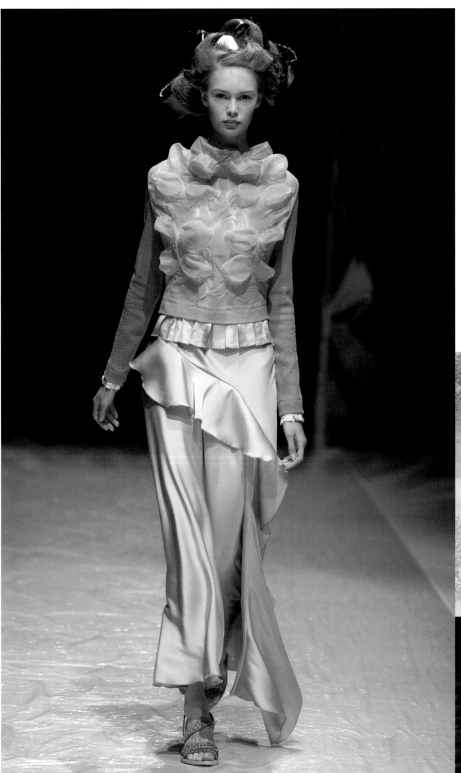

**JUNYA WATANABE
FOR COMME DES GARÇONS
Autumn/Winter 2004/05**

Junya Watanabe frequently uses the latest techno textiles to realize his designs. Like his mentor Rei Kawakubo, his work is very conceptual and points the way to the future. This collection makes reference to a theme of protection with its padded lightweight textiles.

opposite right
**MICHIKO KOSHINO
Spring/Summer 2004**

Michiko Koshino's signature photographic prints are used creatively and enable a new and contemporary look. This asymmetric dress displays palm trees and exotic flowers; the images were taken by Michiko Koshino herself during a trip to Hawaii and have been digitally printed.

left
**YOSHIKI HISHINUMA
Autumn/Winter 2002/03**

Yoshiki Hishinuma works with heat-treated synthetics to achieve wonderful relief surfaces which have the appearance of coming from another world. He is fascinated with the latest materials available with today's technology and gives attention to fabric in his fashion collections.

below
**YOSHIKI HISHINUMA
Heat-treated synthetics**

Yoshiki Hishinuma is passionately interested in textiles and works closely with designers to realize unique cloth. He combines a love for technology with exquisite craftsmanship. Here he exploits the thermoplastic property of synthetics to heat-set them into relief effects with colour adding another dimension.

SCHOELLER TEXTIL AG
Overexposed

Schoeller created a range of textiles
called spirit, intended for fashion
designers, when they noticed that
fashion designers were working with
their highly technical materials but
choosing them mainly for their
appearance. This range is non-
stretch and made of high-tech
synthetics. Various finishes can be
added and frequent use has been
made of coatings and gloss effects,
but their main criteria is aesthetic.
Shown here is an example of such a
decorative finish.

SHELLEY FOX
Autumn/Winter 2000/01

Shelley Fox is interested in surface
embellishment and deconstruction.
She sewed panels of sequins to a
base fabric but on finding the results
too pretty subjected the textile to the
intense heat of a blow torch. The
sequins tarnished and fused
together to create a new, other-
worldly blistered surface. Here, the
semi-destruction of material creates
a new identity.

SHELLEY FOX
Autumn/Winter 2000/01

Innovative cutting works with a
technical material for futuristic
dressing. Fashion designer Shelley
Fox is interested in using non-
conventional materials. Here, she
contrasted a specialist synthetic
membrane architectural material
from A. Proctor Group Ltd with wool
and used her characteristic circular-
cutting. This company supplies the
construction industry with high-
specification technically advanced
materials. The membranes are
extremely strong and resistant but
also breathable, making them
suitable for fashion too.

It is only in the last two decades that textiles and fashion have been closely linked in Japan. Yoshiki Hishinuma, a Japanese fashion designer passionately interested in fabric, controls the look from fibre to garment working with Mr Ishida, his textile designer. He trained at the Miyake Design Studio where he learnt a great deal about experimental textiles and technology. For his own Tokyo-based label, Yoshiki Hishinuma began creating his distinctive fabrics when he could not find the ones he wanted. Sources of inspiration include textiles from all over the world and even eighteenth-century European clothing. Many of the fabrics he uses are synthetic, and he is fascinated with the aesthetics achieved through heat-treating textiles. Heat-setting can create a whole range of textures not unlike the puckered effects created with traditional Japanese shibori. Yoshiki Hishinuma's fashion designs give full attention to his original fabrics which explore ideas of transparency and opacity and flat next to high relief surfaces.

Trained in both textiles and fashion, Shelley Fox is a highly creative designer who has a conceptual approach, producing unconventional, sculptural clothing which redefines femininity. Her sources of inspiration are diverse and include different means of communication, something she has been interested in for some time. Examples include embossed Braille markings and prints with Morse Code messages which have featured in past collections. Based in London, she has, however, a sensibility much in common with the Japanese fashion designers mentioned above. This manifests itself in a real awareness and understanding of materials, an interest in both traditional fabric and the latest technical synthetics and a way of working with the human body, wrapping rather than exposing it. Her modern, uncluttered silhouettes are achieved with unorthodox cutting which often uses the circle as a starting point. Pared down simplicity belies complex construction that necessitate expert pattern-cutting and asymmetry is used, another aspect she has in common with the Japanese aesthetic. Shelley Fox creates her own textiles and experiments with a variety of materials in her studio/laboratory. She has become known for her use of unconventional textiles which have often been achieved by accident. Felted cloth (when she overboiled wool in the washing machine)

Fashion designer Liza Bruce uses the latest in advanced textiles to create beautiful and functional swimwear. She often uses techno-stretch fabrics which include a high percentage of Lycra for its important elastic and shape-retaining properties. This swimsuit is made of a very lightweight synthetic which allows for distinctive ruching without losing the streamlined aesthetic.

and scorched or singed fabrics (when she allowed a press to overheat). Shelley Fox is also interested in technology. 'Technology fascinates me because it is clever and satisfying but also because many of these things are designed to do something to help' (Susannah Frankel, the *Independent* magazine, 3 November 2001). She has worked with synthetic materials including Daltex Roofshield by A. Proctor Group Ltd UK, which is a high specification, triple-layer spun-bonded polypropylene breathable membrane, more commonly used to line and insulate buildings. It was garments made from this technically advanced material which won her the first Jerwood Fashion Prize in 1999. Elastoplast is a breathable, medical fabric by Smith & Nephew UK. Shelley Fox became fascinated with this material and contacted the company to find out more. Textiles she has worked with often feature unusual print and embellishment finishing techniques. Her collections begin with such innovative textiles and are only complete when the form of the human body is in motion. Enjoying working with other creative people, she has collaborated with the photographer Nick Knight for his fashion website SHOWstudio, with the Michael Clark Dance Company, London, and with the sound artist Scanner. Shelley Fox's collections have attracted an international cult following; they are always beautiful and thought-provoking and offer a cerebral approach to clothing for the future.

Liza Bruce is known for her body-conscious collections using quality synthetics with a high percentage of Lycra. She began by making swimwear and this is her main focus, although past collections have also included ready-to-wear. Her work has inspired many fashion designers with designs which are simultaneously glamorous and functional. She is interested in textiles and has developed her materials with the specialist Rosemary Moore – for example, a thick lustre bubble crêpe fabric, a tubular polyamide and Lycra blend developed in 1986, a crinkle crêpe in 1987, and in 1998 a scuba material with 20 per cent Lycra, a very lightweight textile but dense in colour and feel on the body. Her swimwear looks good but also performs well, due to her choice of materials which are often the latest synthetics. Liza Bruce is interested in various treatments to her textiles, including waxed and metallic finishes, subtle glitter surfaces,

LIZA BRUCE
Swimwear

It was with swimwear that Liza
Bruce first became known. She
selects her fabrics very carefully –
ultra-stretch synthetics for
their functional properties and
contemporary appeal. Here, semi-
transparent fabric is used for a
unique look and contrasting colour
to create the illusion of a two-piece.

right
PRADA WOMAN
Autumn/Winter 2004/05

Digitally printed silk Empire line dress features a 'memory' print inspired by classic and romantic motifs. The imagery has been reworked via computer technology and transformed into contemporary, almost abstract designs. Notions of beauty from times past are revived and projected into the future.

far right
PRADA WOMAN
Autumn/Winter 2004/05

This elusively wispy dress is made of ultra-light organza chiffon with digital printing to create both the illusion of the human body and folds and creases.

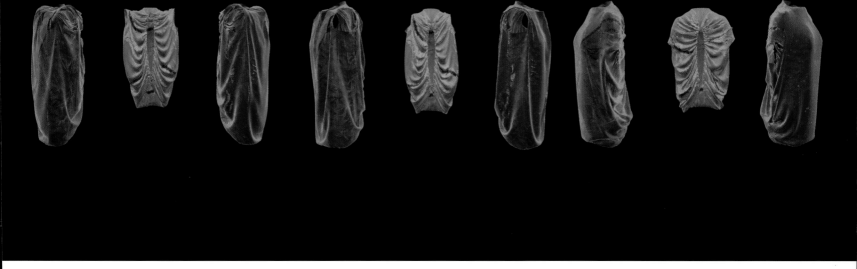

matt/gloss and sheer/opaque synthetics and leather-look polyamide/Lycra. She is not afraid of colour and is inspired by the Indian city of Jaipur ('the Pink City') for fuchsia pinks. With her signature materials she creates hard, graphic, futuristic-looking shapes, including strapless, asymmetric and cut-out designs which redefine what is beautiful and sexy.

Most fashion designers believe that the future of their discipline lies in the textiles themselves and many are working closely with the design and manufacture of new materials. Expert knowledge from scientists, engineers, the textile manufacturing industry, textile practitioners, fashion designers and even sociologists is often pooled to result in innovative surfaces and structures which are then featured on the international catwalks.

One highly creative area, and one which promises a great deal in the new future, is

digital craft. Textile practitioners, fully aware of the inherent properties of a given material, are working more and more with computer technology to create and realize ideas. An example of this approach is the collaboration between textile artist Jane Harris and fashion designer Shelley Fox. Their work demonstrates the power of visually animated textiles, literally bringing the cloth and the garment to life using advanced 3D computer graphic animation together with a real knowledge of both the fabric and the garment's cut, drape and relationship to the human form. Utilization of such newly available technologies has had a very positive effect on contemporary fashion and looks set to continue.

above
JANE HARRIS, SHELLEY FOX & MIKE DAWSON
Balloon Top. 2003/04

This is a collaborative digital work directed by the artist Jane Harris with fashion designer Shelley Fox and 3D computer graphic operator Mike Dawson. The work uses 3D computer graphic animation in relation to textiles and dress. The sequence of images shows a form of simulation that explores the unique construction of a drawstring top by Shelley Fox. It demonstrates the stages from a flat circle to a fully dimensional form. This work had financial support in the form of a grant from the Arts and Humanities Research Board.

Design

Marie O'Mahony

above left
NICHOLAS PRYKE
Carbon fibre table

Commissioned as part of the
Hitec-Lotec project, furniture
designer Nicholas Pryke designed
a carbon fibre table using Formula
One motor racing technology.
The design makes use of both the
carbon fibre composite and its
mould.

above right
SIMON CONDER
Beach house
Dungeness, Kent

This beach house is a good
example of an unremarkable
material being used in an
unconventional context to stunning
effect. The original 1930s
fisherman's hut has been stripped
to its timber frame, plywood
constructed then clad in a matt
black rubber. The finished building
appears like a 'stealth' house
located between Derek Jarman's
timber cottage with its famous
sculpture garden and the
Dungeness nuclear power plant
further down the beach.

Increasingly sophisticated materials and technologies have forced designers to re-examine many of their working practices. It is becoming more common for designers to work as part of multi-disciplinary design teams. Allied to this is the versatility of technologies to transfer from one area to another opening up new possibilities in terms of materials and design. Environmental concerns are making a strong impact on products, with questions being raised about the need for a new product as well as the number of functions it can serve. The energy issue has also forced designers to look to nature as a source of inspiration – honeycomb structures, for instance, which provide weight-saving and strength in many composite structures, and termite mounds, which are a blueprint for natural ventilation systems in architecture. Biomimetics, the extraction of good design from nature, is about as far from traditional floral prints as can be imagined. Scientists and engineers are learning about the creation of energy efficient monomaterials as well as ergonomics and composite structures. Biotechnology is a more controversial area of research, raising questions about the use of human cells and the potential for their misuse. There are significant breakthroughs being made in this area so that moral and ethical questions do have to be addressed now before it becomes too far advanced and impossible to reverse.

Nanotechnology operates at a more conceptual level, though there are a growing number of examples of its use not just in the laboratory, but as commercial products. Serious questions are now being asked about its future role from an environmental point of view but also the desirability of a technology which would have the ability to behave as an autonomous and possibly self-replicating Artificial Intelligence.

MULTI-DISCIPLINARY DESIGN

Advanced tools and materials are making the designer's task ever more complex. As a consequence, we are starting to see some changes in design practice. People from a wide range of disciplines are being included in design teams. Design is no longer regarded as the task of just one person. Even large companies with considerable staff resources bring in outside expertise for product development. One consequence of downsizing during the recession has been the availability of a rich source of freelance expertise.

Holland's Droog Design, along with designer Marcel Wanders, has worked with the Aerospace Laboratory at the Technical University of Delft (TUD) to develop the Knotted Chair. The university usually works with the aerospace industry, producing a range of composite and sandwich structures which use high-performance fibres. These composites are developed for specific functions within the aircraft. For the project with Marcel Wanders, a carbon-aramid hybrid fibre is used. A net is formed with a macramé-like structure. This is draped over a wire frame, then dipped in a solution to harden the net for more structural form. The chair is now in production with Cappellini.

In the West the average working person is cash rich and time poor. This has led to a desire for personalized products that look like they might have been homemade. The attempt to commodify this as a customization service has failed. What is now emerging is an unprecedented interest in craft by high-technology industries. The bringing together of the handmade, using traditional techniques or materials, with the high-tech seems an ideal marriage. Craftspeople at the Haystack Mountain School of Crafts in the US have collaborated with technologists from the wearable technology group at MIT. The idea of the workshop was to explore each others' different ways of thinking, particularly about design and haptics or tactile qualities in particular. The UK Crafts for Now initiative Hitec-Lotec I and II also looked to bring together craft and industry. Here, makers from different disciplines went on placements in materials-led industries with the intention of developing prototypes that could be further developed for production. New work was also commissioned for an international touring exhibition. Though some very good results were achieved, the allocated time was not enough to indicate whether any of the

opposite bottom
TOM DIXON: CHAIR KARINA THOMAS/SALT: FABRIC DESIGN
Rocking Chaise Longue

The metal frame chaise has been upholstered in a tubular knitted fabric that slips over the structure like a sock. The fabric is padded to provide part of the upholstery and the concept originated from a desire to reduce the amount of pattern cutting and sewing needed to cover the chair. The chaise longue was exhibited as part of the 2010 – Textiles and New Technology exhibition.

below left
MARCEL WANDERS/DROOG DESIGN/TUD/CAPPELLINI
Knotted Chair, 1996

The designer developed the carbon hybrid fibre for the chair with the Aerospace Department at the Technical University in Delft. Traditional macramé knotting was used to construct the chair which was then dipped in an epoxy resin to harden and fix it into its final shape.

below right
MARCEL WANDERS
Lace table, 1997

Surplus pieces of Swiss lace are formed into a table and stiffened with resin.

above
GRADO ZERO ESPACE
Oricalco Shape Memory Alloy Shirt

The Oricalco shirt relies on SMA technology from the European Space Agency in order to recover its original shape when subjected to heat. Shape Memory Alloys (SMAs) are nickel and titanium alloys. Because the two metals respond to heat differently, they can be deformed at room temperature but regain their original shape when heated a few degrees higher. Grado Zero Espace have woven SMAs into the nylon fabric so that the shirt can be creased, then regain its former shape by applying low-level heat such as from a hairdryer.

opposite
ZAHA HADID ARCHITECTS
Charleroi Danses, Belgium 1999

In keeping with the urban theme of the dance performance, architect Zaha Hadid decided to use industrial fabrics with a technical aesthetic for the costumes rather than more conventional clothing fabrics. Materials used included polypropylene, shown vacuum moulded in a test piece (top) and geomesh (bottom left and right). The geomesh was used as a large screen manipulated by the dancers during the performance with lighting used to create a dramatic abstract effect

prototypes could be commercially viable. These initiatives are part of a growing trend that sees technology and tradition come together bringing together the benefits of both. New phrases such as 'digital craft' are starting to enter the design lexicon.

TECHNOLOGY TRANSFER

Over the years the space industry has been responsible for the development of some important new materials. Both NASA and the ESA have Technology Transfer Programmes that aim to make potential commercial interests aware of the technologies available, and collaborative ventures are set up to develop commercial products. The space agencies see their links with the private sector as a way to create new jobs and improve economic security. NASA's Small Business Innovation Research (SBIR) programme was set up to increase participation by small businesses. It also stimulates the conversion of government-funded research into commercial applications. Comfort Products Ltd in Colorado have had a working relationship with NASA for twenty years. This began with the adaptation of astronaut's protective clothing to a design for a ski boot. The company used a heating element, which had been originally used by NASA to keep the Apollo astronauts warm or cool in extremes of temperature on the moon. They used it to create a built-in rechargeable foot-warming device which they then supplied to ski-boot manufacturers.

ESA operates a Technology Transfer Programme (TTP) which disseminates such technologies as Shape Memory Alloys (SMAs) and cooling systems embedded in undergarments that blow cool air on the skin. The agency invites proposals from a variety of interested parties interested in working together. Typically this might include a textile manufacturer, designer and research department from a university, often in several different countries. The results are impressive with cooling garments being used by the McLaren Formula One Team and fabrics that block out up to 90 per cent of infrared radiation being used in public buildings like the Toronto Skydome.

Many of today's textile-related products adapt technologies from apparently unrelated

areas, showing how adaptable designers can be, moving with ease between disciplines. Airbags are among the most important driver safety features to emerge in recent years. Driver and passenger airbags are very different in design. While the technology used by product designers differs, the general concept has been a strong influence on some of the latest sports and furniture designs.

The sports industry is always one of the market leaders in using the latest materials and design. Nike Product Design have introduced their Nike-Air technology to many of their sports shoes. The system uses a blow-moulded urethane cushioning in the sole. This provides protection and comfort for the wearer by reducing the shock of impact. After each step the bladder regains its original shape.

GREEN ISSUES

Victor Papanek aptly described the dilemma facing the designer in the 1990s in his book *The Green Imperative* (1995), when he wrote of the need to 'design things that will last, yet come apart easily to be recycled and reused'. The statement indicates a change in our whole way of thinking about green issues. In the 1980s recycling meant bringing empty bottles to the bottle bank. Today the term is used to refer to a greater awareness of how we live. The influence of green issues in design no longer begins with the manufacturing process but with the question of whether there really is a need for the product. Do we need yet another packet of washing powder, where the packaging is effectively the product?

New technology has a long gestation period before it is generally accepted. One of the most common ways of introducing a new technology is to use it to replace an existing material or process. Viscose rayon was first introduced as a replacement for silk. Plastic was marketed as a substitute for ivory. This may seem unbelievable now, but they were viewed simply as more economical alternatives. Both have subsequently suffered from the reputation of being cheap, disposable materials.

The emphasis today is not just on cost but the 'added value' which a technology may bring to a product. One example of this is Shape Memory Alloys, usually nickel and

below
Corrugated plastic roof, Kyoto

Natural materials such as wood and leather are prized for the patination they gain with age. Synthetics and plastics are often discarded as they show signs of ageing. Designers such as Hella Jongerius are now looking at ways of addressing the issue and preventing products that otherwise function well from being discarded simply because they have changed colour. This plastic roof in Japan is no longer as transparent as it once was, but has taken on another aesthetic that has its own beauty.

opposite top
LESLEY SEALEY
Layered and printed nonwoven

It is not always easy to decide what is environmentally good and bad. Lesley Sealey's nonwoven fabric layers it with a floral print synthetic and overprints with glitter. This material would be very difficult to recycle but used to make a coat it will be worn for several years.

opposite bottom
Disposable nonwoven hotel room slipper

The nonwoven hotel room slipper has carbon in the sole to absorb odour but is otherwise made from one material so much easier to recycle. However, the design means that it will most likely be discarded after a single use lasting less than twenty-four hours. Which use of a nonwoven has less impact on the environment?

titanium, which can regain their original shape when heated. This can be done simply through the process of washing. The SMA wires are inserted in shirt collars and as underwiring in bras to help them retain their shape.

Ultimately it is the consumer who decides whether an innovation is worth spending extra money on. But designers have been accused of cynically implanting dissatisfaction in products, forcing people to replace goods with newer versions almost as soon as they have been bought. This could be said of the fashion industry, but it fails to acknowledge that much of fashion's energy and innovation has come from the process of constantly reinventing itself.

One of the most important design approaches in recent years has been the concept of Design for Disassembly (DFD). From an environmental viewpoint, how a product ends its life is a natural extension to considerations of how and from what it is manufactured. The leading contract furniture manufacturer Herman Miller have set an impressive standard in their commitment to the environment. They have set up an in-house Environmental Quality Action Team (EQUAT), to deal with issues ranging from the 'responsible' use of land to choosing business partners and suppliers. Their AsNew Programme allows Herman Miller products (especially office systems) to be repurchased. The company renovates these products, replacing worn or damaged parts. Design for Disassembly (DFD) is further advanced by marking each individual component with a material reference so

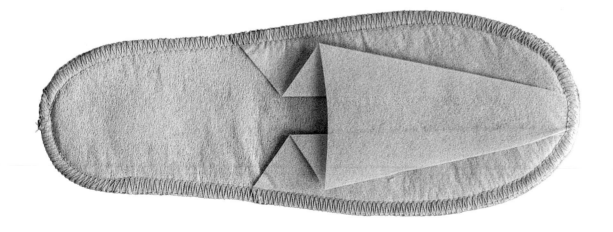

JESSICA OGDEN
Two half dresses
Spring/Summer 2000

These designs (top; and fabric detail, above) use repaired and reconstructed cloth kit and 1940s printed cotton. Each half dress is unique; they are designed to be mixed and matched to create new dresses. There is greater environmental awareness among young fashion designers who try to balance seasonal collections with an appreciation of the need to reuse clothes and fabrics. These were shown as part of the Fabric of Fashion British Council Touring Exhibition.

that it can be identified at a later date for replacement or recycling. The Equa chair also carries a general parts location diagram on the underside of the body to facilitate recycling. This approach highlights the role of the consumer: if they are not involved then such a system cannot work. One sportswear manufacturer has been offering a repair service for their garments. Although advertised, after three years not one customer had taken them up on the offer.

BIOMIMETICS

'Biomimetics is the extraction of good design from nature.' This is the definition given by Professor Julian Vincent at Bath University. Biological materials can often be more efficient in their design than their manmade counterparts. Recognizing this, designers and architects are increasingly looking to nature for more efficient design processes.

Some early attempts to mimic nature were doomed to failure and even hindered the design process. Early inventors thought we might be able to fly simply by attaching a pair of oversize wings to our arms and flapping them. What they failed to realize is that wings only work in this way up to a certain limited size. The solution to manned flight was eventually found in a very different system where wings were fixed and had a separate power source.

Perhaps the most striking difference between manmade and biological materials is the number of components used. Vincent reminds us that much of nature's design revolves around two main types of ceramic, a single type of fibrous protein, a number of non-fibrous structural proteins, and several space-filling polymers. The variety and versatility of their applications lies mainly in their structure at a molecular level. Single component or monomaterials have much less impact on the environment compared with more complex systems that are harder to separate. Nature designs with monomaterials very well and scientists are trying to catch up. Polymers can be constructed in the laboratory to fulfil a wide range of functions by 'genetically' altering their structure at a molecular level. Polypropylene is an example. It can be 'cloned' depending on the function required, and can be soft like a rubber or resistant like a technopolymer.

Researchers at Bell Labs in the United States have been looking at deep sea sponges in the search for a better way of designing fibre optic cables. Researchers have managed to transmit light through the ultra-thin fibres (not unlike glass fibre) of a sponge known as a Venus flower basket. The aim is to discover how the fibres, which grow at near freezing temperatures, can still be flexible enough to be tied in a knot. Glass fibre optic cables are currently manufactured using high temperatures and as a result are very brittle and fragile.

Stomatex Ltd have developed a system that allows us to control our own microclimate. Stomatex mimics transpiration in nature, whereby plant leaves can remove large quantities of water through otherwise impermeable surfaces. The system works by maintaining a temperature above the level where sweat condensation would occur. Trapped vapour is removed from beneath the fabric by the action of tiny pumps formed within the material. The pump is a curved deformable chamber which is formed as part of the fabric and has a small exit pore. When the body is inactive, the system does not operate. It is only with movement that Stomatex starts to work, removing perspiration as the need arises. It is effectively a 'smart material', responding to the wearer's needs and to the environment. The fabric is already used in sportswear. It relies on neoprene and polyethylene because they are elastic and thermoformable.

Speedo's FASTSKIN was the most controversial swimsuit in the Sydney Olympic Games in 2000 as swimmers from all over the world clamoured to be allowed to wear it upsetting other swimwear sponsors in the process. The FASTSKIN FSII took a further four years to develop and was launched at the Athens Olympics in 2004.

The basic design looks to the sharkskin for inspiration, with the fabric surface mimicking the characteristics of the dermal denticles on the skin. The knitted construction uses tiny hydrofoils with V-shaped ridges to achieve this. This is what allows the shark to move through water at such speed. While the original FASTSKIN used the same fabric all over, the second version utilizes three different surfaces. This was in response to more detailed research which showed that rougher dermal denticles were found on the

top
Bamboo in Japan

Materials engineers, designers and architects are increasingly looking to nature for inspiration. Bamboo is providing the composites industry with a blueprint for making materials that are lightweight yet extremely strong. Bamboo is light and flexible enough to move with the wind, yet cut in section it can withstand considerable force from above. Paper and polypropylene tubes have been used in a similar way. Pushed from the side, these materials are easy to distort yet they can withstand considerable pressure directed from the cut section.

bottom
STOMATEX LTD
Stomatex

A neoprene fabric from Stomatex Ltd allows the wearer to control their own environment. Stomatex is based on the idea of transpiration in nature. The fabric is heat-treated so that tiny convex bumps on the surface of the fabric with pinpricks in the top serve to move perspiration away from the body.

SPEEDO
Fastskin FSII

Wearing FASTSKIN FSII, Speedo reputedly offered the American swimmer Michael Phelps a $1 million bonus if he could equal Mark Spitz's seven Olympic gold medal win. He managed six.

Artist Julie Ryder's Scanning Electron Microscopy (SEM) image showing a detail of 'Strand G' which comes from her experiments growing algae on fabric. The image has been further manipulated in Photoshop to add colour, then used as part of her Chromophilia series.

Julie Ryder's Chromophilia is a series of hand-printed textiles framed by embroidery hoops which utilizes the chemical resist technique. The title refers to a love of colour and is described as the property possessed by most cells of staining readily with appropriate dyes. The hoops allude to the circle; found in the petri dish and the view seen through the microscope which form the basis for these digitally altered SEM images. Arranged on the wall they represent growth in colonies of bacteria or cell division.

shark's nose while smoother ones were located further down from the nose. It is this varied surface that scientists now believe optimize its friction drag. The finished swimsuit boasts three different surfaces: the first uses the FASTSKIN fabric, a second uses an ordinary knitted fabric and the third involves tiny pinhead spots of silicone rubber printed on specific areas of the body including chest and shoulder. All are aimed at reducing friction drag as much as possible. Speedo reckon it reduces drag by 4 per cent on the FASTSKIN, which in the world of competitive sports can mean the difference between a gold and bronze medal.

BIOTECHNOLOGY

Biotechnology is the term given to any technological application that uses biological systems, living organisms (or their derivatives), to make or modify products or processes for specialist use. Applications for biotechnology include recycling and the treatment of waste as well as the production of biowar agents. Living organisms are not always used, with DNA chips being used in genetics and radioactive tracers used in medicine.

The use of microbes in textiles is not new; they have long been used as part of the dye process to colour cloth. Indigo, a violet-blue dye derived from a plant, is recorded as having been used as early as 2500 BC. The marriage of bacteria and textile to form a biotechnological material is ideal for several reasons. Textiles are generally non-toxic and are receptive to all manner of coatings, laminates and microencapsulated chemicals. A second reason for their usefulness is that they have the potential to supply perfect living conditions for these bacteria: body heat, humidity and water. While it is easy enough to encourage bacteria to grow on textiles, the difficulty is in controlling the cells so that they can live and function without harm to the user for a prolonged period of time. Researchers from a group of top American universities have been looking at the use of hollow fibres to create biologically activated fibres. The benefit of this method is that the bacteria is enclosed by the fibre serving to protect both the bacteria and user. As well as synthetic fibres, milkweed and cotton are also being considered as suitable (biofriendly) fibres. The group have identified a strain of e. coli that produces bioluminescent luciferase which makes it glow. It is bioluminescence that makes fireflies and plankton glow. The benefit of this method as opposed to the use of fluorescence is that ultra-violet light is not needed. The down side is that the bacteria have a limited lifespan.

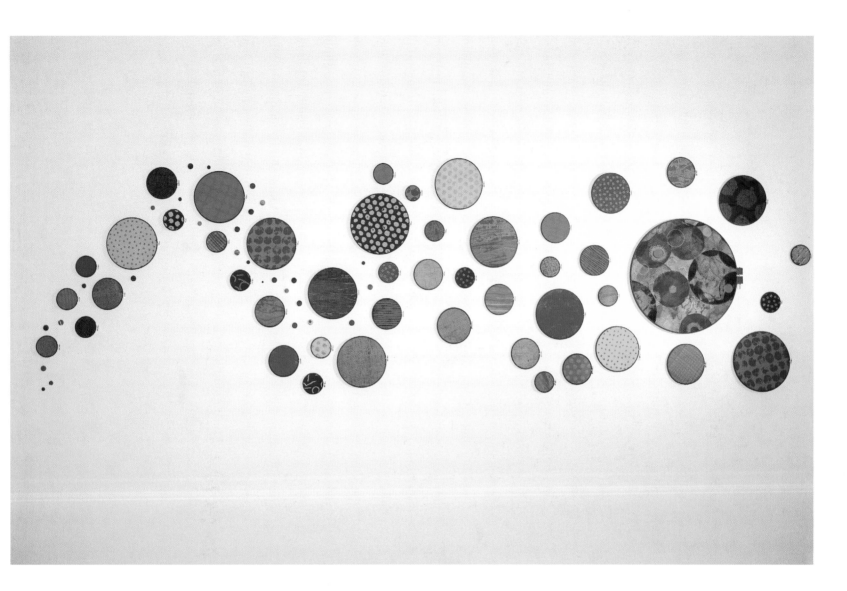

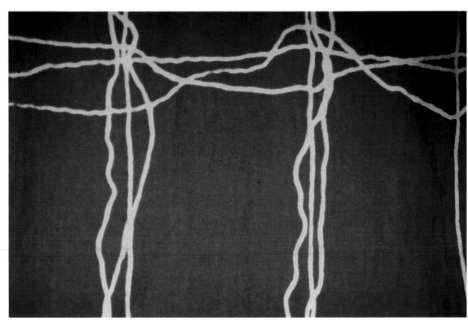

above
Goat

With new scientific advances such as biotechnology, a new relationship is being forged with nature. From the use of human DNA to transgenic goats, the possibilities are tremendous, and the responsibility of scientists, designers and citizens alike is considerable.

below
TISSUE + CULTURE
Victimless Leather

'Artificial leather' has featured in shops for a number of years. It is essentially plastic, usually PVC. Kind to the animals it may be but kind to the environment it is not. Victimless Leather points towards the creation of a leather-like material using biotechnology that relies on neither animal nor environmental cost.

opposite
TISSUE + CULTURE
Semi-Living Seamless Jacket

The jacket is one of Tissue + Culture's most controversial artworks because it uses human cells. The artists are a reminder that these technologies are here to stay and we must decide how we want them to be used. Much of their work is conducted in collaboration with scientists as part of the SymbioticA Research Lab at the University of Western Australia. The centre helps forge links between artists and scientists, particularly in the area of biotechnology.

The Israeli company Cellaris have developed a lightweight ceramic foam that is over 90 per cent air in volume. It can withstand temperatures up to 1700°C (about 3100°F) making it ideal for thermal and acoustic insulation though it has also been used for biotechnology applications. Special crystals are used in the manufacture of the foam that contain the metal components and all the foaming ingredients. On heating, the crystals form a solution within which a reaction takes place forming polymer chains. Further heating sees the creation of a residual ceramic metal oxide foam. Foam wood is under development using residual materials produced during wood processing. Using biotechnology, micro-organisms such as yeast and bacteria transform the wood dust or chippings using a fermenting process. The initial outcome is a paste, similar in consistency to bread dough. Once dried, the material looks and behaves like chipboard. The main difference is that no chemical additives have been used in its production.

The British-based company CellTran have developed Myskin biological bandages made from patients own skin cells. Initial tests show that they speed up the recovery process of patients with severe burns and long-term wounds. A sample of the patient's skin is taken under local anaesthetic then expanded in the laboratory before being placed on the bandage. The process is undertaken at 37°C (98.6°F) but once prepared the bandage can be handled and transported at room temperature. Additional cells from the patient can be cryogenically frozen in liquid nitrogen for future use.

A more controversial use of human cells comes from Australia. Artists Oron Catts and Oinat Zurr comprise Tissue + Culture. Their work explores the area of tissue culture, using it to create art works that provoke questions about the future of the biotechnology industry. Their *Victimless Leather* does not involve the death of any animal. Layers of cells are coated onto a biodegradable polymer until the required thickness and strength is achieved. The 'leather' grows in its petri dish and once removed from this environment it ceases to 'live', just as natural leather is no longer alive once taken from an animal. Because the *Victimless Leather* is biological the artists argue that it is a natural system and biodegradable. Art works such as this undergo a burial ritual at the end of their lifespan. *The Semi-Living Seamless Jacket* is also grown on a biodegradable polymer inside a specially designed profusion pump. The

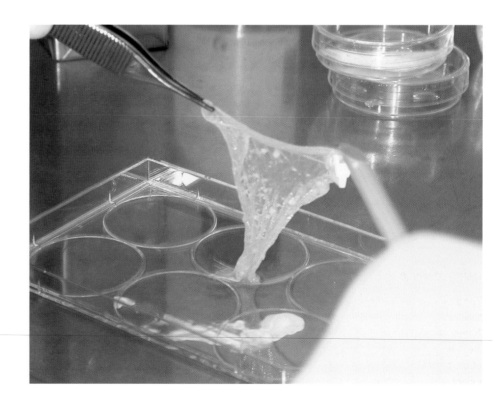

cells used include mouse connective tissue and human cells. The latter are pre-oseoplast cells that can become either muscle or bone. The jacket is quite tiny, no more than a few inches long. Even cocooned in its special micro-climate and housed in its protective bell jar the jacket cannot survive a week before it becomes contaminated by bacteria.

Silk is admired not only for its aesthetic qualities, but also for its strength and elasticity. It absorbs large quantities of mechanical energy before it breaks. Spider's silk can combine rigidity and flexibility in a single web. This makes it much stronger than silk produced by the silkworm, than nylon, rubber or even steel which is brittle and can snap under strain. Scientists have attempted to make artificial silk since the middle of the last century. Viscose rayon was developed as the original artificial silk. Kevlar is a more recent development by DuPont. The aramid is used in applications where strength is important, for instance in protective clothing. While it has strength it is lacking elasticity. The Canadian biotechnology company Nexia have developed BioSteel, a recombinant spider silk. Its intended applications are expected to be in the medical and industrial fields. The first patent disclosure appeared in 1999 for the production of recombinant spider silk protein in the milk of transgenic goats. Two transgenic goats, Peter and Webster, were born in 2000 with the spider silk gene incorporated into their genetic composition. Both animals were used to propagate a herd which now produce BioSteel in their milk yield. The protein is isolated from the milk and developed into spun fibres. It has proved very difficult to produce bulk, cost-competitive spider silk fibres with superior mechanical properties, especially strength. The growing interest in nanotechnology has also prompted the company to examine ways of producing the fibre as a biopolymer on a nanotechnology scale. Applications are unspecified, but could include medical implants.

NANOTECHNOLOGY

The prefix 'nano-' denotes a factor of one thousand-millionth in units of measurement. Nanotechnology operates at a molecular level. It combines some of the principles of molecular chemistry and physics with engineering and computer science. The

SCHOELLER
Nanosphere

The Swiss company have produced one of the first commercial textiles using nanotechnology. The technology is used to apply a very fine layer of the coating engineered to resemble the structure of the lotus leaf that makes it difficult for dirt to stick to the fabric. Dirt is easy to wash off using the force of water alone rather than relying on detergents. The design is inspired by the surface of the lotus leaf which combines a bumpy surface with a wax-like coating that causes rain droplets to bounce off, taking with them dust or other dirt particles.

technology has the potential to produce goods and services for little cost, though some sectors of the scientific community have expressed concern about the environmental impact of some of the manufacturing processes.

The earliest reference to nanotechnology can be found in a lecture to the American Physical Society in December 1959 by Richard Feynman entitled 'There's plenty of room at the bottom'. To those who reasoned that nanotechnology was not possible, he gave an example from nature. He made the comparison with the small number of atoms encoded with countless bits of information in DNA, which could provide all the instructions necessary to 'manufacture' a human being. The concept of nanotechnology, however, was not developed for a further twenty years until K. Eric Drexler took an interest founding the Foresight Institute

to further its development in California's Silicone Valley. Drexler's idea is to manufacture products from the molecule up, manipulating individual atoms one at a time until the object is formed. The work could be done by tiny robots, 'assemblers'. Because manufacturing would take place at a molecular level by rearranging existing atoms, Drexler argues that the raw material could be almost anything, making the whole process of great economic and environmental benefit. Asked in 1992 when he expected to see production in place, Drexler replied, 'I commonly answer that fifteen years would not be surprising for major, large-scale applications' (quoted in *Nano! Remaking the World Atom by Atom*, 1995). While we are still some way off this optimistic prediction, there is a trickle of commercial products on the market. Textiles, it seems, are one area particularly suited to the technology.

A consortium comprised of the US Air Force, researchers from Georgia Institute of Technology (Georgia Tech), Rice University and Carbon Nanotechnologies Inc. have been looking at how they might incorporate carbon nanotubes (first discovered in 1991) into fibres and films. Carbon nanotubes can provide thermal and electrical conductivity yet allow the fibres to maintain the touch and feel of typical textiles. The main difficulty is in getting the nanotube molecules into centimetre lengths without loss of strength. The single-walled nanotubes are produced in bundles thirty nanometers in diameter and containing more than a hundred tubes. These are then dispersed in an organic solvent to produce composite fibres. Polymeric materials can then be dissolved with these dispersed nanotubes, going on to produce fibres using standard textile manufacturing methods and equipment.

The main use of nanotechnology in textiles is as a coating. Schoeller have developed a coating that makes it difficult for dirt to stick and easy to wash off. The design is inspired by the surface of the lotus leaf. The ESA have developed Polymet, using a potentially endless three-dimensional polymer. It has a microporous metal structure that can be adapted in size as needed. Based on the system of galvanizing, the space agency maintains that completely new metallized surfaces are possible. The ESA are also promoting Polymet as a fashion and advanced textile applications. In America, Gentex are developing reactive nanotechnology for use in chemical warfare. Intended to provide protection against chemical or biological attack, the system uses nanoscale clusters of atoms and molecules with unique morphologies. These can potentially absorb and render harmless hazardous chemicals by breaking their molecular bond.

Researchers at Virginia Commonwealth University (VCU) have developed a nanothread mesh for use in bandages that reduce patient pain and speed up the healing process. The mesh uses fibrinogens just 80 nanometers thick that makes them comparable in size to natural fibrinogen fibres in human blood. Human or bovine fibrinogen is dissolved in a solution before being forced through a narrow nozzle towards a metal plate. While in the air, the threads are twisted and dried, reaching the metal plate as a mesh of fine threads. Initial tests show that clotting can begin in a matter of seconds of being applied to the wound. Another American university is looking at the use of nanotechnology to create fire-resistant fabrics based on natural rather than synthetic fibres. Scientists at the Agricultural Research Service in New Orleans, part of the government Department of Agriculture, are developing a nano-composite fibre using cotton and clay. The cotton is first dissolved then mixed with particles of Montmorillonite clay (more commonly used as cat litter) at a molecular level. The mixture is dried and the solvent removed to leave a natural material with a heat tolerance of 20–30°C (68–86°F) above that of unbleached cotton.

David R. Forrest of the Institute for Molecular Manufacturing is optimistic about the ability of molecular manufacturing to provide an energy-efficient and environmentally benign way to produce textiles. The process is conceived to allow the parallel-processing of individual molecules on a large scale in order to fabricate large atomically exact products. The system would rely on the use of several trillion molecular robotic subsystems working in parallel to process simple chemicals into new materials and devices. Forrest sees it as having the future potential to allow clothes to increase or decrease in size as needed, or change colour and pattern on demand. Robot components could be introduced to the fabric at a molecular level enabling it to be self-cleaning and repairing, while molecular fasteners could create new possibilities for a truly seamless garment.

The role of the designer has never been more complex as advances in new materials and processes continue to appear. The traditional notion of the designer as an isolated individual working alone in a studio is gone. Now we see designers as part of a team, usually multi-disciplinary, working together with technologists, engineers, material scientists, artists and craftspeople to realize a product. It is an exciting time which sees the designer involved as never before in the development of new materials and technologies. With it comes attendant responsibilities – not only that the design is good and fit for purpose, but that moral and environmental issues are considered in the way these brave new textiles develop.

Architecture

Marie O'Mahony

Stone reliefs carved during the Assyrian, Egyptian and Roman civilizations depict army tents made from animal skins, or woven fabric pulled over a framework of bars. Traditionally tents or canopies changed shape to carry different loads, sagging under snow and billowing up in wind. Today's tented or membrane structures satisfy a growing demand for permanent tensile systems which are expected to last twenty years, and for temporary designs that can be easily erected, yet remain robust.

In 1917 the English engineer F. W. Lanchester registered an ambitious patent for 'An Improved Construction of Tent for Field Hospitals, Depots and like purposes'. The design was for a pole-free tent that would rely on a difference between the internal and external pressure for support. This was an early air structure, but the design was never realized. It was not until the 1950s when more advanced materials became available that tensile membrane structures were developed in earnest. By 1980 fabric structures were being hailed in the journal *Progressive*

Architecture as 'a mature building technology'.

John Thornton, a director at structural engineers Ove Arup and Partners, reflected on the demands placed on contemporary membrane structures in the *Architects' Journal* as early as 1992: 'We expect them to perform with the same reliability as a conventional structure.' This is by no means an unrealistic expectation because much of the material technology and design know-how is already in place.

TYPES OF FABRIC

The majority of fabric membranes used in architectural applications are based on either a glass fibre or polyester fabric. A coating enhances their performance, protecting the membrane against pollution and grime. In the early 1970s DuPont developed a polytetrafluoroethylene (PTFE) resin under the trade name Teflon. It contains microscopic glass beads that can be coated on to a woven glass cloth. The fabric provides strength, with PTFE adding durability.

J. O. SPRECKLESEN A/S WITH PAUL ANDREU/ADP: ARCHITECTS RFR/OVE ARUP AND PARTNERS: ENGINEERS
'Nuage Léger', La Défense, Paris, 1984–89

Visitors are often surprised by the scale of the 'light cloud' (le nuage léger) close up. From a distance it appears almost flimsy. The cable supports are made into a feature, while the free edge of the membrane makes it seem as if it is floating.

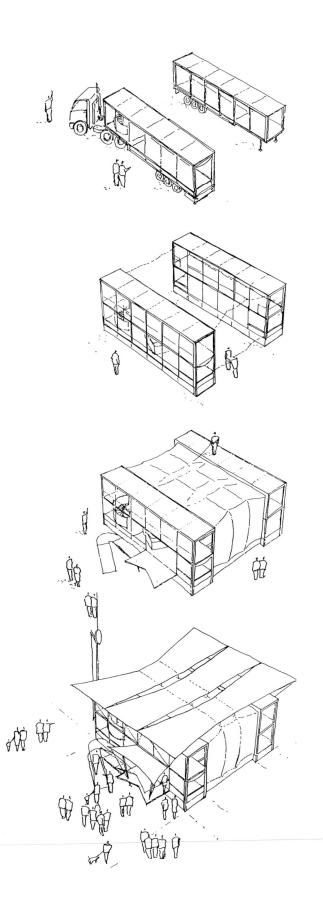

Coated glass-fibre membranes are hydrophobic (water-repellent), chemically inert and non-combustible. They are best suited for permanent rather than demountable structures.

The PVC-coated polyester is more resilient to handling and ideal for demountable structures. It is not as long lasting, with the plasticizers in the vinyl coating eventually rising to the surface and creating a sticky base that attracts dirt. However, it is a less expensive alternative to fibreglass and for that reason is used for both temporary and permanent structures. The main issue about the use of PVC is concern about its environmental impact. The problems with PVC appear at every level: it is toxic in manufacture, produces toxic dioxins in a fire situation and is not biodegradable.

Woven polypropylene is emerging as a possible alternative to PVC-coated membranes. Two companies, one Australian and one British, have already launched products. Gale Pacific Ltd in Australia have developed two polypropylene membranes. Landmark is available in a small range of colours and is generally used for agricultural and animal shelters. Aspect is available in white but used in the banner industry because it is highly suitable for printing on. The Landmark range allows little light through, but the Aspect range includes a translucent version. BP have developed Curv, a woven polypropylene that can be used for composite or membrane structures. The advantage of all three products is that they can be recycled and produced at a low cost. In theory, polypropylene is UV-stable, or can be made so by the addition of a film to the surface of the material or dye at liquid stage before the tape is pultruded. Thepolypropylene products available have yet to undertake industry-standard tests for UV-resistance. Until these tests are available to architects they are unlikely to be used in medium- or long-term structures.

SPECIALIST FABRICS

There are a growing number of speciality fabrics and coatings on the market. W. L. Gore have launched a sunscreen fabric, Tenara. This woven fabric uses PTFE not as a coating, as is usual, rather as high strength fibres. Dyneon, a division of the 3M group, produce a range of fluoropolymers including PTFE coating and Ethyl Tetrafluoroethylene (ETFE) foils. The latter can be extruded and processed into multi-layer cushions making it possible to produce both convex and concave forms.

While translucent membranes used in architecture are usually appreciated for the quality of the soft light they allow into the building, transparency is sometimes a requirement. Hoechst supply fluoroplastic films, Hostaflon ET and TF, which can be coated on to glass fabrics. When two or more layers are used, air cushions are formed which provide thermal insulation. One very unusual application of this technique is demonstrated in the roof of transformer stations. The roof forms a protective shell over a parabolic mirror which has been designed using a metallized Hostaflon ET. The film intensifies the sunlight over a thousand times, transforming it into electricity. Alpha produce a wide variety of coated glass fibre membranes including coloured and colourless and ranging from blackout to highly translucent membranes. The Screen line products are an example of the latter. The weave appears slightly open as stripes of white glass fibre with a transparent silicone coating. Although giving the appearance of water permeability, because the coating is all over, the fabric is in fact water-resistant.

While textiles have long been used in interiors to absorb noise, they have been more lacking in providing thermal insulation, particularly in roofing membranes. Manufacturers and designers are responding to these needs. Companies such as Sweden's Snowcrash are combining the performance of acoustic-absorbing fabrics with a new aesthetic. The result is that architects and interior designers are specifying their product for use as part of the overall visible design, not a technical textile to be hidden from view. The issue of thermal insulation is seeing some interesting design solutions from architects. Climate control is an issue at both ends of the spectrum, for cooling a building and keeping heat in.

opposite
**APICELLA ASSOCIATES:
ARCHITECTS
ATELIER ONE: ENGINEERS
Pavilion, Hong Kong 1994–95**

In this design for the Hong Kong Tourist Authority, the aluminium frame is roofed by a double-skinned inflatable membrane. The combination of structure with means of transportation achieves economies of function and space.

left
**KIYONORI KIKUTATE: ARCHITECT
TENSYS: ENGINEERS
Resort Centre, Japan**

Woven glass fibres are coated with a fluoroplastic film, Hostaflon, for this transparent roofing membrane.

**AMALGAM ARCHITECTS
B CONSULTANTS: MATERIAL
CONSULTANTS
Money Zone, Millennium Dome,
London**

The walk-through exhibition used
giant walls of tensioned perforated
fabric that combined with lighting,
translucency and printing to create
a layered three-dimensional effect.

TYPES OF STRUCTURE

In parallel with the development of materials, there is an increased understanding of the behaviour of these structures. Pioneers in the field, such as Frei Otto, advocated a design approach based on natural systems. The use of advanced computer programmes assists in converting three-dimensional shapes into two-dimensional cutting patterns, as well as plotting stress loads on the structure. The relationship between the architect and engineer has changed considerably, and an increasing number of specialist engineers are now being brought in on the design process at a much earlier stage.

Perhaps the simplest membrane structure is a hyperbolic paraboloid roof that uses four straight boundaries, masts or cables. A supporting structure, such as a cable net, can be placed below the membrane. This can be particularly useful when a large clear span is needed, such as in the Munich Ice Stadium. The structure of 'Nuage Léger' at La Défense in Paris makes a feature of its cable supports, while the free edge of the membrane gives it a floating appearance. Conical forms are also popular and can be created by pushing or pulling with rings or reinforced areas. Umbrella structures are used in many outdoor sites to provide protection from the elements.

TEMPORARY AND MOBILE STRUCTURES

One of the most common designs for temporary or mobile structures consists of a series of aluminium portal frames between which fabric is stretched. Simplicity of erection and the robustness of the fabric are key design factors. Architects Apicella Associates, with Atelier One as engineers on the project, have designed an ingenious system for the two-storey mobile Hong Kong Pavilion. Two trailers use hydraulic lifts to level the chassis and raise the first floor frame. Floor panels open out to provide an atrium space. The aluminium frame bridges brace the two structural frames, while a double-skinned inflatable membrane forms the roof. Warm air is pumped in during winter months to prevent heat loss and condensation, with air-conditioning and heating powered separately. Speed of installation time was an important consideration: it is estimated that it takes twenty-four hours to set up or dismantle.

Christo and Jeanne-Claude's *Wrapped Reichstag* was planned and developed over a 24-year period. Yet when the artwork was completed in June 1995, it stood for just two weeks before being dismantled. Around 100,000 square metres (1 million square feet) of silvery polypropylene (enough to cover fourteen football fields) were draped over

below
SERGE FERRARI SA
Soltis screens, Banque Populaire de l'Ouest, Rennes, 1990

Soltis membrane screens provide protection from the sun for the façade. The fabric uses a high tenacity polyester coated with PVC.

**GRIMSHAW: ARCHITECTS
ANTHONY HUNT ASSOCIATES:
ENGINEERS
Eden Project, Cornwall, 2001**

The panels on Grimshaw's Eden
Project are made using inflatable
ETFE foils. The computerized
construction process allowed the
panels to be cut to size, each fitting
their own allocated slot on the
structure. The foils are three layers
thick and heat-sealed before being
inflated to create a 2 metre (6 feet)
deep panel.

Berlin's Reichstag. It was secured using
a further 15,600 metres (50,000 feet) of blue
rope. Specially constructed steel cages
covered the delicate ornamentation on the
façade of the building. Fire precautions had
to take account of possible arson attacks.
Large numbers of visitors came to see the
wrapping in progress, which almost became
a performance as professional mountain
climbers bounced around the structure
attached from the roof by ropes. The
immense amount of technical planning was
made worthwhile by the beauty and simplicity
of the finished work.

AIR-SUPPORTED STRUCTURES

Air-supported structures can provide
a complete environment, whether permanent
or temporary. These structures are used
by architects for sports complexes, mobile
housing or stage sets. Artists and fashion
designers are also making use of the
technology with some dramatically different
results. Typically, a double layer of fabric is
inflated, and pressure is maintained by the
air supply system which replaces any air lost.
Three-dimensional inflatables work on much
the same principle, using a lighter fabric such

as polyurethane-coated polyester.
Mark Fisher has worked on a number of
spectacular stage sets for pop concerts
including giant inflatable pigs for Pink Floyd
and Indian priestesses for the Rolling Stones.
The fabrics are sewn by lock stitch technique,
with a web to support more detailed shapes.
The figures are painted or silk-screen printed
with vinyl etching inks. The British architects
Nicholas Grimshaw and Partners have used
an inflatable membrane solution for the Eden
Project, a series of biomes each with its own
unique climate. Glass proved too heavy
for the large structures so that ethylene
tetrafluoroethylene (ETFE) provided a
lightweight, transparent alternative, weighing
less than 1 per cent of its equivalent in glass.
Housing thousands of plants, the use of ETFE
allows crucial photosynthesis to proceed
much more efficiently than a glass equivalent.
The Swiss artists Lang and Baumann
create inflatable site-specific installations.

Commonplace words, such as SPORT or
UNDO, are often used precisely because they
are so familiar yet open to different readings.
The oversized scale, bright colours and art
gallery context invite the viewer to bring their
own interpretation to the works. Their earliest
installation, *Breathing Pillows*, 1996, remains
one of their most successful. The sky-blue
outsize pillows are nearer in scale to a
mattress as they occupy the gallery floor.
Each is equipped with a ventilation device as
the pillows are slowly inflated and deflated
in sequence to suggest a room full of people
breathing in a deep and peaceful slumber.
An American company, appropriately
named Larger Than Life Inc., manufacture
inflatable costumes mainly for advertising,
and a giant Babar and Tyrannosaurus Rex
are just two of their designs. Each of their
costumes has its own fan and battery pack
that inflates the costume and cools the
person inside.

LANG AND BAUMANN
Breathing Pillows
De Fabriek, Eindhoven

In a room reminiscent to the artists
of Dutch greenhouses, a number
of large pillows are set up to inflate
and deflate rhythmically, evoking
breathing forms.

ARCHITECTS OF AIR
Archipelago in Antwerp

The Architects of Air is a group of artists – based in Nottingham, UK – who travel the world with their amazing 'Luminaria'. The Archipelago is entirely constructed of tailor-made coloured plastic. The pieces have been cut and glued together by hand. Its creator, Alan Parkinson, calls his installations 'ephemeral architecture'.

G.H. MERZ: ARCHITECTS
IPL: ENGINEERS
Golden cloud

An architectural sculpture made
from an air-supported structure
celebrates the opening of a new
theatre building.

ENERGY AND WELL-BEING ISSUES

It is estimated that half our consumption of energy is accounted for by buildings. The advent of cheap energy and mechanical air-conditioning has diminished our ability to use building form and mass effectively. The energy crises, an awareness of green issues and sick-building syndrome have combined to focus architects' attention on design solutions which are more compatible with our environment. This means using less fossil fuel, and concentrating on a more dynamic use of the building itself.

Climatic control was one of the main problems faced by the organizers of Expo '92 in Seville. The event was staged between April and October, the most popular time for visitors, but soaring temperatures brought the climate well above comfort levels. Conscious of environmental concerns, the organizers decided to try and improve the environment making use of passive or natural methods.

Architects Lippsmeier and Henninnormier used a mixture of tensile shade structures, water, concentrated vegetation and devices to promote air movement. The Avenue of Europe was bordered by pavilions for the twelve EC countries, with a central pavilion for the EC itself. Visitors wandered freely between the garden, covering and the Cool Towers. The 30-metre (100-foot) towers consisted of a 5-metre (16-foot) high mast with a tensile covering made from a white plastic fabric.

left
VEECH.MEDIA
The Language Pavilion
Vienna, 2000–2001

Mobile pneumatic structure designed to reflect the fluidity of communication and information technology.

opposite
**LIPPSMEIR AND HENNIN-
NORMIER: ARCHITECTS
ESII SEVILLE : ENGINEERS
Cool towers, Expo '92, Seville**

The towers consisted of a 5m (16ft) mast with a tensile covering made from a white plastic fabric. The system was inspired by ancient Middle Eastern wind towers.

The environmental control system of the towers was inspired by ancient Middle Eastern wind towers which circulated cool air by wind or gravity flow. The ancient towers relied on air passing through evaporative cooler panels, whereas the Cool Towers at Expo '92 used atomizers as fogging devices. Included in the interior cooling system were micronizers (high-pressure nozzles) and a device for catching breezes at the top of each tower. The evaporative cooling of the air inside allowed large-scale treatment of the air in the Avenue. This finely regulated system provided a comfortable outdoor environment, as well as some ground-breaking research into the difficult area of outdoor climate control using passive energy systems.

SMART MATERIALS

The concept of a smart, or responsive building system is undoubtedly very attractive. Many of the issues which are now being addressed in relation to Information Technology (IT) could equally be applied to responsive architecture. The most fundamental question relates to the cognitive element: what will it be like to live in a smart building? Early attempts have often ended in disaster, with executives having to jump up and down during meetings to persuade the light system that there really is someone in the room and that light is needed. Many architects adopt a more tempered approach; they include a system override whereby the occupants can take full manual control of their environment.

As demographic trends indicate that people are living longer, enabling technologies, such as smart materials, become increasingly important. These technologies, consisting of wires, computers, gels and inks, all need an accessible user interface. Textiles are ideal in many instances, providing both a flexible conduit and aesthetic. While much of the technology is already available, its use in architecture is most restricted by material and development cost factors.

There have been some prototypes developed, mainly by students or as competitions. These give clues as to the way architects would like to use the technologies and what we may see in the near or distant future. While a student at London's Architects Association, Nigerian architect Ade Adekola developed a Surface Kinetic Integral Membrane (SKIM). This was an explorative design for a responsive textile composite that would monitor the mood of the human occupants in the room and adapt accordingly. The design had three layers. The first was a flexible fabric embedded with piezoelectric sensors. The second, and most complex, contained contact electrodes, current-carrying coils and the electrorheological (ER) fluids. These are non-conducting fluids containing polarized particles that stiffen when exposed to an electric field. The third layer mirrors the first, acting as a control interface. The intention of this system is that it would monitor its surroundings and adapt to it, providing a smart or responsive environment. Whether having a flexible ceiling move and adapt to the mood changes of the occupants would provide a calming or irritating environment is open to question.

The use of advanced textiles in architecture has been driven by some of the most creative minds in architecture, engineering and textile manufacturing. The results are changing the very appearance of our temporary, and increasingly, permanent buildings. As leading artists employ the fabric and engineering know-how to create sculpture on an architectural scale, this serves to further open the eyes of architects to the possibilities of the material. The use of advanced textiles in architecture has moved far beyond changing the shape of architectural roofing. What we are now seeing is the use of fabric in every conceivable aspect of building and structural design on a monumental scale.

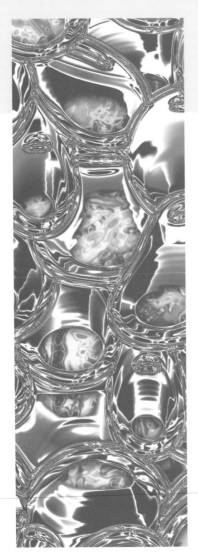

Art

Sarah E. Braddock Clarke

above left
MALGORZATA SKUZA
Quasifractal 5 (detail) of a series.
2004
208 (height) x 120 (width) cm

above right
Quasifractal 3 (detail) of a series.
2004
188 (height) x 120 (width) cm

right
Quasifractal 2 (detail) of a series.
2004
160 (height) x 120 (width) cm

opposite
Quasifractal 4 (full-view) of
a series. 2004
180 (height) x 120 (width) cm

Digital printing on cotton canvas.
The inspiration for this series of
textile art works are fractals, digital
space and interference of the virtual
and real world. Malgorzata Skuza
works with Photoshop software and
digitally prints her striking layered
imagery.

In the last decade, many practitioners
within the textile art world have been
utilizing the new technologies available.
Advanced technology can enable the artist
to think and work differently and plays a role
within contemporary textile art practice that
is both provocative and inspiring. In order to
comment effectively on today's technological
environment, contemporary artists are
making full use of the sophisticated materials
and techniques which science has provided.

Textile art is generally distinct from the
creation of fabrics with applications for
fashion, interior or industry. Free from the
limitations which the design world or industry
might impose, such as the commercial
market, the season and imposed deadlines,
the textile artist can experiment fully with
their chosen medium.

The vast array of materials, increasing all
the time as research adds new inventions,
includes different combinations of traditional
and the state-of-the-art textile and non-
textile. Working towards an environmentally
friendly future, textile artists can recycle and
transform materials while the use of new
non-pollutant dyes, eco-solvent printing inks,
chemicals and finishing treatments can also
contribute. Textile artists are often intrigued
by the latest developments and many are
even incorporating industrial and technical
textiles into their work – exploring them for
their visual and plastic qualities. In the search
for creative expression they may take purely
functional materials and transform them
to give an unexpected aesthetic. A variety
of surfaces and forms with unique
characteristics and properties can be created
which present exciting challenges to the
practitioner. The same material through
manipulation can be soft, hard, flexible, rigid,
free or controlled; it can be folded, rolled,
formed and moulded.

Weaving, knitting, dyeing, printing and
various methods of embellishment all are
used in textile art. Frequently such artisanal
skills are being combined with sophisticated
engineering technology, and technical skills
once considered appropriate only to one
discipline are being applied to another.

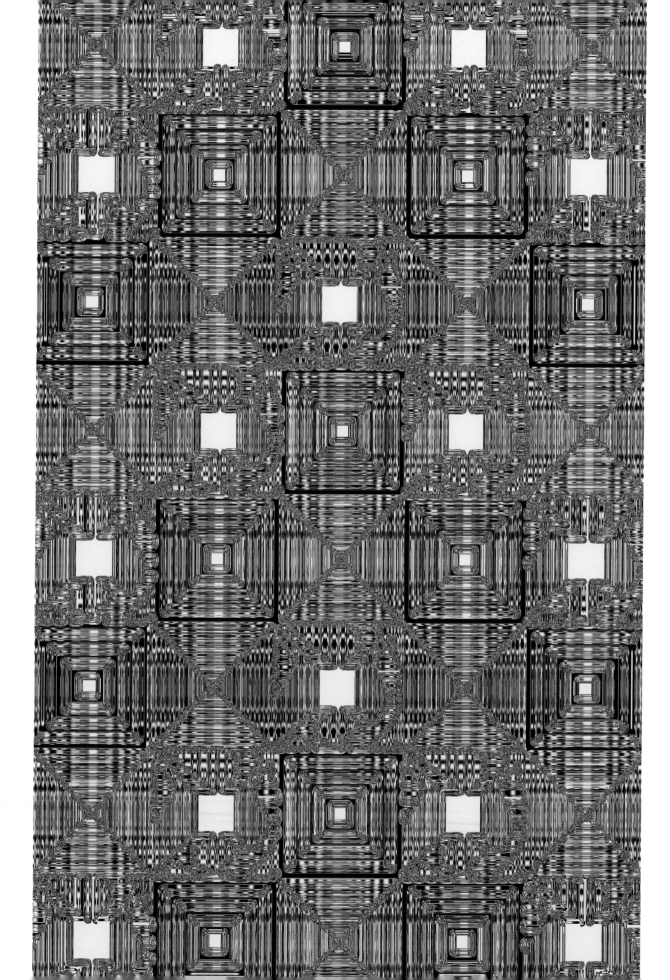

above
PETERIS SIDARS
Passion-2. 2003
180 (height) x 80 (width) x 70 (depth) cm

Hot melt glue and plexiglass. This art work explores the thermoplastic material of hot melt adhesive and the technology of lamination. Pēteris Sidars is interested in the changing nature of a material and in his experiments discovered the beauty of the glue itself to create textile-like structures.

opposite
JANIS JEFFERIES
Disolved I. 2004
130 (height) x 180 (width) cm

Jacquard weave from an original photograph, worked through Photoshop and woven at the Centre for Contemporary Textiles, Montreal, Canada. The photograph is one of a series Janis Jefferies took of a rope and sisal-making factory near Poznán in Poland which was about to close down. The image is digitized and broken down through scanning and Photoshop until it nearly disappears but is then materialized as a complex weave structure.

In addition, digital advances in many areas of construction and embellishment are now widely employed.

The use of a new or unconventional material/technique can challenge perceptions, and therefore the way we define beauty may need to change. Materials and techniques taken from outside the normal arena of textiles means that they can be decontextualized, to be seen afresh and therefore need to be assessed using different criteria. Areas in art and design are being broken down by the flexibility of both medium and technique and the future is possibly in the questioning of such boundaries. Instead, the choice of materials and the methods of making are being made through the textile artist's concept which may be more conducive to the creative process. Contemporary textile art with its interdisciplinary ideas and methodologies is capable of successfully demonstrating the leaps in science and technology. Resulting work can be seen to offer future potential outcomes with its manipulation of material and choice of technique while simultaneously communicating a powerful message.

TEXTILE ARTISTS

Many textile artists, while recognizing that a large part of this art form's history revolves around fundamental traditions and cultural identities, are experimenting with the new aesthetics and properties offered. By incorporating advanced materials and techniques with craft traditions their scope is enlarged and new perceptions created. This co-existence of tradition and technology is often considered the way forward. Much contemporary textile art engages with the resonance of textiles, updating it for a new audience.

Textile art began as an art form in its own right in the late 1950s, coming from Eastern Europe in the form of monumental, three-dimensional fibre constructions, and from the USA as hand-woven art works. It was with these early works, free from commercial constraints, that the full potential of this medium began to be realized.

There is a key difference between the textile artist and the artist who uses textiles. With the former, materials and techniques

chosen are fundamental to the expression of their ideas and a vital component. The essence of the art work cannot be translated into any other medium without changing its meaning and context. Contemporary practice is incredibly diverse and the ways in which individual expression is achieved are as many and as various as the textile artists themselves.

However, two main considerations are clearly evident. One approach is where creative experimentation is through the physicality and intimacy of the textile medium itself, with the material's formal and sensual qualities frequently providing a starting point. The potential of textile is fully engaged with and subsequent end results demonstrate visual and tactile effects made possible by such free experimentation. The work of Latvian textile artist Pēteris Sidars, for example, investigates the characteristics of diverse materials and techniques. He is particularly interested in ideas of transformation and in the possibilities of merging nature and technology. Another, more conceptual approach is also prevalent, where a textile artist explores intellectual processes to arrive at pieces which ably illustrate their ideas. UK-based textile artist Janis Jefferies examines critical issues of the textile medium and is interested in imagery and its translation. She questions the relevance and meaning of materiality and uses both traditional and new technologies to realize her works.

For many, the direct handling of yarn and fabric and an intuitive response to their inherent properties are crucial to the early stages of an idea's development. A thorough understanding of material together with expert technical knowledge is brought to the making of a successful piece. The use of computers sometimes involves less hands-on, and textile artists intrigued by the new possibilities are looking at connecting these sometimes very different ways of operating. Similarly, when working with the results of advanced textile technology with its myriad of new materials, the textile artist may explore them in much the same way as the traditional. In this chapter a range of approach is illustrated and a fantastic international diversity. The latest inventions and novel methods found within the world of textile art can in turn feed back into design

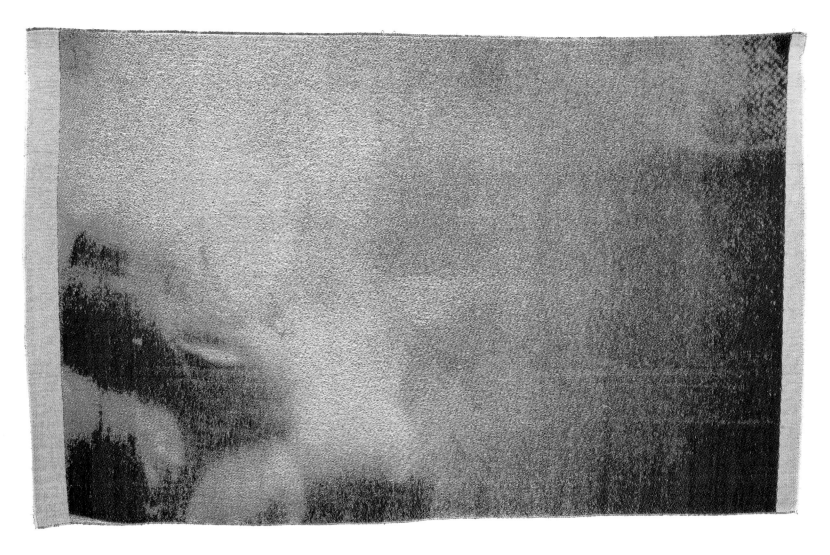

This handwoven golden tapestry was commisioned for the facade of a new store, a leading Buddhist altar fittings company in Japan. Pure gold threads were used to create two tapestries which are installed 250 mm apart to create a depth and wonderful moiré effect. The front tapestry is a plain weave and uses chained warps of pure gold and gold alloy. Gold threads are used for the weft together with acrylic sticks. The back or inner tapestry uses specially processed gold threads. The tapestry is heat-processed and mounted on the inside of forty-five metal panels. Due to varied lighting conditions the art work has different characters by day and by night.

This work demonstrates that textiles do not always have to be viewed inside. Here, Swedish textile artist Eva Best dresses an avenue of trees and creates a powerful and memorable image. Polyester and linen are prepared with a polyurethane dispersion and bonded together and then, using the thermoplastic properties of the synthetic textile shrunk to achieve a relief surface. The fabric is coloured, painted and printed before and after manipulation. All the trees had unique costumes which were formed and sewn by hand and special lighting added to the dramatic impact at night.

and industry and be of mutual benefit between art and science.

Artists who use textiles move towards the realization of an idea in a different way. Their training and background may vary to that of textile artists and the incorporation of textile material and technique will often be from a different angle. A work might use yarns or fabrics and demonstrate their various tactile, flexible and draping qualities and even make reference to the rich cultural heritage and traditions of textile, but this is not usually the artists' main concern. Instead, their concept is crucial and often overriding.

Many contemporary textile artists are not only working with large-scale installations but are also relating them to actual interiors and creating site-specific work. Across the globe, artists wishing to create their own environments are collaborating with galleries, museums and shops to create potent expressions. Responding to certain spaces, the artist works creatively within the confines of a given area, often being sensitive to a building's history and atmosphere. It could even be an exterior space. Where possible, the viewer can be encouraged to move through the setting to fully experience a work. Then the advantages that the medium of textiles offer can be appreciated and their

fluid nature and ability to drape can be observed. The form seen from afar can be contrasted with the subtle nuances communicated through construction and embellishment when seen up close. As the audience passes by the work it might move with the passing of air and can create a beguiling and seductive atmosphere.

Japanese textile artists frequently create pieces which can take over an entire space. Machiko Agano has created expressive site-sensitive work for galleries. Often inspired by the natural world, she communicates her ideas in large-scale pieces which exude presence and power. Australian-based textile artist Ainsley Hillard has also created work which responds to very particular locations. She is interested in communicating a spatial experience and her work often explores Eastern concepts of space, where importance is given to the intervals between objects. The results, with their ethereal imagery, make subtle reference to the environment in which they are hung. *Parallax*, a solo exhibition held at the Fremantle Arts Centre, Perth, Western Australia, consisted of fourteen freely suspended tapestries. This exhibition coincided with an international conference called *The Space Between* held in Perth, April 2004, which demonstrated the

creative blurring of boundaries between various art and design disciplines including textiles. *In Passing*, a work from Ainsley Hillard's graduate exhibition, was made up of several panels hung together as an installation while another piece, *Reminiscence*, consisted of three woven panels displayed to relate and work together. In the final installation the viewer interacts with the art work by moving through and leaving their traces. Ainsley Hillard uses digital photography, and some work, for instance *In Passing*, incorporates video stills. She uses computer software such as Photoshop to process digital images, Pointcarré Jacquard Software to help translate images into woven structures and

Final Cut pro, a film/video editing package. However, technology is merely a tool for her working process and is mainly used in the preliminary stages of developing her ideas.

Communication by email and accessing information on the Internet are now commonplace. Many textile artists are exploring creative ways of using Internet sites – showing live and interactive performances. Some artists are creating websites for their unique art works, inviting viewer interaction and debate. The worldwide network is standing by for more textile artists to discover it. Artists are now able to show their work to vast new audiences, collaborate in real time with other artists and even use the Web as a means of creative expression.

above left and right
AINSLEY HILLARD
Parallax. 2004
Fremantle Arts Centre, Perth,
Western Australia during April to
May 2004
Installation of fourteen tapestries each 300 (height) x 34 (width) cm

Textile artist Ainsley Hillard took a series of digital and manual photographs of the architectural space (a former mental asylum), enlarged them, and then heat-transferred this imagery onto transparent viscose yarn in a tape form prior to weaving. When combined with transparent polyamide monfilament and hand-woven the result is fragile-looking and thought-provoking with its emerging and shifting images. Moving between the piece, the viewer connects with the objects and the spaces between.

below
JULIE GRAVES
Underground, Overground. 2001
29 (height) x 3760 (width) cm

This textile art work was created specially for the exhibition, *Messages and Meaning: The Narrative of Print* at Bankfield Museum in Halifax 2001. It was inspired by a soft toy made for McDonalds, Womble Wellington. Julie Graves is interested in how things are constructed, their materials, where they are made and by whom, such questions are often the starting point for her work. For this piece, images of factory workers were scanned and manipulated using Photoshop to produce a repeat pattern which was then silk-screen printed onto the warp of a loom and woven using silk. The repeated image becomes integral to the woven structure. This toy, fabricated in China had travelled all the way to UK and ended up as a free gift to children in a fast food outlet. Off the loom, images of maps and travel routes were then printed on the textile's surface. In 2003 Julie Graves extended this work with an interactive website.

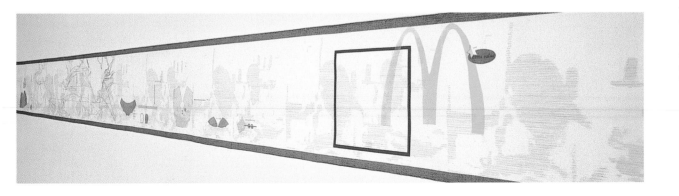

above
MACHIKO AGANO
Untitled
The Modern Museum of Art,
Gunma. 2003

This installation uses stainless
steel wire, polyamide monofilament
and silk thread hand knitted in
garter stitch. Machiko Agano uses
very long needles (almost 1 metre/
3 feet in length) to make the pieces,
evoking forms found in nature such
as the ocean, clouds and wind.

opposite
MACHIKO AGANO
Untitled
Gallery Gallery, Kyoto. 2003

Taking inspiration from air, wind and
light, Japanese textile artist Machiko
Agano creates a site-specific work
in this gallery in Kyoto. She explores
the potential for three-dimensional
textiles using stainless steel wire,
polyamide monofilament and kozo
(Japanese paper) with techniques
of hand-knitting in garter stitch and
paper-making.

**PLEATS PLEASE ISSEY MIYAKE
Guest Artist Series No. 2**

In 1996 Issey Miyake started this series where he invites different artists to use the Pleats Please collection as their starting point. The results show a dialogue between fashion and the arts. Here, the work of the photographer Nobuyoshi Araki has transformed the Pleats Please canvas into garments which communicate his theme of memory. This vest top shows a self-portrait of the photographer (far left). The print on the long figure-hugging dress (left) is of a woman which disappears when worn, leaving the image in the memory.

opposite right and far right
**PLEATS PLEASE ISSEY MIYAKE
Guest Artist Series No. 4**

For this series Issey Miyake invited the artist Cai Guo Qiang who was interested in the polyester textile as a flammable material. He took eighty items of the Pleats Please clothing and laid them in the shape of a dragon and then made a trail of gunpowder over the garments. An audience was invited to see the event. Photographs were made of the burnt and charred garments and these images printed on to the Pleats Please clothes.

EAST AND WEST

In the late 1950s, textile art from Eastern Europe and the USA made a great impact on Japanese textile artists. They looked to the USA for a narrative approach, bold use of colour and hand-woven structures, and to Europe for social and political comment, large scale tapestries and three-dimensional installations.

Generally speaking, Western textile artists take issues of gender, society, politics and the urban and natural landscapes as their themes. The concepts behind this issue-based work is much debated by the artists and the press. In Japan, however, craft practitioners have traditionally enjoyed a status akin to fine artists. In addition, much investment has been made into research and development into new textiles in Japan. Textile artists in the East have utilized these two strengths, finding their voice from looking back at their rich craft tradition and forward to a technological future. Textile art is a recognized art form in Japan and its lyricism and spirituality are distinctive. The style is often minimalist with a meditative, contemplative quality, experimenting with repetition of form and contrasts of symmetry with asymmetry.

The Japanese textile artist works with all textile techniques, including dyeing and weaving (intrinsic to Japanese craft traditions) and three-dimensional construction – manipulating both yarn and fabric. Often the works are large in scale and free-standing installations, allowing full appreciation of the textile. In contrast to the Western artist, the Japanese tend not to discuss their work so much. The cultural differences between East and West are valuable and it is good to see that both can continue to learn from each other and yet preserve their unique identities.

Due to the popularity of Pleats Please and also demonstrating his interest in the fine arts in general, in the mid-1990s Issey Miyake launched his Guest Artist Series, produced in a limited edition. His aim was to collaborate with various international artists who use diverse media from painting to photography with Pleats Please as a canvas. Each artist has treated the project in his or her own creative way and the results exist in the area between fashion and art.

As well as the international catwalk shows Issey Miyake displays his work in the context of the art gallery or museum and has had

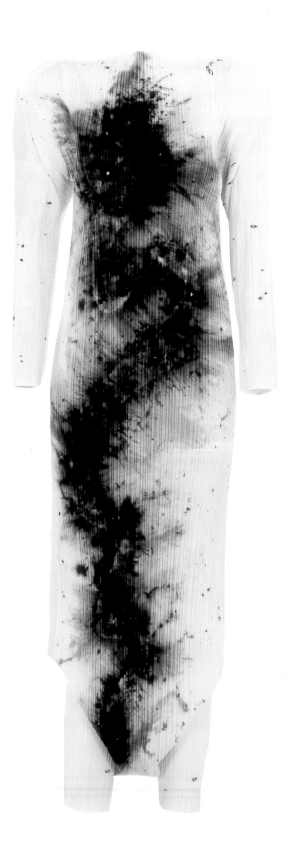

above
KYOKO KUMAI
Wind Blowing over the Grass. 2002
C-square, Chukyo University,
Nagoya

Stainless steel filaments are used
to create this art work which takes
nature as its source of inspiration.
One of Kyoko Kumai's most
powerful memories since
childhood has been the image of
wind blowing over the fields. Using
a technique similar to that of
making ropes, she creates this
powerful and evoocative piece.

many exhibitions, the first being in 1963
at the Seibu Museum of Art in Tokyo.

Issey Miyake has also worked in the area
of contemporary dance, creating costumes
for Maurice Béjart and for William Forsythe
and the Ballet Frankfurt. He has enjoyed the
design challenge of creating clothing which
is visually stunning, lightweight and very
flexible; in fact it was on stage that his
famous pleats first appeared.

Japanese textile artist Kyoko Kumai uses
stainless steel in her art works which
comment on the power of nature. She often
invents her own construction techniques
such as interlocking and transforms this
industrial material into compelling pieces
that appear to be light and soft. Kyoko Kumai
conveys the temporal forces of air, wind and
light. Subsequent art works can be two-
dimensional and wall-based or, as was the

case with her 1991 exhibition at New York's
Museum of Modern Art at the invitation of the
Architecture Department, can take over
a whole room. Her use of metal promotes
a new aesthetic and a fresh vision. Conveying
aspects of nature in the form of large three-
dimensional installations, her works are
dramatic and yet subtle, imaginative and
thought-provoking. She has also exhibited
her work at London's Science Museum in
their 'Challenge of Materials' gallery which
looks at the world of materials and
challenges the audience's perceptions.

Grethe Wittrock is a Danish textile artist
and designer who became fascinated with
paper when she was studying in Japan. She
primarily uses this material with textile
techniques to fully explore the beauty and
variety of it as a medium. Her work has been
exhibited internationally and draws from both

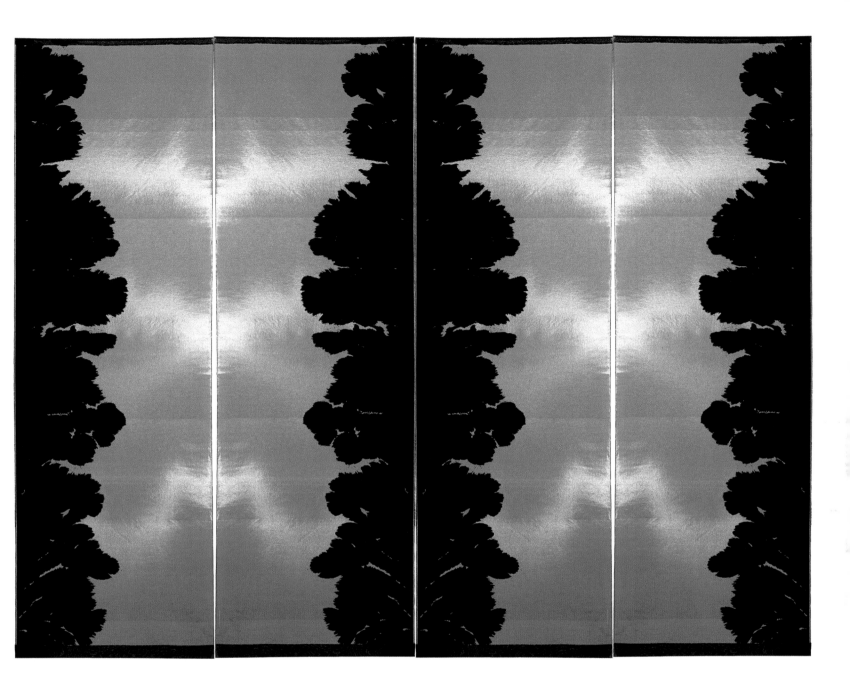

Eastern and Western cultures. It was when she spent time in Kyoto that she was made fully aware of this city's very rich textile tradition and in particular the use of paper. Traditionally, tightly coiled paper is used in the weft of a complex Jacquard textile to create stiff obi (the sash worn around the kimono). Paper is also used for shoji (interior room dividers and screens). Grethe Wittrock has her textiles machine-woven in Japan – for example, a polyamide warp and paper weft which creates a wonderfully translucent surface. This is then dyed and printed on. Her

inspiration comes from a variety of sources, frequently from the natural world. She demonstrates a sensitivity to both occidental and oriental cultures and brings the aesthetics from both worlds together while communicating a message about the world in which we live.

Visual artist Lucy Orta is internationally known for her powerful and original works of art which comment on the fragile nature of the world and our survival as the human race. She addresses political concerns and the problems of society such as the unemployed

above
GRETHE WITTROCK
Obsidian, 2003
4 panels each 400 (height) x 125 (width) cm

The inspiration for this art work came from lava formations in Iceland. Polyamide/paper is machine-woven in Japan (polyamide warp and paper weft), dyed and then hand silkscreen printed with Expandex paste. It was made at the National Arts & Crafts Workshops in Copenhagen.

and homeless. Her work promotes working together as a team to overcome adversities. Lucy Orta has created numerous site-specific pieces and often stages her works in the urban environment – the streets, the underground, train stations and even live within museums. Installation-based ideas such as clothing/temporary, portable and mobile shelters/habitats/site-specific performance-based works, are her signature. Lucy Orta originally trained in fashion and textiles and uses her knowledge to select the most appropriate materials for her works. Advanced technological textiles she has utilized include ultra-microfibres, chlorofibres, the latest synthetics, nonwovens, extremely fine specialist coatings and environmentally friendly textiles with biodegradable membranes, selected for their futuristic aesthetic as well as their functional capabilities. She has also used reconditioned army surplus alongside techno textiles. Such previously used fabrics bring with them a history, both real and symbolic, which can deliver a potent message in today's difficult political climate.

Lucy Orta is interested in new ways of showing her work and has streamed multimedia, interactive performance on the Internet as live webcasts. She has also staged installations in museum galleries and choreographed participants to create formations as a series of live works. The work of Lucy Orta stands between fashion, art, architecture and installation/performance art. It asks questions about the way we live, both as individuals and as part of social groups, and demonstrates the strength of interaction – offering hope for the future.

DIGITAL TEXTILE ART

Advances in technology are rapid and computers have become ever more sophisticated and play an increasingly important role in the work of textile artists. The software available to artists and designers is a growing market but the most satisfactory programmes encourage free experimentation in generating and manipulating visual ideas. Flatbed scanners have enabled all kinds of two- and three-dimensional imagery (made or found) to be downloaded into specialist software for further manipulation. Digital cameras and video equipment linked to computers allow for artists to work with images they have captured.

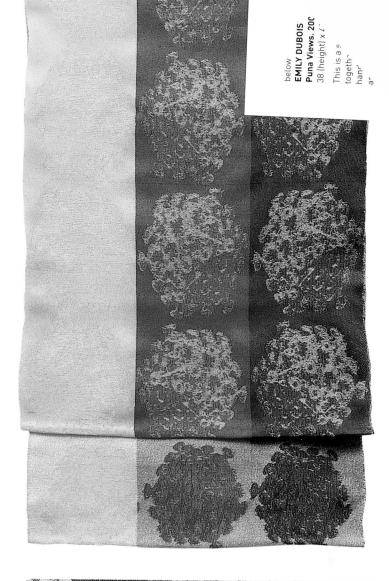

below
EMILY DUBOIS
Puna Views. 20(
38 (height) x ∠́
This is a s
togeth
han
a

opposite
LUCY ORTA
N.U.O. No. 0303 (left) and 0307 (right). 2003

N.U.O. stands for Non-identified Urban Objects. Military stretcher beds support silkscreen printed body-related pieces which comment on our precarious world. In No. 0303 aluminium-coated polyamide is contrasted with the raw quality of ex-army surplus linen. In No. 0307 high-resistant coated cotton is used.

above left
MITSUKO AKUTSU
Seeking a Land of Rest No. 22. 2001
109 (height) x 79 (width) cm

In making this work, two photographs (red and white arrows) are scanned and manipulated by computer before being ink-jet printed onto two pieces of polyester.

Each cloth is cut into strips for either the warp or weft and then woven to create overlapping imagery. The warp and weft interlacing makes further reference to the pixellated process.

above right (full view in daylight) and right (detail in artificial light)
CAROL WESTFALL
Aids. 2003
59 (height) x 36 (width) cm

This art work is made of a cotton warp and glow-in-the-dark weft yarns. The complex imagery is made possible by a computer-aided Jacquard loom. It is the latest part of a trilogy by the artist – Anthrax, 2000; Pox, 2001 and Aids.

...[width] cm

...ries of works pieced
... from ikat and shibori dyed,
...-woven fabrics from her studio
...d power-loom Jacquard fabrics
from the Bridging Worlds, Jacquard
Project. This work shows
inspiration taken from the district
Emily DuBois lives in on the big
island of Hawaii with its wonderful
views of ocean, lava rock and sky.

opposite left
EMILY DUBOIS
Zero and One. 2004
153 (height) x 33 (width) cm

This fabric was Jacquard power-
loom woven at Philadelphia
University as part of the Bridging
Worlds, Jacquard Project in 1995. In
2004 Emily DuBois pieced together

sections of the fabric to create this
art work. It is a unique piece even
though the fabric is woven in
repeats.The inspiration for her work
comes from patterns of harmony
found in nature, in weaving and in
t'ai chi. In this piece she relates the
zero and one of computer code to yin
and yang, which combine in endless
permutations.

opposite right
EMILY DUBOIS
Diatoms. 2004
84 (height) x 84 (width) cm

This woven art work combines
an image of diatoms (single-celled
organisms) seen through
a microscope with two close-ups
of the inside of a basket. The two
repeats of the image (above) create
a figure of eight or an infinity
symbol. The work is both suggestive
and mysterious.

With the computer, layers of visuals, including
text, either created directly on the screen or
scanned in, can be built up. Many possibilities
can be rapidly tested at the touch of a button,
including changes of form, background,
foreground, colour relationships and scale,
making further experimentation possible and
giving the artist more time to devote to the
content, meaning and communication of their
ideas. The textile artist becomes a selector
or an editor, though the limitless variations
offered by the computer can make this
a daunting prospect. The computer, however,
is merely a tool, and aesthetic decisions can
only be made by the artist. The ultimate
challenge is to combine pure creativity with
technology – this is where the huge potential
for digital textile art may lie.

Much has been written about the links
between the digital coding of computers and
the woven textile as means of expression.
The intersection of warp and weft are
considered similar in principle to the essence
of pixellation. Particularly relevant to the
complexity of the computer is the Jacquard
loom which enables individual threads to be
lifted to create complex imagery, such as
smooth curves from horizontal and vertical
lines, and an almost photographic realism.
Textile artists who have previously undertaken
Jacquard weaving, tapestry and canvas
embroidery seem to possess a natural affinity
for working with the computer. The
computerized loom allows complex weave
structures which would otherwise be far too
time-consuming. Double, triple and quadruple

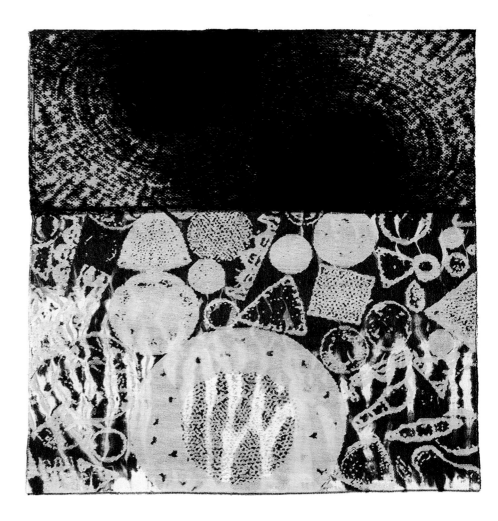

layered cloths with varying textures and surface interest can be created.

Weavers have a rich past to draw from, and balancing this with advanced technology can create thought-provoking work. American textile artist Emily DuBois works with both ideas taken from this strong tradition and the latest technologies on offer. She relates the zero and one of computer binary code to the concept of yin and yang, and warp and weft. Her woven art works demonstrate how a simple system can produce infinite configurations. A deep interest in patterns of energy which reveal growth and the elemental forces of nature, observing wind and water in motion, are often translated into woven structures. The idea of collage is important to Emily DuBois and original drawings, paintings and photographs are reinterpreted in fabric for her art works. She combines many techniques including dyeing and/or painting the warp/weft, stitching, hand-weaving (both

dobby looms and Jacquard, the latter enabling unique threading) and the electronic Jacquard powerloom. CAD-based imagery is converted into CAM Jacquard software which translates it into the appropriate interlacing of the warp and weft threads. However, it is her expression and not the technique which is fundamental. Her compelling and visually powerful work balances traditional hand weaving with the mechanical process of the computer-assisted loom. Emily DuBois is very interested in surface design as well as structure, and has used traditional Japanese resist-dyeing techniques to achieve beautiful visual effects. Sometimes optical illusions and moiré patterning appear as lines converge – horizontal (weft), vertical (warp) and diagonal (twill weave). Her woven art works sometimes seem to flicker and move like the images on a computer screen. The work of Emily DuBois is extremely complex in structure and yet has visual unity.

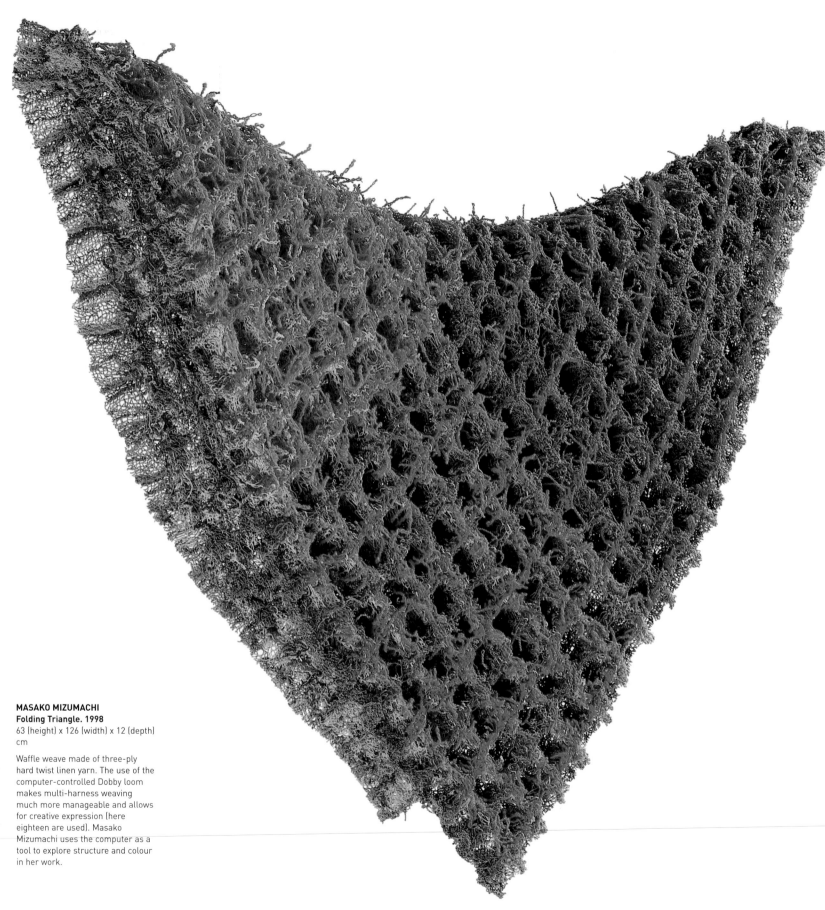

MASAKO MIZUMACHI
Folding Triangle. 1998
63 (height) x 126 (width) x 12 (depth)
cm

Waffle weave made of three-ply
hard twist linen yarn. The use of the
computer-controlled Dobby loom
makes multi-harness weaving
much more manageable and allows
for creative expression (here
eighteen are used). Masako
Mizumachi uses the computer as a
tool to explore structure and colour
in her work.

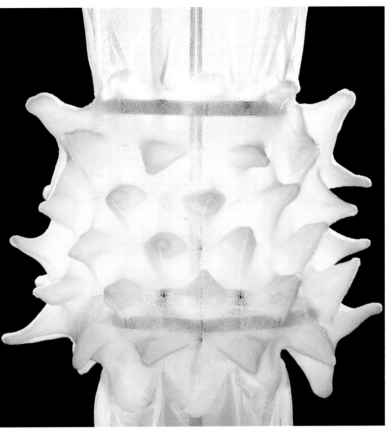

left
ULLA E:SON BODIN
Snowball

Polyamide monofilament and polyester are used to create this striking costume with dramatic three-dimensional forms. Such complex construction is made possible by the use of a computerized flat knitting machine. The garment is knitted in two pieces and sewn together at the sides and shoulders.

below
ULLA E:SON BODIN
Collage

Produced on a computerized flat knitting machine, these costumes are knitted in two pieces with side seams. The metallic look of the main textile is polyester, polyamide monofilament and lurex, and at the waist polyamide monofilament and an iridescent yarn.

HIDEO YAMAKUCHI
Shisen. 1997
120 (height) x 240 (width) cm

The art work begins with a
photograph taken by the artist. It is
then interpreted in a textile medium
using a digital weaving technique.
Parts of the imagery of this piece
are digitally woven in individual
shirts which combine to form the
work, like a picture puzzle – it looks
as if an image is being projected on
to clothes. The computer enables
him to achieve this photographic
realism – the vast amounts of
information processed would not
be possible without it. This is made
of 100 per cent rayon and is in
the permanent collection of the
Metropolitan Museum of Art,
New York.

Hideo Yamakuchi is a pioneer in his field. In
Japan, he grew up surrounded by traditional
textiles: his family were weavers from an area
where fabrics for traditional kimonos were
made. He has also worked closely with
computers. He experiments with the new
possibilities in art afforded by the latest
digital fabric technology and his particular
aesthetic often achieves a larger-than-life
photographic realism. Hideo Yamakuchi's
images are technically superb and startling
in their power. Beginning with the taking of
photographs which record his own
experiences, he then works with them on the
computer linked to electronic Jacquard looms
in order to create unique art works. He sees
the loom as a kind of printer; the digital
image data can be read as warp and weft in

a woven structure. The Jacquard technique
allows for sophisticated patterning and it is
the development of the computer that has
enabled the processing of the vast amounts of
information needed to weave images so close
to the original. He uses colour in the same
way as a printer, mixing them pixel by pixel
or thread by thread to achieve incredibly
accurate results. Traditional colour printing
on paper produces all colours by mixing four
coloured inks: cyan, magenta, yellow and
black (white is not needed for printing since
inks are usually on a white paper). He uses
a similar approach to create three different
kinds of fabric. Two-colour monotone weave
has black and white in both warp and weft
and produces a lightweight fabric. Five-
colour weave has cyan, magenta, yellow,

black and white in both the warp and the weft and gives a slightly thicker fabric. However, the eight-colour weave gives the most vivid colours and the most high-fidelity textile. It uses only black for the warp and eight colours – cyan, magenta, yellow, red, green, blue, white and black – for the weft. The fabric is quite dense (maximum density is 240 yarns per cm) and can therefore be heavy but it communicates imagery with a three-dimensional illusion and is ideal for fine art expression. He explores the future potential of textiles and shows us the possibilities for digital cloth. Hideo Yamakuchi's work comments on the world around us and illustrates a creative and challenging way of working with technology.

A computer-controlled loom has been invented that has incredible potential in the creation of three-dimensional textile art forms. The results are interesting both from a visual and a technical point of view. Instead of removing two-dimensional cloth from the loom, you take off a contoured or fully formed textile. This loom gives a freedom similar to working with tapestry, and allows for sophisticated weave structures such as multi-layers and tubular forms. The textile artist creates directly on a computer screen, and converts the information to a grid (warp and weft). The type of yarn and other specifications are fed in, and the programme will work out the fabric construction. Different shapes can be produced to give a dense, irregular textile, and diverse weave patterns can be designed to occur at certain places along the length or width of the piece, much like Jacquard technique. Seaming is not necessary and distortion does not happen with a stretch fabric. Time and labour are saved as there is no assembly and waste is minimal. In the near future it is hoped that textile artists will be able to work with such equipment to create new and exciting work.

Computerized knitting machines allow great control of the way the threads are linked. Complex relief or three dimensional forms and sophisticated patterning are all possible. In both woven and knitted methods of construction random effects can be programmed in to produce totally unpredictable imagery and subtle and gradual changes in a series are easier to make.

CAD and solvent ink-jet digital printing are changing the look and methodologies of printed textiles in new and dramatic ways. The technology has improved considerably in recent

right
SIMON CLARKE
Designs for digitally-printed art works. 2004

Digitally generated designs inspired by the language and culture of the Cornish and Swahili coasts, both recurring themes for Simon Clarke's work. The marks and colours are formed by intuitive and reflective actions based on visual ideas suggested by these particular environments. The imagery has been entirely generated in Photoshop and illustrated here is the computer screen stage. They are then digitally printed on cotton using the Japanese technology of a Mimaki TX2 1600.

years. Since very expensive pieces of equipment are needed, the textile artist might only have access to such machinery within the textile department of a university. Some companies have developed textiles specially for digital printing – the substrates need to be of high quality and often weaves are dense so the inks will not bleed. Ink manufacturers are putting much research and development into pigmented dyes and the technology is advancing fast. When pigment dyes can be used with digital print techniques many artists will use them as they do not need pre-treated fabric and therefore allow for much experimentation.

Traditional screen printing is being affected by digital printing as there are many advantages to working with digital ink-jet print techniques. Before, a fifty pure-colour print needed fifty separate screens. Now, with digital textile printing, the artist has much more creative freedom. The use of photographic imagery was previously notoriously difficult, despite being a four-colour process. This is now significantly easier with the digital printer. Very wide pieces of fabric can be printed on and extra long lengths too, whereas before there was a limitation imposed by the size of both the screen and print table. Experimentation can be made using digital imagery to convey both two- and three-dimensional layered imagery with a strong illusion of space and depth and extremely detailed textures. From an ecological stance, digital printing can be less

damaging than traditional screen printing. In the latter, on completion of the print process, there is always ink left behind on the screens which is blasted off and washed away. And to prevent having to mix more dye halfway through a print, the artist will often initially mix too much which is thrown away afterwards. With digital working there is far less waste of ink/dyes as you only use what you need.

A disadvantage is that certain print techniques are still not possible digitally although technology is advancing fast in this area. For example, dévoré must be done in the traditional way using screens. Discharge printing, where light colours are printed on a dark background, cannot be done as the ink jets are not compatible with the special inks; this also applies to metallic dyes. However, there are creative ways of getting around such problems by using mixed media, combining old techniques with the new and utilizing both machine and hand processes. For example, digital printing can be done on to a dévorable fabric (which usually needs a cellulosic and other yarn in both the warp and the weft) and then chemically treated after the digital print has been fixed. Also, heat-reactive or patination processes can be used in conjunction with the digital. Many consider the future of digital printing to be alongside traditional techniques, not replacing them, and textile artists are paving the way with their pure and free experimentation.

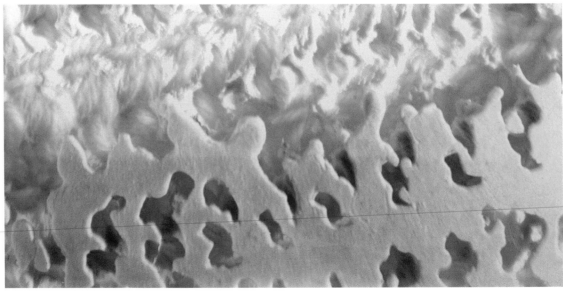

MUSEUMS AND GALLERIES

Special textile museums and galleries may be found internationally, and almost all major cities have a particular space for displaying contemporary textile art, although still too few compared with the great number of exhibition spaces for fine art. Places known for their rich past for textiles, such as Kyoto and Prato, often have a museum dedicated to textiles.

These days, many universities have their own gallery spaces or have long-standing links with interested gallery and museum owners. Many different types of venue are also interested in staging exhibitions of textiles and fashion, possibly ones not normally associated with these mediums. Textiles, fashion and art are very closely linked and many curators are exploring these ideas with subsequent events demonstrating the connections with stylishly evoked artistic concepts. As ideas about textiles are changing, fashion and textile art are increasingly being exhibited in galleries of contemporary art and museum departments of design, architecture and science.

It is at international forums for textile art that textile artists from all over the world are exposed to and influenced by each others work. Historically, the International Lausanne Biennale was of great importance in the world of textile art. Begun in 1962 and held every two years in Lausanne, Switzerland, this event has been instrumental in showing European, American and Japanese work together. Japanese textile art, for example, was shown for the first time in the West at the first 1962 exhibition, and soon afterwards work from Japan was to be seen in galleries and museums worldwide. Originally demonstrating the most creative ideas within tapestry art, in 1992 it opened up to other techniques in textile art besides tapestry. Its title reflected this change – from Biennale de la Tapisserie Internationale (International Tapestry Biennial) to International Lausanne Biennale Exhibition: Contemporary Textile Art. The last exhibition for this Biennale was held in 1995 but its influence over the years has been felt internationally. Experimentation in its truest sense has always typified the work shown at the Lausanne Biennale and this is still continuing today at other venues.

Several important exhibitions during the 1970s brought international textile art works to Japan for the first time, making a lasting impact. The first major museum in Japan to

above left
NORMA STARSZAKOWNA
Transmutations **Exhibition, the Netherlands Textile Museum, Tilburg. 2004**

Art work on display. *Blue Wood* is second from the left.

above right
NORMA STARSZAKOWNA
Blue Wood (detail). 2004
350 (height) x 50 (width) cm

Silk organza, digitally printed and then screen printed with mixed media and heat-reactive inks, partially glazed and rust-patinated. This textile art work combines a use of digital imagery with with manual processes. The rust patination technique is created by using liquid iron on the cloth and then applying patination fluids.

above
SONJA WEBER
Sky Moment. 2001 (left)
170 (height) x 240 (width) cm
Sky Moments. 2001 (middle)
32 (height) x 32 (width) cm each
Sky Moment. 2001 (right)
65 (height) x 170 (width) cm
Augenblicke **Exhibition, Constance,**
Germany. 2002

Polyester warp and acrylic weft.
Nature is the main theme for artist
Sonja Weber and here she has made
works which depict various changing
moments of our skies. The end result
is achieved through combining
photography, painting, computer
technology and weaving. Using
computer programmes minute detail
can be captured and created to then
be interpreted into Jacquard woven
structures. As the viewer looks at the
work from a distance it may appear
two-dimensional but on moving closer
and passing by the work a different
impression of the picture results from
the relief structures of the fabric.
Depending on the lighting a new
surface develops.

opposite
MARK DION AND J. MORGAN PUETT
In collaboration with The Fabric
Workshop and Museum. 2003
(above) The Post Apocalyptic Nurse
(c. 2130) and (below) details of The
Intergalactic Nurse (c. 2206)

From the exhibition *RN: The Past,*
Present and Future of the Nurses'
Uniform

Two of four proposed futuristic
uniforms: in a time of anarchy
everything has to be recycled as
nothing is being produced. The
uniform becomes the nomadic
hospital in situations of large-scale
conflict. (above) The architectural
fabric, polytetrafluoroethylene (PTFE)
has been salvaged and used for its
abrasion-resistance and protective
qualities against acid rain, ultraviolet
radiation and environmental
pollution. Fabrics used include
Tenara woven with expanded PTFE
fabric supplied by Gore, nonwoven
fibres and aramids in thermoplastic
film by Honeywell Performance
Polymers and a synthetic latex by
Scott Materials Group, Inc.
(below) Fibre panels contain
receptor-transmitter devices. The
skintight uniform shown here is made
of many highly technological
materials, including various silver
and nickel plated synthetics by
Sauquoit Industries, 3M reflective
film, synthetic latex by Scott
Materials Group Inc. and no-stretch
suede and a co-polymer on polyester
knit both by Harrison Technologies.

show textile work was the National Museum of
Modern Art, Kyoto in 1971 with the exhibition
New Textile Artists. The National Museum
continues to support textile art, and to
demonstrate that textiles are an integral
part of Kyoto's past, present and future.
Kyoto is a city where the applied arts are given
a particular reverence. The first exhibition
devoted to contemporary Japanese textile art
was held by Takeo Uchiyama in Kyoto in the
mid-1970s. Prior to this, Japanese expression
in the textile medium had no recognized
identity. Now there are many significant and
emerging textile artists from Japan, some
receiving art education in the West and
responding to both cultures.

Since the 1970s the number of Japanese
museums and galleries showing textile work
has increased, and this can be related to the
growing number of textile artists in Japan.
Gallery Gallery in Kyoto was originally set up
by three textile professionals in 1981 (two
textile artists and one critic), and regularly
shows contemporary textile art. Keiko
Kawashima, who took over as director in 1988,
is deeply committed to encouraging the work
of new textile artists, often providing them with

their first gallery space. In 1993 she established the Kyoto International Contemporary
Textile Art Centre (KICTAC). Keiko Kawashima
herself trained as a textile artist and has
shown her work in Japan and Europe.

The Kyoto International Textile Competition
(KITC) was first held in 1987 and then every
two to three years. Their aim is to promote
the textiles of the future with an emphasis
on the new technologies available, while still
acknowledging traditional techniques and
fabrics. KITC is open to both textile artists
and designers, and textile art and industrial
textiles are shown. Creativity and technical
accomplishment are high on the list of criteria
with a particular interest in the area of textile
art and technology.

The Fabric Workshop and Museum (FWM)
in Philadelphia, USA, does much to promote
contemporary gallery textiles. Established in
1977, one of its main aims is to bring
contemporary art and textiles to a wide
audience. The FWM works directly with
international textile practitioners, both artists
and designers, collaborating with them by
commissioning the creation of innovative
textile-based works. Artistic experimentation

is invited and their artist-in-residence schemes actively encourage those from disciplines other than textiles such as fine art painting, sculpture and performance/installation art. A positive and open-minded approach, this enables those not familiar with textiles to test out new ideas using fibres and fabrics, and unexpected results are often revealed. Such exchange can prove to be of mutual benefit to textiles and the broad world of contemporary art and design. Important international textile art exhibitions are staged – the result of these specially commissioned projects. Their programme also extends to education which includes workshops, apprenticeships, tours and publications.

Flexible is an international European biennial exhibition of contemporary art organised by the Textile Museum, Tilburg. Established in 1993 and the second in 1996 (due to difficulties 1995 was not possible), it is concerned with the broad world of visual art made from flexible materials such as textiles or work which makes reference to such materials. Many saw *Flexible* as continuing where the Lausanne Biennale left off. *Flexible* pushes the boundaries of what has been traditionally accepted as textile art, and includes technical composites and plastics. The museum stages touring exhibitions which are often hosted in venues known for showing textile work.

Through The Surface is a touring exhibition of textile art which showed the work of collaborating artists from UK and Japan. It opened at the Sainsbury Centre for Visual Arts, University of East Anglia, Norwich in 2004 before touring the UK and being held at the Museum of Modern Art in Kyoto in 2005. Curated by Lesley Millar, this is the third event in a series which explores the Anglo-Japanese textile arena. The first exhibition, *Revelation* (1996), showed the work of artists who use textiles and their related techniques. It toured the UK, and in 1998 was exhibited at the Museum of Modern Art, Kyoto. The second, *Textural Space* (part of *Japan 2001*), displayed contemporary Japanese textile art at venues throughout Britain. This third venture examined cross-cultural collaborations between fourteen Japanese and British textile artists which took place throughout 2003. Keiko Kawashima of Gallery Gallery in Kyoto was Project Co-ordinator in

Japan. Established artists were paired with lesser known artists. The work of Jun'ichi Arai, Machiko Agano and Frances Gessin were included and the resulting work encompassed both high and low technologies and worked within the areas of art, science and fashion.

The exhibition *Artists at Work: New Technology in Textile and Fibre Art* at the Textile Museum in Prato, Italy, in the autumn of 2003, is considered very important. A collaboration between Prato's Textile Museum and the European Textile Network – Textile Forum, it was curated by the textile artist Patricia Kinsella. Prato is known for its textiles and holds the Prato Expo, the textile trade show. The exhibition showed how industrial and technical textiles are being used in creative ways. The Textile Museum in Prato has a Contemporary Section which displays textiles produced in Prato (the largest textile area in Europe) over the last fifty years. Every season, contemporary textiles are acquired which demonstrate new fibres and technology and an exhibition is put on which reflects the previous season's trends from the world of fashion textiles.

The textile artists discussed here all have contemporary visions that draw from a rich culture and history while accepting the challenges of the new technologies. When given access to the very latest materials and equipment, textile artists experiment freely, unconstrained by commercial considerations. They often impart a soul and a meaning to the slick computerized mechanics of a process and the work of the textile artist can inspire creative textile design for fashion or interior applications. Welcoming advanced materials and techniques, these artists are creating works that demand to be judged by new aesthetic criteria. The conventions and preconceptions within the world of textiles are changing radically as they are being questioned by today's textile artists with their inspiring and thought-provoking work – a true comment on the technological age in which we live.

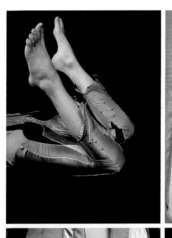

right
FRANCES GEESIN
Dispersion. 2004
Arranged multiples. Each section measures approximately 30 cm

The outer circle of this art work uses conductive fibres, metallic organza and silver shielding fabric which have been manipulated and electroplated with copper. The inner circle uses zinc electroplating to create a colour contrast. This art work was made specially for the exhibition *Through the Surface*.

bottom left
KOKO TOSHIMA LARSON
Chiaroscuro. 2004

Handmade and hand-dyed wool. Parts of the bodice and the sleeves of this piece are made from woven stainless steel with a silk warp. A retro-reflective sheet is applied and the sleeves and lower back of the coat are felt mixed with Angelina – a sparkling polyester fibre from Meadowbrook Inventions Inc. The artist contrasts the natural with the synthetic, ancient woollen felt with technical materials and makes reference to both Eastern and Western cultures.

below right
ANJA MADSEN
Trace of the Human Body, 5. 2000
76 (height) x 86 (width) cm

This work, shown here under artificial light, was included in the exhibition, *Artists at Work: New Technology in Textile and Fibre Art*. Polyamide monofilament and phosphorescent yarn have been knitted in a simple tubular form to create this body-related piece which maintains a three-dimensional volume. The phosphorescent yarn is manufactured by the Lurex Company Ltd and is a polyester-based textile. After being charged by a bright light source it will glow in the dark for up to twenty minutes.

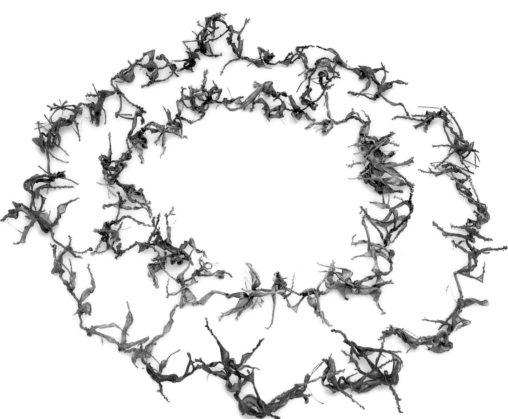

opposite top
FRANCES GEESIN
Time Reveals. 2003
Circumference of each sphere 52 cm

Included in the exhibition *Artists at Work: New Technology in Textile and Fibre Art*. Polypropylene fibres melt when subjected to heat. They are formed around a metal sphere and harden on cooling. The sphere is then removed. The resulting forms are partially electroplated with copper and then patinated. The product reveals the process: the five spheres are rigid but retain a sense of their former fluidity.

opposite bottom
JANE HARRIS
Potential Beauty. 2002–03

The artist Jane Harris generated an asymmetric garment form and digitally hand-painted the textile element working with the 3D computer graphic operator Mike Dawson. The piece presents a fashion or body-related idea as an art statement. Interested in textiles, both physically and digitally, Jane Harris uses her prior knowledge of fabric to demonstrate how a material drapes and moves. The result is a very realistic simulation of a garment turning in space.

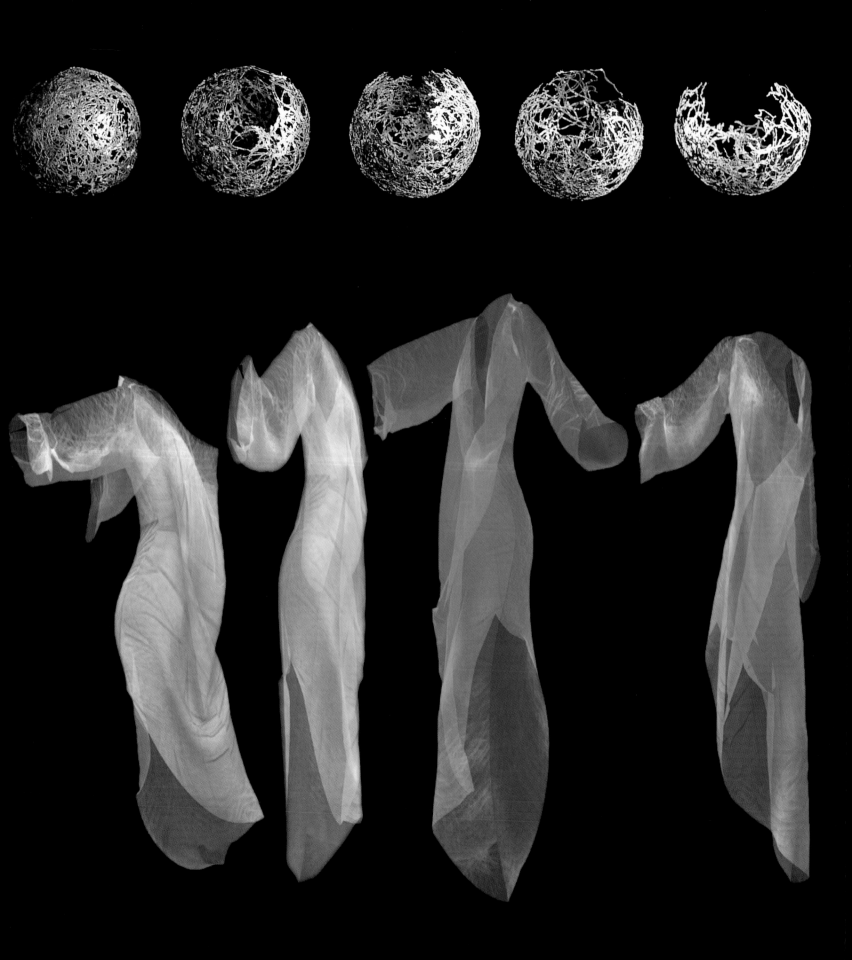

Glossary of Technical Terms

aramid Highly oriented organic polymer derived from polyamide with high density and low modulus, used where strength and stiffness is required in a fibre. Examples: Kevlar and Nomex.

biomimetics Design extracted from nature.

biotechnology Term given to any technological application that uses biological systems, living organisms (or their derivatives), to make or modify products or processes for specialist use.

braiding Weaving of fibres into a tubular shape.

butyl rubber Copolymer of isobutylene and isoprene.

carbon fibre Produced by the pyrolysis of organic precursor fibres, such as rayon, polyacrylonitrile (PAN) and pitch, in an inert environment.

cellulose, cellulosic Substance made from a natural source with many glucose molecules, examples being cotton and rayon.

chemical bonding Process by which fibre surfaces are made sticky with chemicals and passed between compression rolls that consolidate the web and form a bond at crossover point. The textile is then passed through a chemical bath to neutralize excess stickiness.

composite Combination of two or more identifiable materials usually with improved performance characteristics.

compression moulding Process by which material, introduced into an open mould, is shaped by closing the mould and heating.

copolymer Long-chain molecule formed by the reaction of two or more dissimilar monomers.

creep Change in fabric length or thickness when subjected to prolonged stress.

crêpe Fabric with distinctive matt appearance and bouncy texture from its woven structure, often made with high-twist yarns. Traditionally used for black mourning clothes, commonly made with wool and silk yarns.

deformation Change in fabric size under load.

dévoré From the French *dévorer* (to devour, eat up), a technique by which a fabric is etched or eaten away by chemicals (such as sulphuric acid), printed or painted on. It is then baked at a high temperature to 'burn out' the designs. The fabric must either contain a proportion of cellulosic fibre, such as cotton or viscose which is susceptible to the chemical, or be treated in certain places with a resist paste. It produces a fabric with partially or totally removed areas.

elastomer Material which substantially recovers its original size and shape at room temperature after removal of a deforming force.

electroplating Technique for fixing a very fine deposit of metal to a material. The material to be coated is made electrically conductive and put into an acid bath, allowing a build up of metal.

embossing Permanent relief surface made with a heavy metal press which translates a pattern to the textile. A thermoplastic fabric can be heat-treated, making the result even more dramatic. Embossed printing uses special dyes and pigments to create a relief surface.

engineered print Design printed directly onto fashion garment, usually for catwalk designs, by the textile designer. It can be placed with exactness, avoiding seams, etc. A successful design that goes into production is reworked and printed on a continuous length of fabric.

extrusion Polymers are produced by chemical and petrochemical companies in the form of solid pellets, flakes or granules. These are then heated to melting point before being extruded, or drawn, through a cooling process to form yarn or flat sheets (see also monofilament).

fatigue Failure or decay of mechanical properties after repeated applications of stress.

felt One of the oldest nonwovens, made by the interlocking of the woollen fibres with the application of water and friction.

fibreglass Filament made by drawing molten glass.

fibril Small fibre.

filament Continuous length of fibre. Silk is a continous filament, giving the fabric its beautiful drape and lustre. The fibres run parallel to each other, with no tangles or breaks in length. Most synthetics are made into continuous filaments to obtain smooth yarns.

flocking Fabric finish usually combined with printing whereby minute powdered fibres are fixed to the fabric surface using static electricity or glues.

geogrid Flat structure in continuous length or sheet form, mainly used for soil reinforcement and usually made from a polymer with rectangular or square apertures.

geomat Three-dimensional multilayer structure mainly used for the control of soil erosion and to provide vegetative cover.

geomembranes Can be made from a number of polymers with low permeability to provide a barrier to fluids.

holographic Effect achieved on foils, plastics, fabrics etc., by applying a hologram, a photograph of a pattern (produced by interfering with a laser beam) that appears three-dimensional under ordinary light.

honeycomb Sheet material (paper, metal foil, etc.) formed into hexagon-shaped cells. The material is usually impregnated with a resin and the structure, valued for its strength, is used in the manufacture of composite sandwich structures.

hydrophilic Water-attracting. Molecules of a hydrophilic polymer attract water molecules and pass them along the polymer chain. Water molecules always travel from a high to a low temperature.

hydrophobic Water-repelling.

Jacquard Complex weave structure relying on perforated paper patterns or wooden pegs to control the lifting of the warp threads for the weft insertion. Damasks, brocades and tapestries are made by this technique. The patterning often results in many floating threads on the reverse of the design. Computer-aided looms have speeded up this technique.

junihitoe Formal, decorative Japanese garment, made up of twelve kimonos worn in layers, the contrasting colours and patterns only visible at the neck, sleeves and hem.

Kevlar Trade name for aramid fibre developed by DuPont.

kimono From the Japanese kiru (to wear) and mono (thing). Traditional loose Japanese costume based on the 'T' shape, one size, tied left over right around the body. Now mostly worn for ceremonies and other special occasions.

knitting/knitted fabric Fabric construction consisting of a chain of looped yarn, each row dependent on the last, made by hand or machine. Has a natural elastic quality and resilience. The vertical rows in a knitted fabric are the 'wale' and the horizontal rows are the 'course'.

laminate Two or more materials united with a bonding material, usually with heat pressure.

latex Viscose liquid with rubber particles suspended in it. The resulting material can be moulded into many configurations which once dried are permanent.

Lurex Tradename for fibre invented in the 1950s by Dow Badische Company, made from thin strips of aluminium. Blends well with other fibres for a subtle or dramatic shimmering effect.

Lycra Tradename for spandex fibre, a synthetic rubber, developed by DuPont, Delaware, USA, in 1958. Originally developed for lingerie, it became popular for sportswear and fashion in the 1980s. Blends well to make stretch fabrics whose elasticity and excellent stretch recovery allow tailored shapes without seaming, darting and complex cutting.

mercerization Finish given to cotton for a smooth polished appearance. A 20 per cent solution of sodium carbonate causes the fibres to swell, become rounder in cross-section and more lustrous. Fibre-strength is also increased, and the finished fabric absorbs dye well.

microfibre Extremely fine yarns of one denier or less. These fibres, being so fine, can be specifically engineered to create a wide range of aesthetics and revolutionary performance characteristics.

moiré Finish given to fabrics (usually silk taffeta but also the new synthetics) for a wavy watermark effect, achieved using heat and engraved metal rollers.

monofilament Synthetic fibre made by extrusion process from a single polymer.

needlepunch Mechanical bonding widely used in the production of nonwovens. Needles are used to consolidate and entangle a loose web made of continuous filament or staple fibre to produce a stable bond.

neoprene Trade name for a synthetic rubber compound made from polychloroprene which is vulcanized with sulphur or metal oxide.

nonwoven Fabric with no formal structure, such as weave, knit or braiding. Instead the yarn is laid in a loose web before being bonded by heat, by adhesives, by high-pressure jets of water, or by needlepunching. With synthetics, heat and pressure are used to fuse the fibres. Nonwovens do not drape, stretch or fray and can be specifically engineered for different applications.

obi Decorative stiff sash worn around the traditional Japanese kimono, constructed using complex Jacquard weaving.

organic solvent spinning Organic solvents mix organic chemicals with water. Solvent spinning entails dissolving and spinning to obtain the fibre without any by-product.

phenolic resin Thermosetting resin produced by an aromatic alcohol condensed with an aldehyde.

pilling Balls of soft fibre formed by friction with the stronger fibre plied with it. These are trapped on the surface of the fabric by the stronger fibre. Blends of natural and synthetic yarns have a strong tendency to pill, but it can also happen with purely natural yarns. The only remedy is to 'shave' or comb off pilling. The prevention of pilling is under research. New microfibre blends seem to stay smooth despite constant wear.

ply Fabrics or felts consisting of one or more layers, or number of fibres that make up a yarn (such as 4-ply).

polyester Thermoplastic fabric produced from the polymerization of ethylene glycol and dimethyl terephalate or terephthalic acid.

polyethylene Group of semicrystalline polymers mainly based on ethylene monomers.

polymer Material formed by the chemical combination of monomers with either the same or different chemical compositions. Plastics, rubbers and textile fibres are examples of high-molecular-weight polymers.

polypropylene (PP) Semicrystalline thermoplastic textile.

polyurethane Thermosetting resin prepared by the reaction of diisocyanates with polyols, polyamides, alkyd and polyether polymers.

polyvinyl chloride (PVC) Polymerized from vinyl chloride monomers and compounded with plasticizers and other additives.

preform Preshaped fibrous reinforcement formed by distribution of chopped fibres or cloth by air, water flotation or vacuum over the surface of a perforated screen to the approximate contour and thickness required. Used in the manufacture of composites.

prepeg Ready-to-mould material in sheet form or ready-to-wind material in roving form, which can be cloth, mat, unidirectional fibre or paper impregnated with resin.

pultrusion Process by which fibre-reinforced material is pulled through a resin-impregnated bath and a shaping die where the resin is cured. This is a continuous process (see also extrusion).

regenerated 'Natural chemical' yarn from a natural source, such as wood pulp, chemically treated to create a new fibre. The first was viscose rayon and could be described as half natural and half synthetic. Different from pure synthetics, which are made from petrochemicals.

resin Solid, or pseudo-solid, organic material with the ability to flow when subjected to stress.

sanding/sandblasting Process of mechanically abrading fabric with a series of sandpaper

covered rollers to remove the immediate surface layer of the fibres, making the fabric softer in feel, drape and colour.

sandwich construction Composite made from a lightweight core material, such as honeycomb, foamed plastic, etc., to which two thin, dense, high strength or high stiffness skins are adhered.

sashiko Traditional Japanese quilting for peasant wear. Formerly stiff in quality, and expensive. For general wear, uniforms and Japanese martial arts.

shearing Process giving a thermoplastic fabric a new form. On heating, the fibres shift, deform and take on a different shape when moulded. Critical factors include the size of the fibres and their spacing in the fabric construction.

shibori Traditional Japanese resist-dye technique. Fabric is tied in a regular pattern, stitched in place, then dyed and the stitches removed, resulting in a puckered appearance and a pattern formed from the areas of dyed and undyed fabric. The time-consuming technique is traditionally used for obi.

shot fabric Iridescent effect from using yarns of two different colours in a woven fabric, one in the warp and the other in the weft.

Siroset Abbreviation of Commonwealth Scientific and Research Organization describing a chemical treatment applied to wool in conjunction with hand pleating to fix permanent pleats. The bonds of the wool fibre are broken down, and a new structure is formed, which is fixed by pressing.

slit film Flat yarn made by cutting a sheet of material (usually synthetic) into fine slits.

slub Yarn that varies in thickness throughout its length. It has a fleecy core around which a finer yarn is twisted, tightly for thinness and loosely for thickness.

solarization Photographic process by which a halo of light is produced around the subject when the print is exposed to light for a very short time before being completely fixed.

spattering technique for fixing very fine particles of metal, such as stainless steel, copper or titanium to a synthetic textile (the fabric must not contain water). Metals are broken down into microscopic particles in a vacuum using ionized argon gas and then fixed to the surface of the fabric. This happens at molecular level, and the finish remains permanent. The 'metal' fabric is fluid, and its texture is not altered by the thin coating.

spun bonding Continuous or staple monofilaments are spun to form a sheet before being subjected to heat-pressurized rollers which weld the filaments together at their contact points.

staple Short length of a fibre, also referred to as 'spun'. The most common natural staple yarn is wool. The shorter the staple length the more hairy and matt the yarn. The short fibres go in many directions making an uneven, broken

texture. Synthetics can be produced in staple as well as filament yarns.

stitch bonding Process of bonding together fibres (particularly multifilaments) by stitching.

stretch In a 'warp stretch' the elasticity runs parallel to the selvedge of a woven textile. A 'weft stretch' runs horizontally from selvedge to selvedge. 'Bi-stretch' or 'two-way stretch' runs in both directions. A stretch fabric normally incorporates an elastic yarn, such as Lycra. Cutting a woven fabric on the bias, or diagonal, also imparts stretch. Knitted fabrics have natural stretch from their method of construction. Nonwovens do not stretch unless made from an elastic yarn.

substrate Background or base to which a finish or treatment is applied.

thermal bonding Process of heat-bonding in which the outer surface of filaments is melted allowing crossover points to be fused together. Used for bonding polypropylene continuous filament.

thermoplastic Quality of a fibre whose molecular structure breaks down and becomes fluid at a certain temperature, making it possible to reshape the fabric by pleating, moulding, vacuum-forming or crushing. The fabric is 'fixed' on cooling and cannot be altered unless heated to a temperature greater than the one at which it was reshaped. Most synthetics are thermoplastic; of the natural textiles, wool possesses this characteristic.

thermosetting polyester Group of resins produced by dissolving unsaturated (generally linear) alkyd resins in a vinyl-type active monomer such as styrene.

trilobal Rounded triangular cross-section of a fibre, which catches and reflects light.

Tyvek Tradename for spun-bonded olefin, a nonwoven, paper-like material manufactured by DuPont, USA. Also known as 'envelope paper'. Strong, durable and resistant to most chemicals, originally developed for protective clothing, now also used for fashion.

ultra-violet degradation Breakdown of fibres when exposed to sunlight.

vacuum forming Process by which plastic sheet film is heated to a liquid state, placed in a mould in a vacuum former; all air is removed so that the plastic takes on the shape of the mould. This becomes permanent on cooling. Used for subtle relief textures or dramatic three-dimensional forms.

warp Vertical threads fixed on the loom before weaving begins. A warp yarn needs to be strong and should not stretch.

weaving/woven fabric Textile structure made by interlacing warp threads with weft threads. The three primary weave structures are plain, twill and satin.

weft Horizontal threads in a woven fabric. Weft yarn can be softer and weaker than the warp.

Biographies and Histories

3M

3M is a $18 billion diversified technology company with leading positions in health care; industrial; display and graphics; consumer and office; safety, security and protection services; electro and communications; and transportation. With headquarters in St Paul, Minnesota, the company has operations in more than 60 countries and serves customers in nearly 200 countries. 3M is one of the 30 stocks that make up the Dow Jones Industrial Average and also is a component of the Standard & Poor's 500 Index.

Helle Abild

Textile designer, b. Denmark, 1964
Studied Textile Design, then Product and Furniture, The Danish Design School, The Royal Academy of Fine Arts, Copenhagen. 1992–2001 worked in New York and San Francisco. Experiments with new technology and has been the co-ordinator since 2004 for a new Research Centre for Innovation and Digital Design Technology in Copenhagen. Uses digital textile printing for exhibition work and for fashion and interiors. As a freelance designer, has worked for DuPont, Jhane Barnes and Maharam in New York and licensed print designs for Esprit, Walt Disney and Warner Brothers. Her gallery textiles have been exhibited in USA and Europe.

Machiko Agano

Textile artist, b. Japan, 1953
Studied weaving at Kyoto University of Arts at post-graduate level, 1979. Currently Professor of Textile Department at Kyoto Seika University. Her textile art work is inspired by nature and works with stainless steel wire, nylon monofilament, silk and Japanese paper using knitting technique for large scale installations and site-specific works. Has had many solo shows and group exhibitions of her work throughout Japan and also in Europe, China and Australia. Took part in Through the Surface UK exhibition, 2004. Her work is in many public collections.

Mitsuko Akutsu

Textile artist, b. Japan, 1952
Graduated with BFA in Industrial Design from Tokyo National University of Fine Arts and Music,1977. Assistant Professor in Aoyama Gakuin Women's Junior College. Has attended workshops in computer-aided Jacquard weaving at the Montreal Centre for Contemporary Textiles and uses this technique to create tapestries with unique patterns. Mitsuko Akutsu also employs heat-transfer printing on synthetics and digital printing to convey her imagery. She has had many solo and group exhibitions of her work mainly in Tokyo but also in Seoul and Helsinki.

Akzo Nobel

Leading European manufacturer of technical textiles since 1930s. In the late 1970s began manufacture of nonwoven textiles mainly for industrial and technical sectors, including carpets and geosynthetics. Started production of aramid and carbon fibres in the 1980s. Manufacturer of Enka Viscose, and microfilament polyester fibres such as Diolen Micro for high-performance outdoor fabrics and for fashion. Research into high-tech membranes resulted in Sympatex, microfibre used as invisible weatherproofing laminate.

Alpha

Business division of P-D Interglas Technologies AG. Specializes in the coating and laminating of fibreglass and other synthetic fabrics. The range includes coating with silicone, polyurethane and neoprene, as well as lamination with aluminium foil and aluminium vaporized polyester foil as well as a number of film laminates.

Architects of Air

Alan Parkinson, lead designer with Architects of Air, is intrigued by the quality of light and colour and has been building luminaria for 20 years. The company is inspired by monumental architecture such as cathedrals and mosques, and also cites Buckminster Fuller and Frei Otto as major influences. The approach is one of traditional engineering coupled with a deep understanding of the nature and behaviour of flexible structures. Each luminaria is unique and the practice build approximately one each year.

Jun'ichi Arai

Textile planner, b. Japan, 1932
Born and now lives in Kiryu, north of Tokyo, an area famous for its Jacquard weaving and high-twist yarn production. In the 1950s he pioneered new techniques working with metallic yarns in which he is considered an expert. There are 36 patents on his textiles. In the 1970s he experimented with computers and in the 1980s explored finishing techniques including heat and chemical treatments. Set up his first company, Anthologie, working with plastics, synthetics and metallics. In the early 1980s he worked with Makiko Minagawa and Issey Miyake and has supplied textiles for avant-garde fashion such as Comme des Garçons. In 1984 he founded Nuno Corporation with Reiko Sudo creating innovative fabrics for fashion and interior. He was one of the first to combine traditional Japanese techniques with sophisticated technology, using computers in both design and manufacture for Nuno. Now works independently in the creation of one-off textiles. His work is in many permanent collections including the Victoria and Albert Museum, London, and the Cooper-Hewitt Museum, New York. In 1987 he was made Honorary Member of the Faculty of Royal Designers for Industry by the Royal Society of Arts in Great Britain. In 1992 he gained an award from the Textile Institute, UK. He has taken part in numerous exhibitions including Through the Surface, UK, 2004.

Helen Archer

Textile designer, b. UK, 1973
Studied Textile Design at Loughborough University College of Art & Design (1995) specializing in Printed Textiles. Has used techniques such as printing, embossing, heat-treating and laminating textiles mainly intended for interior applications. Has worked with Astor Universal Ltd who have supplied her with holographic foils. Exhibited her work in the UK. Now based in Auckland, New Zealand and designs textile prints for the US market.

Nigel Atkinson

Textile designer, b. UK, 1964
Textile Design, Winchester School of Art specializing in Printed Textiles, 1986. In 1986 pioneered the use of heat-reactive inks to create raised surfaces, a process he has developed over many years. Created fashion fabrics and has also sold designs to international designers including Azzedine Alaïa, Issey Miyake, Romeo Gigli, Alberta Ferretti and John Rocha. Has also created fabrics for the Royal Shakespeare Company and The National Theatre. In 1997 established Nigel Atkinson Interior Textiles and his designs are now all for luxury furnishing fabrics. He has worked with architects, interior designers and galleries. His work has been included in many exhibitions including Fabric of Fashion, a British Council touring exhibition (2000–2) and with Kyoko Wainai for Hagoromo: Floating Fabrics as part of Milan Design week, 2004. His textiles are in the collections of the Victoria and Albert Museum, London, Stedelijk Museum, Amsterdam, The Fashion Institute of Technology, New York, and The Fashion and Textile Museum, Barcelona.

Savithri Bartlett

Textile designer, b. Sri Lanka
Studied Printed Textiles at Edinburgh College of Art, 1992, MA at the Royal College of Art, 1995, MPhil, 1997. Her area of research is functional and decorative nonwovens and she has also worked with theromplastic materials such as silicone, resin and surgical latex. She is currently engaged in PhD research at Loughborough University College of Art & Design where she is looking at the use of lasers for etching and cutting on textiles for fashion. She has created moulded hats for Chanel's Autumn/Winter 1997/98 collection shown on the Paris catwalk. Savithri Bartlett has collaborated with the London avant-garde duo Boudicca on several collections, the first for Spring/Summer 1998. Her work featured in the British Council touring exhibition Fabric of Fashion, 2000–2 and she collaborated with Deborah Milner for Great Expectations in New York City, 2003.

Walter van Beirendonck

Fashion designer, b. Belgium, 1957
Studied fashion at the Royal Academy of Fine Arts in Antwerp. Has been showing under his own label, Walter van Beirendonck, since 1983. First came to international attention as part of the 'Antwerp Six' at the British Designer Show in 1987. Influences range from art, music and literature to ethnic culture, nature and safe sex. Humour, strong graphics and innovative cuts are a constant in his work. He has set up his own store in Antwerp and teaches regularly at the academy there. He was curator of MODE2001 LANDED-GELAND fashion project, Antwerp, and has been included in major fashion exhibitions in museums worldwide.

Eva Best

Textile artist, b. Sweden, 1947
Studied at the Textile Institute, Boras, 1971, the Gerlesborgs Art School, 1974 and the Stockholm School of Art and Crafts, 1977. She has had solo and group exhibitions of her textile art works which often employ both natural and synthetic materials together with polyurethane and painting/printing/bonding techniques. Mainly exhibited throughout Sweden, but also in the Salon de Arte in Caracas, Venezuela. Best has worked to several public commissions in Gothenburg and Stockholm and her work is represented in Swedish collections including the Textile Museum, Boras and the Rohs Museum, Gothenburg.

BFF Nonwovens
Specializes in nonwovens for a range of industries: smart fabrics, wipes, interlinings, medical and automotive. Manufacturing processes include spunlace as well as chemical and thermal bonding.

Maria Blaisse
Textile designer, b. the Netherlands, 1944
Studied Textile Design specializing in Constructed Textiles at the Gerrit Rietveld Academie in Amsterdam. She worked in Jack Lenor Larsen Studio in New York City and spent two years researching textile techniques in South America. From 1974 to 1987 was Professor in Textile and Flexible Design at the Gerrit Rietveld Academy. She has been Guest Lecturer in many institutions worldwide. Since 1982 she has worked with industrial materials and has worked with many different textile and non-textile materials.She researches into fibre engineering, rubber, nonwovens and synthetic foams creating unusual forms for fashion accessories and dance costumes. Maria Blaisse explores various heat treatments of her materials including laminating, vacuum forming and moulding to create new shapes. In 1987 she went to Japan where her interest in Japanese craft was strengthened. She has created innovative hats for Japanese designer Issey Miyake for two collections. Her excellent technique is due to her close research and she has explored the rubber inner tube as a design for many years, interpreting it in knitted and felted works and even in ceramics. She has run several international workshops, including in Perth, Australia, 2004. Maria Blaisse had a solo exhibition of her work at the Centraal Museum in Utrecht from August to September 2004.

Ulla E:son Bodin
Textile designer and artist, b. Sweden, 1935
Studied Textile Design at the Textile Institute, Boras, 1955 and HDK School of Design and Craft, Gothenburg, 1958. Since 1958 has worked as a consultant in textile and fashion design for many Swedish manufacturers. Acting Professor in Textile design at HDK and the Swedish School of Textiles, 1996–2001. Costume designer for opera, Vadstena Academy, 1995, 1997, 2000, 2001 and has also run costume summer courses at the University of Linkoping,1998, 1999. She initiated the Knitting Academy there for young designers to work with Swedish companies. She experiments with relief and three-dimensional forms using computerized knitting machines. She received a grant from the Artistic Faculty Board at the University of Gothenburg and has exhibited her costumes at exhibitions in Sweden. She has also exhibited her textile designs in Europe, USA and Japan and examples of her work can be found in museum collections in Sweden and Mulhouse, France. She is now Consulting Professor in Textile and Fashion Design, Artistic Supervisor at the Swedish School of Textiles, University College of Boras.

Boudicca
Fashion label established in 1997 by Zowie Broach and Brian Kirkby, both b. UK, 1966
Zowie Broach and Brian Kirkby trained at Middlesex University; Kirkby also studied Womenswear Fashion at the Royal College of Art, London. They are known for their use of interesting materials, precision cutting and impeccable tailoring. They have worked in collaboration with textile designers including Savithri Bartlett and accessory designers including Paul Murray Watson. Boudicca is non-conformist, conceptual couture which has acquired a strong cult following. Boudicca present their highly choreographed catwalk shows at London Fashion Week, their Autumn/Winter 2000/2001 collection being the first on the official London schedule. Their work frequently crosses over from fashion into art and they have been included in several exhibitions including Jam at the Barbican (1996), the British Council's touring shows Lost and Found (1999–2000) and Fabric of Fashion (2000–2), and Fashion Creation in Fabrics 1960–2000 at the Galleria Museum, Paris (2000).

Liza Bruce
Fashion designer, b. USA, 1955
Went to school in London and from age 14 to 18 to an American College in Mexico run by nuns. She lived in Northern California and bred horses. On a visit to Mustique she made her first bathing suit when she could not find one she liked. She moved to New York and started to make swimming costumes which became very popular in the late 1980s. Known for her use of quality synthetics with high Lycra content, her designs support and flatter the female form and challenge expected notions of beauty. Liza Bruce creates swimwear, cruise wear and a range of leisure wear, often using techno textiles. Her silhouettes are influenced by sportswear with their streamlined, body-conscious silhouettes which are sexy too. Liza Bruce has shops in Belgravia, London, and SoHo, New York.

Critz Campbell
Furniture designer, b. USA, 1967
BFA, School of the Art Institute of Chicago, USA (1990). Also studied in Portugal and at Penland School of Crafts, Penland, North Carolina, USA, before completing post-graduate course in furniture design and fabrication at Parnham College, Beaminster, UK, in 1999. Set up b9 Furniture in Chicago in 2000.

Luisa Cevese
Textile designer and artist, b. Italy, 1955
Self-taught designer based in Milan. From 1993 to 1998 she was Director of Research for Centro Richerche Mantero, a large Como-based textile company famous for its quality woven silk scarves and ties. She then experimented with turning the waste material into beautiful fabrics. She was in charge of special projects for Mantero Seta such as internships and competitions for international art and design educational institutions 1993–97. In 1994 founded Riedizioni (Italian for recycling) and she is now Creative Director. She continues to use industrial waste, often fabric selvedges, immersing them in polyurethane and working with crafts people to create accessories. She works with all types of textile, naturals and synthetics. Each design is similar, but never identical due to the recycling process. Riedizioni products such as bags and cushions are put into production but have an appealing handmade look. They are sold in stores and galleries worldwide. Luisa Cevese also creates gallery textiles and has shown her work in international solo and group exhibitions since 1994.

Hussein Chalayan
Fashion designer, b. Cyprus 1970
Studied at the Central St Martin's School of Art, graduating in 1993 with his now infamous buried silk dresses. His design combines minimalism with sophisticated tailoring. His treatment of the garment as a three-dimensional form reflects his interest in architecture (he almost studied architecture instead of fashion). He collaborates with creatives from other disciplines for many of his catwalk showpieces including architects, sculptors and filmmakers. He has been awarded Fashion Designer of the Year several times and has designed for other labels such as TSE alongside producing his own collections.

Simon Clarke
Artist, b. UK, 1963
Studied Printed Textiles at Middlesex University, 1986, and Textiles at Masters level, Birmingham Institute of Art and Design, University of Central England, 1987. He was Textile Fellow at the University of Plymouth, 1990, where he explored the relationship between painting and printed textiles. He is a Senior Lecturer in Printed Textiles at University College Falmouth. He is currently engaged in PhD research into Eastern African printed textiles and the production of studio work, registered with Birmingham Institute of Art and Design. He was a Lecturer in the Department of Fine Art, Kenyatta University, Nairobi 1990–93 and taught as a Visiting Lecturer at Goldsmiths College, University of London 1996–99. He was Senior Lecturer in Textiles for Fashion at University College, Northampton. Clarke's current area of research is digitally printed textiles and Eastern African visual arts. He has exhibited his work internationally including at the exhibition Artists at Work: New Technology in Textile and Fibre Art, Prato (2003).

Clothing+
Part of the Reima group, the company Clothing Plus Oy specializes in developing and producing wearable technology. Their aim is to provide innovative approaches to everyday problems, by creating wearable solutions that are easy and logical to operate. The company strives towards a multi-disciplinary work team including industrial and clothing designers, hardware, software and textile engineers, production designers and marketing specialists, who combine their knowledge and skills to create wearable products for both leisure and work.

Daniel Cooper
Designer, b. 1972, based in England
Degree in Three-Dimensional Design (1995), Leeds Metropolitan University and MSc, Industrial Design, University College, Salford (1996). Has worked for both Daniel Poole and Paul Smith Ltd.

Courtaulds
Textile company, established UK, 1816
Samuel Courtauld III founded Courtaulds as a silk company; in 1911 Courtaulds USA was founded. In the 1950s it was the first company to manufacture a regenerated cellulosic fibre, viscose rayon, patented in 1894 by Clayton Beadle, Edward Bevan and Charles Cross, who sold it to Courtaulds. In 1978 the company started research which led to the development of Tencel; production began in the UK in 1988 and in the USA in 1992. In 1992 Tencel was officially launched for the top end of the fashion market. In 1995 Courtaulds introduced Tencel as a filament yarn for nonwovens. Intended applications include protective clothing, coated fabrics, medical and hygiene products and specialist papers.

Diesel
Fashion label, founded Italy, 1979
Diesel was founded by Renzo Rosso and soon became known for its functional clothing in quality materials with a distinctive edge to them. DieselStylelab, a more experimental line for both men and women, was launched in 1998. Diesel often use the latest developments in technical textiles and sophisticated finishing treatments and adopt them for their fashion collections that have achieved a cult following. They work closely with specialist textile mills who frequently produce fabrics for them. Diesel mix traditional natural materials with the latest synthetics and combine inventive choice of materials with expert cutting and styling.

Mark Dion
Artist, b. USA, 1961
BFA and Doctor of Arts from Hartford Art School, University of Hartford, Connecticut. Also studied at the School of Visual Arts in New York and at the Whitney Independent Study Programme, New York, 1985. Has had many solo exhibitions in the USA and Germany. Received the Larry Aldrich Foundation Award in 2001. He collaborates with J. Morgan Puett on the creation of art works.

DLMI (Dorures Louis Mathieu Industrie)
Established in 1888, the company makes yarns and fabrics for industrial, decorative and fashion applications.

Isabel Dodd
Textile designer, b. UK, 1966
Studied Multi-Media Textile Design at Loughborough University School of Art and Design (1993) and Embroidered Textiles at the Royal College of Art (1995). Now works at Chelsea College of Art and Design, University of the Arts, London, as Stitch Tutor and at the Hampstead Insitute as Embroidery Tutor. She uses rubber as a printing ink to create textural fashion fabrics and experiments with chemicals on embroidered textiles to create unusual surfaces. She collaborates with designer Ray Harris to create garments for the label Isabel & Ray and accessories such as shawls and scarves for her own label, Isabel Dodd. Inspired by organic forms, her work was included in Natural Forms, Crafts Council Shop at the Victoria and Albert Museum, London, 2002. She has exhibited at Chelsea Craft Fair, London, since 1996.

Hil Driessen
Textile artist and designer, b. the Netherlands, 1963
Graduated 1990 from the Academy of Visual Arts, Maastricht from the department of Fashion Design. Her work involves the transformation of a textile and employs various materials including

synthetics and laminates and techniques such as digital printing, stitching and Jacquard weaving. Subsequent textiles have many applications which include fashion and interior and as textile art in its own right. In 2002 she experimented with crochet dipped in porcelain at the European Ceramic Work Centre in 's-Hertogenbosch and digital print. Exhibitions of her work include Artists at Work: New Technology in Textile and Fibre Art, Prato (2003), a duo-exhibition with spatial designer Toon van Deyne Orangerie at Gallery Ra, Amsterdam (2004), and the exhibition of Dutch Textile Designers at the Fashion Institute of Technology Museum, New York City in 2005.

Droog Design
Co-founded in Amsterdam by product designer Gijs Bakker and design historian Renny Ramakers in 1993. Championed the careers of such designers as Hella Jongerius and Marcel Wanders, defining a new approach to design by mixing materials and interacting with the user.

Emily DuBois
Textile artist, b. USA, 1946, based in Hawaii since 2002
BFA from the School for American Crafts, Rochester Institute of Technology, New York (1970) and MFA at the California College of Arts and Crafts in Oakland (1980). She h as won several major awards for her work including the National Endowment for the Arts Individual Artist Fellowship, 1984. She spent time in India studying loom technology. She makes complex weaves with richly patterned surfaces and layered imagery using the computer-controlled loom. Also uses traditional Japanese techniques such as shibori, ikat and various other resist-dyeing methods. Inspired by the natural world and Taoist philosophy. Emily DuBois has had work in both group and solo exhibitions of contemporary textiles and new technology. She took part in e-textiles, an exhibition at the Museum of Contemporary Art, Montreal, also touring Canada and Australia 2000–3, and had a solo exhibition, Emily DuBois: The Richest of Nature, at Taiwan College of Art Gallery, 2004.

Dunne & Raby
Anthony Dunne and Fiona Raby are partners in the design practice. They also lead studios in the Design Product and Architecture & Interiors departments at the Royal College of Art. BioLand, their current research project, investigates design as a tool for critical reflection on the social and ethical implications of biotechnology. Design Noir: The Secret Life of Electronic Objects was published in 2001.

DuPont
Multinational company, founded USA, 1802
Originally founded as E. I. du Pont de Nemours and Co., DuPont are known for their production of synthetic textiles which they have been researching since the 1930s. In 1958 they introduced Lycra which has made a huge impact on the fashion and sportswear markets. In the 1970s DuPont invented Teflon, which is used as a coating on fabrics. Research in the 1980s led to Tactel (a microfibre brand name), a Polyamide 6.6 fibre with many different qualities made possible at the finishing stage. Other fibres by DuPont include Kevlar, Supplex, CoolMax, Cordura and the nonwoven material Tyvek.

Rebecca Earley
Textile designer, b. UK, 1970
BA in Printed Textiles from Loughborough University School of Art & Design (1992), MA in Fashion specializing in Printed Textiles from Central Saint Martins, the University of the Arts, London (1994). Currently Senior Research Fellow on the Textiles Environment Design project and Associate Lecturer on BA and MA Textiles, Chelsea College of Art and Design. She established her own label of printed textiles, B. Earley, in 1993 creating womenswear and accessories such as large wraps and scarves. Her signature textile is the heat photogram technique which she began exploring while studing for her MA. B. Earley has shown catwalk collections 1994–98 and received a New Generation Award in 1996. In 1999 she was a winner of the Textiles category for the Peugeot Design Award and in 2003 was on the Textiles shortlist for her recycled tops. She has designed textiles for Donna Karan and Karl Lagerfeld and for the Italian textile/fashion company Etro. She has been involved in many group exhibitions including Fabric of Fashion, a British Council touring show (2000–2) and Great Expectations, a Design Council touring show (2001–3). Her textiles are in major collections including the Victoria & Albert Museum, the Constance Howard Research Centre, the Crafts Council, London, and Pitt Rivers Museum, Oxford.

Ecotextil Ltd
Founded in 1994 in Central Bohemia, north of Prague. Specializes in the manufacture and processing of melt-blown nonwovens. Annual output is around 450 tonnes. Makes microfibres of thermoplastic polymers, mainly propylene. A major part of the company's output is aimed at preventing and dealing with environmental accidents, particularly those caused by dangerous liquid leaks. Air filtration is another area for melt-blown nonwovens where applications include operating masks, respirators, industrial filters and vacuum cleaner filtration bags.

Eley Kishimoto
Mark Eley b. UK, 1968; Wakako Kishimoto b. Japan, 1965. Textile and fashion label established in 1992
Eley studied Fashion and Constructed Textiles at the University of Brighton (1990) and Wakako studied Fashion and Printed Textiles (BA and MA) at Central Saint Martins College of Art and Design, University of the Arts, London (1992). Eley Kishimoto have supplied innovative printed textiles to Givenchy, Yves Saint-Laurent, Alexander McQueen and Hussein Chalayan. In 1995 they set up their own textile and fashion label. They create distinctive print designs for a variety of media and have produced accessories such as umbrellas, boots, scarves to complement their collections. Not content just to print on textiles, they have created wallpaper and even printed on ceramics for tea-sets. They have a cult following for their distinctive print designs. Eley Kishimoto contributed to the exhibition Fashion at Belsay and collaborated with 6a Architects (Stephanie Macdonald and Tom Emerson) to create bold print patterns and trompe l'oeil effects to transform an interior space by printing on plywood and cement board.

Ellis Developments Ltd
Incorporated in 1985 to exploit a patented design for an artificial ligament, the Leeds-Keio Ligament, now amongst the best-selling knee replacements in the world. Specializes in industrial textiles, embroidery, weaving, knitting or braiding, in particular for surgical implants.

Foresight Institute
Public interest organization focused on nanotechnology, formed in 1986 by K. Eric Drexler and Christine Peterson. Provides education, information, and public policy development on molecular nanotechnology and molecular manufacturing. The organization's goal is to guide emerging technologies to improve the human condition and environment.

Shelley Fox
Fashion designer, b. UK, 1965
BA Honours (1993) and MA in Fashion with Knitwear (1999) from Central St Martins, University of the Arts, London. Her graduating collection was bought by Liberty, London. In 1996 she won a Crafts Council Development Award and in 1999 the Jerwood Fashion Prize. She is currently a Research Fellow at Central St Martins and teaches at many institutions throughout the UK including the Royal College of Art and Goldsmiths College, University of London. Shelley Fox launched her own label in 1997 and creates conceptual clothing which demonstrates a particular interest in unusual materials and finishes. She has worked with various technical and industrial textiles cut into abstract geometric shapes to create distinctive collections which have attracted a cult following. She has also worked with the Michael Clark Dance Company, London, 2003 and 2004. Her work lies in between fashion and art; Fox has exhibited her work in many international museums and galleries. Exhibitions include the British Council's Fabric of Fashion (2000–2) and Fashion at Belsay (2004) with English Heritage and Northern Arts.

Frances Geesin
Textile artist and researcher, b. UK, 1941
Studied painting at West Sussex College of Art with Woven Textiles as an additional area (1963), Woven Textiles (1966) and PhD (1995) from the Royal College of Art, London. Senior Research Fellow at the London College of Fashion, University of the Arts, London, since 1999. Her PhD research explored the electroforming of textiles. In 1995 she won the British Standards Award and in 2003 was granted the Arts Foundation Fellowship for Textile Design. Consultant to Philips Design 1997–2000 and since 1997 has been a consultant in synthetic fabrics electroplating to Surface Engineering Consultant Group. She has also worked with Akzo Nobel and collaborated with Brunel University. Commissions include Palm Aura, an interactive sound and light panel with Ron Geesin for London's Science Museum. Frances Geesin has exhibited her work widely, including Artists at Work: New Technology in Textile and Fibre Art, Prato (2003), for which she was a member of the jury, and Through the Surface at the Surrey Institute, Farnham and the Sainsbury Centre, Norwich.

W. L. Gore and Associates
Textile company, founded 1958, USA.
Established to develop fluorocarbon polymers and polytetrafluoroethylene (PTFE). The company is well-known for its weather-proof and breathable invisible laminate Gore-Tex, which was launched in 1976. Originally developed for space travel, Gore-Tex is now used for protective outdoor wear and footwear. W. L. Gore and Associates are constantly refining the technology for this membrane and have collaborated with Italian company Raumer spa to create Windstopper, a fabric which insulates against wind while remaining breathable.

Grado Zero Espace
Within the framework of the Technology Transfer Programme of the European Space Agency, D'Appolonia supported innovative Italian clothing manufacturer Karada Italia, owner of the brand Corpo Nove, in spinning off their R&D department Grado Zero Espace. The research laboratory is active in the area of textile and garment innovation with its aim to build on the parent company's existing expertise to provide contract research services and innovation consultancy. Their aim is to integrate new technologies and materials into wearable garments. They have collaborated with the European Space Agency as part of their Technology Transfer Programme, which included developing garments for the McLaren-Hugo Boss F1 mechanics.

Julie Graves
Textile artist, b. UK, 1959
Graduated in Textiles with a first class Honours Degree from Goldsmiths College, University of London, where she is currently employed as a Digital Archivist at the Constance Howard Resource and Research Centre in Textiles. Combines the latest technology with traditional techniques in her textile art pieces which often look to the future while making reference to the rich history of textiles itself. Photoshop software is used to manipulate imagery and she frequently combines weave with print in the creation of her one-off works. Technology is just one part of her creative process. A major commission in 1996 for the Corn Exchange Arts Centre, King's Lynn, comprised ten woven hangings relating to themes of local agriculture and industry. Her work has been exhibited throughout UK and Europe, including Messages and Meaning – The Narrative of Print at Bankfield Museum, Halifax (2001).

Green-Tek Inc.
US company established in 1986 as a convertor, fabricator and distributor of packaging materials, greenhouse coverings and thermal glazing.

Griffin
Founder Jeff Griffin set up Griffin Laundry in 1993 which served as a prototype for Griffin. The label is primarily men's clothing but for the spring/summer 2004 season it launched a very small women's collection. Specializing in combat

design, the garments are at the cutting edge of technology with a touch of handmade. The philosophy is about discovering new dimensions, getting the wearer to rethink clothes, the way they are worn and why. The garments are being sold all over the world. At present Griffin has two concept stores, in London and Tokyo.

Sue Gundy
Textile designer and artist, b. Canada, 1967
Studied Textile design at Rhode Island School of Design, 1989. She has worked as a textile designer since 1989 including for the prominent New York firm Jhane Barnes Inc. as Menswear Designer (1990–94); then moved to the West Coast and worked in Men's Product Development for Nordstrom (1994–96). Based in Seattle, she set up her own Design Group – Sue Gundy Textiles – in 1996. Since 1999 she has used the latest digital technology to print her textile designs, inspired by both nature and architecture. Gundy creates fashion and accessories for both men and women, home accessories and limited edition art works. Her work was included in the 6th International Textile Competition 1999, Kyoto, and her work has won several awards.

Grimshaw
Architectural practice established in London in 1980, now with offices in New York and Melbourne. The company works in many design areas including Arts and Leisure, Research and Education, Transport and Infrastructure. Winner of over one hundred awards including the RIBA Building of the Year and the Mies van der Rohe Pavilion Award for European Architecture.

Zaha M Hadid Architects
Hadid studied at the Architects Association in London and was awarded the Diploma Prize in 1977. She went on to lead her own studio there until 1987. The practice consistently pushes the boundaries of architecture and urban design. Their work experiments with spatial quality, extending and intensifying existing landscapes in pursuit of a visionary aesthetic that embraces all fields of design, from urban scale through to products, interiors and furniture. Major buildings include the Vitra Fire Station, Land Fomation-One and the Strasbourg Tram Station.

Jane Harris
Artist, b. UK, 1965
Studied Woven and Embroidered Textile Design at Glasgow School of Art, PhD research at the Royal College of Art, 1995–2000. Her research included the aesthetic fabrication of digital textiles. Jane Harris is Senior Research Fellow at Central Saint Martins College of Art and Design, University of the Arts, London and Visiting Lecturer in Textiles at Goldsmiths College, University of London. Her work has received awards from the Arts Council (2002), the Arts Humanities Research Board (2001) and the Hi-Tech Award, the Arts Council and Channel 4 (1996). She has served as an advisor to the Scottish Arts Council and the Arts Council of England.

Kyoko Hashimoto
Textile artist, b. Japan, 1945
Graduated in Textiles from Tama Art University,

1968 where she has been Professor since 1976. In 1978 established Hashimoto Textile Art Design Studio, designing tapestries for public buildings, carpets for hotels, chapels and private houses, and woven textiles for interiors. Member of Japan Craft Design Association. Her commissioned works are installed in many important buildings in Japan. In 2002 she won the Excellence Prize at Japan Sign Design Association – Shop section for Façade Design by Golden Tapestry and this work also won at the Japan Architecture Art Craft Association. Kyoko Hashimoto is currently working on a five-piece art work for the international airport in Nagoya.

Anke Henig
Textile designer, b. Germany, 1978
Has worked in the Italian textile industry and is a qualified tailor. In 1998 she began to study textile design at the University for Art and Design-Burg Giebichenstein, Halle. Her main area of interest is in CAD Jacquard weaving. She has exhibited at the Talente 2002 show in Munich and Artist at Work: New Technology in Textile and Fibre Art in Prato, Italy (2003).

Ane Henriksen
Textile artist, b. Denmark 1951
Graduated from School of Applied Art, Kolding, Denmark in 1974. Uses many unusual materials in her art works. Has exhibited worldwide, including France, Germany, Japan, Scandinavia and USA. 1992 Outstanding Award, 3rd International Textile Competition in Kyoto. A monograph on the artist's work has been published by Rhodos in 1998.

Herman Miller Inc.
Research, design, manufacture and distribution of office furniture systems and furniture and related products and services. Products include modular systems, seating, storage and freestanding furniture for environments ranging from offices to healthcare facilities. Products are marketed worldwide by the company's own sales staff, dealer network, independent contract office furniture dealers and the Internet. The group has international operations in Canada, Europe, Asia and Central America.

Hexcel Corporation
Manufacturer of advanced structural materials. Operates in three divisions – Reinforcements: manufactures and sells carbon, glass and aramid fibre fabrics, decorative blinds and soft body armour. This division also weaves electronic fibreglass fabrics as a substrate for printed circuit boards. Composite: manufactures and sells prepegs, honeycomb, structural adhesives, sandwich panels and specially machined honeycomb parts. Structures: manufactures and markets a range of lightweight and high-strength composite structures. The group's products are used in commercial aerospace, space and defence, electronics, general industrial and recreation markets. It operates in the United States and Europe and has sales offices in Asia, Australia and South America.

Ainsley Hillard
Textile artist, b. Carmarthen, Wales, 1978
Graduated in Constructed Textiles at Middlesex University, London with a first class BA Honours

Degree in 2000. Awarded the James Pantyfedwen Scholarship (2001 and 2002) which enabled her to undertake her MA in Visual Arts at Curtin University, Perth, Western Australia (2002) where she is currently Research Fellow. Her work uses computer technologies together with textile printing and weaving techniques. She has exhibited her work in Australia, Ireland, UK, Germany and at the Artists at Work: New Technology in Textile and Fibre Art, Prato (2003).

Yoshiko Hishinuma
Textile and fashion designer, b. Japan, 1958
Trained in textiles and fashion at the Miyake Design Studio. This gave him insight into the world of experimental textile technology for fashion. Based in Tokyo where he has his own studio, he launched his own label in 1984. Awarded the New Designer's Prize at Tokyo's Mainichi Fashion Grand Prix. He has acquired a reputation for creating innovative fabrics which push the boundaries of fabric and fashion. He often explores the thermoplastic property of synthetics to create fantastic new forms.

Michael Hopkins and Partners
Established in 1976, Michael Hopkins and Partners have become a major force in British architecture. Based in Marylebone, London, their design approach brings together creative imagination and rational logic. Their aim is to produce buildings that have a popular public appeal. The practice comprises approximately one hundred people, and has three partners – the founders and RIBA Gold Medal laureates Michael and Patty Hopkins, and Bill Taylor.

Hybrids + Fusion
Designer and manufacturer of advanced textiles for interior design applications. The company produces three-dimensional weave or spacer fabrics in various synthetic and metal yarns, as well as healthgiving fabrics.

Inoue Pleats
Textile company, founded 1953, Japan
Originally Marukei Fabric Trading Company, Tokyo. President of Inoue Pleats Tsuguya Inoue leads a small team of around thirty Inoue family members including daughter Mika and son Katsuhiro. Mainly synthetic textiles, pleated by hand or by machine for fashion garments and accessories. Also pleated objects from paper such as lanterns and interior screens. The Tokyo showroom displays exquisite folded paper for pleating its fabrics.

International Fashion Machines
Design and research company whose broad mission is to understand and transform the aesthetic and material properties of technology. Dedicated to creating technology, art and design that is aesthetic, physically unexpected, intimate and humorous, by merging design and art-making with experimental, technological and smart material research. IFM's projects in this area range from one-of-a kind interactive textile artworks to research for the military and design and strategy for the fashion industry.

International Cellulose Corporation (ICC)
Develops and manufactures cellulose spray-applied thermal insulation and acoustical

finishes. Has developed high performance cellulose products such as K-13®, SonaSpray 'fc' ® and Celbar®. Many provide thermal and acoustic insulation for architectural applications.

Janis Jefferies
Textile artist, b. UK, 1952
Trained as a painter at Maidstone College of Art (1974) before working in Art Textiles. Postgraduate studies at Camberwell College of Art (1975) and at the Department of Woven Construction at the Poznan Academy of Fine Arts, Poland (1977). She has taught textiles, fine arts and cultural studies in a number of art schools in the UK, Australia, Canada and America. Professor and Head of Visual Arts at Goldsmiths College, University of London; set up the Postgraduate Textiles Courses at Goldsmiths. Her work has been exhibited in numerous exhibitions all over the world including Artists at Work: New Technology in Textile and Fibre Art, Prato (2003). She is well known for her critical writing concerning textiles and is co-editor for Textile: The Journal of Cloth and Culture, first published March 2002 by Berg. Two special issues on Digital Textiles were edited by Janis Jefferies in November 2004 and January 2005.

Hella Jongerius
Designer, b. the Netherlands
Started in the early 1990s with products mainly for design platform Droog Design. Since 2000 her design studio JongeriusLab has been based in Rotterdam. Aims to find a balance between an industrial made serial product and a handmade unique piece. Renovated combinations between materials and techniques in archetypal shapes are typical for products which appear as one off and limited edition pieces. Commissions include Maharam, Swarovski and Hermès. Her work has been widely exhibited and is in many international private and public collections. The first monograph on the designer was published in 2003.

Kanebo Co. Ltd
Textile spinning firm, founded Japan, 1887
Major Japanese producer of cotton, silk, wool, polyester, polyamide and acrylic fibres, based in Osaka. Research into microfibre fabrics has resulted in textiles for high-performance sportswear and fashion. They have also explored microencapsulation techniques, mainly perfumed fabrics for lingerie, hosiery and fashion.

Anish Kapoor
Artist, b. India, 1954
Fascinated by darkness and light, presence and absence. These themes translate to his use of materials where he also explores opposites as well as the extremes of what they are capable of achieving, physically or through light and colour. He won the Preimo 2000 prize when he represented the British Pavilion at the XLIV Venice Biennial. His work is in numerous private and public collections such as the Tate Gallery, London, the Museum of Modern Art, New York and Reina Sofia in Madrid.

Donna Karan
Fashion designer, b. USA, 1948
Studied at Parsons School of Design, New York,

trained with US fashion designer Anne Klein, known for her contemporary sports-inspired fashion. In 1985 she started her own line, mainly dark colours with good quality fabrics, classic lines and a clean aesthetic, with immediate success. Her simplified dressing often relies on the fabric properties to create flattering, comfortable clothing. Her first collection utilized stretch textiles for a base layer called a body, a leotard-type garment which gave a streamlined silhouette. In her collections she uses a combination of naturals and synthetics and designs wearable and desirable clothing for today's contemporaray woman.

Rei Kawakubo
Fashion designer, b. Japan, 1942
Studied Fine Art at Keio University, Tokyo where she specialized in philosophy and aesthetics. Worked for Japanese textile company Asahi as a freelance stylist in their advertising department. Created the Comme des Garçons label in 1969 with a womenswear line and founded the company in Tokyo officially in 1973. Since 1975 has shown twice-yearly collections in Tokyo but it was on showing her experimental clothing in Paris in 1981 that her work received international recognition, despite the press's failure to understand it at first. In 1984 Rei Kawakubo created the first Comme des Garçons Homme Plus collection and later in 1987 a diffusion line, Comme des Garçons Noir. Launched a twice-yearly conceptual magazine, Six, to promote her particular aesthetic, which included widely sourced images that indirectly inspired her fashion work. In 1993 she was nominated Chevalier de l'Ordre des Arts et des Lettres by the French state. Her designs have been shown in museums and galleries worldwide.

Christine Keller
Textile artist, b. Germany
New media artist who juxtaposes traditional textile design with state-of-the-art techniques and materials to produce innovative visual and tactile experiences. Born and educated in Hamburg, Germany, she was trained as a hand weaver before going on to study product design and Jacquard weaving at the University Gesamthochschule Kassel. In 1996, she moved to Montreal, Canada, where she completed a Masters in Fine Arts at Concordia University. She is research assistant at the Hexagram Institute of New Media in the Arts at Concordia University, where she specializes in technologically enhanced textiles and textures.

Michiko Koshino
Fashion designer, b. Japan
Worked as apprentice in her mother's boutique, then for Stirling Cooper in London, 1973. In 1975 she opened a small shop in London. Michiko Koshino is now a large and successful business, encompassing labels which cater for different markets. The mainline collection is for womenswear and is shown at London Fashion Week. Yen Jeans is innovative jeans wear for both men and women, Yen Jeans Orange Label is produced in Italy and Yen Jeans Red Label is produced in Japan. One Hundreds is a smaller women's and menswear collection. Introduced in 1999, this is a limited edition range of clothing with great attention to detail. Diffusion collections have included the Motorking range established in 1987, clubwear inspired by biker-wear, now revered by collectors. Stages fashion and music events all over the world and is involved in many projects including customizing an environmentally friendly scooter for Honda. Known internationally as an avant-garde designer who experiments with both modern technological materials and the traditional and explores many techniques including unusual cutting and digital printing to create signature photographic prints. Past collections have shown inflatable clothing and she has pioneered the use of reflective fabrics. In 2002 she celebrated 21 years in the fashion industry. Michiko Koshino is based in London and continues to push the boundaries of fashion with her unique vision.

Kyoko Kumai
Textile artist, b. Japan, 1943
Graduated in Visual Design from Tokyo National University of Fine Arts and Music (1966). She then studied weaving on her own and worked with more traditional textile materials. Since the mid-1980s her work has used industrial stainless steel which she manipulates in many ways, often using textile techniques of twining, wrapping and interlacing. In this way she uses highly advanced technology to express her sources of inspiration which are to be found in nature – earth, water, fire, wind and air. Wall-based works constructed of many forms bound together comment on ideas of continuity and infinity within nature, and installations capture fleeting moments of nature's temporal changes. In 1991 she exhibited Air at the Museum of Modern Art, New York. In 1997 her work was included in the opening of the Challenge of Materials Gallery, Science Museum, London. Examples of Kyoko Kumai's work have been acquired for many collections including the Victoria and Albert Museum, London (1995) and Tokyo National Museum of Modern Art (2004). She has also undertaken many commissions for work in public buildings, in Japan and worldwide. She is Professor in Textile Design at Nagaoka Institute of Design.

Kuraray Co. Ltd
Textile company, established 1926, Japan
Known as Kurashiki Kenshoku Co. until 1970, when it became Kuraray Co. Ltd. Introduced the first regenerated fibre, viscose rayon to Japan. Uses the latest textile technology to create sophisticated textiles; active research into polymers, synthetics and chemical engineering. In 1964 they launched Clarino, a synthetic leather, and in 1980 Sofrina, as an alternative for the fashion world. They are pioneers in ultra-fine microfibres which can be specifically engineered to create a range of aesthetic, tactile and performance properties.

Yayoi Kusama
Artist, b. in Japan, 1929
Studied at the Arts and Crafts School in Kyoto before moving to Seattle in 1957. Has exhibited widely with solo shows at the Los Angeles Museum of Modern Art, the Museum of Contemporary Art in Tokyo and Serpentine Gallery in London. Her work is in numerous public collections worldwide.

Helmut Lang
Fashion designer, b. Austria, 1956
He had no formal fashion training but instead wanted to be an artist. He went to business school and then launched his own fashion label in 1977. In 1986 he was invited by the Austrian government to take part in a national exhibition at the Pompidou Centre in Paris and in this same year he had his first catwalk show in Paris. He moved to Paris for a while but then back to Vienna, and has taught at the Beaux-Arts in Vienna. His clothes for both men and women are inspired by the street and he uses the latest high-performance synthetics and advanced finishing treatments. His pared down shapes achieved by simple but perfect cutting have secured a cult following. After twelve years of showing in Paris he now shows in New York. In April 1998 he showed his first New York collection on the Internet, being one of the first fashion designers to do so. He now lives and works in SoHo in New York City.

Lang and Baumann
Sabina Lang (b. Switzerland, 1972), Daniel Baumann (b. USA, 1967)
The artists' work uses a strong graphic element and includes inflatables. Exhibited widely with solo exhibitions worldwide including Bell-Roberts Gallery in Cape Town, the Swiss Institute in New York and Centro d'Arte Contemporanea in Eindhoven, the Netherlands.

Lee Lapthorne
Textile artist, b. UK
BA Art and Design, MA specializing in the use of photographic imagery within textiles and fashion as installation, University of Central England, Birmingham. Freelance producer, director and artist. Has completed successful commissions for clients including Camper Shoes, Film Four and the Woolmark International Company.

Koko Toshima Larson
Textile artist, b. Japan, 1969
Studied Textiles at Goldsmiths College, University of London (1994). Textile and accessory designer for Pleats Please Issey Miyake in Tokyo, 1996–98. Moved to USA in 1998 and creates one-off clothing ideas to be exhibited. Her work combines traditional materials and high technology, including use of metals and reflectives. Designed the catalogue for the textile exhibition Tradition and Innovation: Contemporary Textiles from the Nuno Studio, Tokyo at the University of California Santa Barbara Art Museum and the University of California Los Angeles Flower Museum. CD-ROM package design for Nuno Corporation, 2001–2.

Barbara Layne
Textile artist and researcher, b. USA, 1952
Studied Painting at the University of Colorado (1979), MFA in Textile Design at the University of Kansas (1982). Associate Professor of Studio Arts at Concordia University in Montreal and founding member of Hexagram, the Institute for Research and Creation in Media Arts and Technologies. Hexagram brings together around sixty researchers working at the intersection of art, science and technology. She is the Principal Investigator of a grant from the Canadian Foundation for Innovations and her work has been supported by the Canada Council for the Arts and the Council of the Arts in Quebec. Her main interest is the development of intelligent cloth structures for the creation of artistic, performative and functional textiles. Her textiles incorporate LEDs, microcomputers and sensors that respond to external stimuli. Exhibitions include Electronic Textiles: Hacking the Museum, The Glass Box Gallery, Salford, 1996; Webs://Textiles and New Technology, University of California Art Gallery, Davis, 1998.

Jürgen Lehl
Designer of textiles and clothes, German, b. 1944 Poland
Worked in France 1962–69, moved to Japan in 1991 and now based in Tokyo. Founded Jürgen Lehl Co. in 1972 designing and selling women's and menswear, accessories and jewelry. Classically simple lines and beautifully draped fabrics include references to East and West. Uses computer-controlled Jacquard looms and knitting machines to create rich textures and sophisticated patterning. His textiles are in the permanent collections of the Cooper-Hewitt Museum, New York, and he has exhibited in Germany, the Netherlands and Japan.

Lenzing AG
Textile company, based in Austria
Manufactures the regenerated fibre viscose rayon and has undertaken much research into this natural chemical fibre group. In 1986 the development of viscose fibres led to Lenzing Lyocell, a wonderfully soft and fluid fabric. In 1990 Lenzing set up a pilot plant in Austria and larger scale manufacture began in 1995. It is an advanced cellulose-based fibre capable of taking various visual and tactile effects for a range of applications, mainly fashion fabrics.

Anja Madsen
Textile designer, b. Denmark, 1971
Graduated from the Design School in Copenhagen in 2000 with an MA in Textile Design. During this time she studied one semester at the University of Industrial Arts, Helsinki, as an exchange student. Based in Paris since 2000 working for the styling agency Peclers Paris, and working for haute couture designers. Explores new and innovative yarns and both natural and synthetic combinations in order to create refined textures and forms. Inspired by architectural structures, she sculpts her textiles in dialogue with the body. She has exhibited her work in group shows – Fibre Art at the Museum of Art and Industry in Copenhagen (1996) and at Artists at Work: New Technology in Textile and Fibre Art, Prato (2003).

Meadowbrook Inventions, Inc.
Textile company, established 1938, New Jersey, USA
Glitter, plastic films and metallic foils used for many applications including cosmetics, toy, paper and textile industries. Innovations include Angelina, a polyester-based fibre available in many different colours and effects including luminescent, iridescent, metallic and holographic. This can be used as yarn to make a conventional textile or heat-bonded for a nonwoven. Using the heat from an iron and a small amount of Angelina, a nonwoven fabric can be made – from fibre to fabric instantly.

Johanna Mills Rose
Textile artist and designer, b. 1972, UK
Studied Multi-Media Textiles at Loughborough University, 1992–95. Graduated with MA in Mixed Media Textiles from Royal College of Art in 1997. Exhibited widely including Contemporary Applied Arts and SOFA. Works to commission for clients such as Louis Vuitton, Donna Karan and Marc Jacobs.

Makiko Minagawa
Textile designer, b. Japan, 1947
Studied at Kyoto University of the Arts where she specialized in Textile Dyeing and opened her studio for dyeing while still a student. In 1970 she met Issey Miyake and helped him found the Miyake Design Studio, where she has since worked creating many highly original textiles, often rich in texture and surface pattern. She selects the fibres and designs the innovative fabrics which have completed Issey Miyake's vision of retaining traditions of ancient handcrafts as well as forging new paths for fashion textiles. While always looking for modern technologies to make new fabrics, she shares Issey Miyake's respect for the environment. She is widely recognized as one of the world's most innovative textile designers and in 1990 she won the Mainichi Fashion Grand Prize. Her fabrics have been included in both group and solo exhibitions. Makiko Minagawa is currently producing the Haat collection under the Issey Miyake umbrella and collaborating with manufacturers in India.

Mitsubishi Corporation
Mitsubishi Corporation (MC) is Japan's largest general trading company (sogo shosha) with over 200 bases of operations in approximately 80 countries worldwide. Together with its over 500 group companies, MC employs a multinational workforce of approximately 48,000 people. MC has long been engaged in business with customers around the world in energy, metals, machinery, chemicals, food and textiles.

Issey Miyake
Fashion designer, b. Japan 1938
In 1965 he moved to Paris after graduating from Tama University, Tokyo. He studied in France, and was apprenticed to a designer of haute couture. In 1970 he returned to Japan where he founded Miyake Design Studio. He showed his first collection in New York in 1971, moving it to Paris in 1973, where he has continued to show ever since. In 1977 he started Issey Miyake Men's line, which began to show independently in Paris in 1985. In 1988 he began work on his pleated clothing, later expanded to include pleated items from main women's collection, as well as a line of pleats only, called Pleats Please Issey Miyake. This proved such a phenomenal success that free-standing Pleats Please shops now exist, in addition to Issey Miyake Collection Stores, in Tokyo, Paris, London, and soon in New York. He uses textiles that include natural materials as well as the most advanced synthetics; he believes that any material can be used for clothing. As widely respected in the art world as in the world of fashion, his work is also shown in museums and galleries. He no longer creates the mainline collections but has given himself more time to concentrate on one-off textiles; he

still works on Pleats Please Issey Miyake and A-POC (A Piece Of Clothing).

Masako Mizumachi
Textile artist, b. Japan, 1928
Studied in Sweden, Stadmissichen Vavskola, Stockholm. Professor at Tokyo Kasei University, 1980–99. Now retired, she writes articles on the structure of weaving. She uses the computer-controlled loom to create complex and beautiful weaves. She has exhibited her work throughout Japan and has made many important commissions for public buildings.

Montefibre
Textile company, founded Italy, 1972
In the early 1980s Montefibre produced Terital Silklike with a very fine denier. They realized then that the way ahead was research into new synthetics and to reduce the denier of a fibre to allow for engineered effects. Montefibre's developments include an extremely fine microfibre, Terital Zero.4, and Terital Microspun, blended with cotton. Known for its acrylic and polyester fibres used in fabrics for fashion, interior and technical applications.

Helen Murray
Textile designer, b. UK 1980
BA Textile Design, Chelsea College of Art (2002). Murray has developed a new way of manipulating fabric to achieve a 3D surface effect without using chemicals. Won the Oxo Peugeot Design Award in 2003 for her sculptural fabric. First winner of the NESTA Prize for Innovation, 2003.

Netlon Ltd
See Tensar.

Nexia Biotechnologies Inc.
Federally incorporated in July 1992 as Turner Research Inc., based in Montreal, Canada. Founded by Dr Jeffrey Turner, then a Professor of Animal Science at McGill University. In September 1993, two venture capital groups provided $2.5 million towards exploiting the company's two patents. The biotechnology company now develops and manufactures complex recombinant proteins for military and civilian applications. Products include BioSteel, a recumbent spider silk. Protexia, Nexia's lead pharmaceutical product, is being developed as a military battlefield protection system and a medical countermeasure (rescue therapy) for civilian homeland security.

Karen Nicol
Textile designer, b. UK, 1952
Trained in Embroidered Textiles at Manchester Metropolitan University (1973) and in Textiles at the Royal College of Art (1975). Since 1990 she has been Senior Lecturer at the Royal College of Art on the Mixed Media Textiles course and she is a Fellow there. Contributing editor of Selvedge magazine. Embroidery and knitwear designer for the German fashion house Cissule-Uta Raasch 1979–95. Established her own design studio in 1986 and undertakes design and production of mixed media and embroidered fashion textiles. Karen Nicol Embroidery and Mixed Media has created textiles for Clements Ribeiro, Chloe, Julien Macdonald, Matthew Williamson, John Rocha and Betty Jackson. Karen Nicol also

produces textiles for furnishing and theatre as well as offering a consultancy and analysis of embroidery. Since 1990 she has worked for John Boyd Textiles and her interior fabric design clients include Zimmer Rhode, Brunschwig Fils, embroidered seating for the Washington Museum, dining chairs for President Bush, King Gustav of Sweden, upholstery for the Thai Royal Family, 2002 and for the King of Norway, 2004.

Nuno Corporation
Textile design company, established Tokyo, 1984
Co-founded by Jun'ichi Arai and Reiko Sudo. Jun'ichi Arai now works on the creation of one-off textiles. The main designer, Reiko Sudo was born in Japan in 1953 and studied Painting and then Textile Design, Hand Weaving and Art, Musashino Art University, Tokyo (1975). She worked as assistant to Professor Hideho Tanaka at the Kawashima Textile School, Kyoto 1975–77. Until 1984 she worked as a freelance textile designer for textile companies, including Kanebo, Nishikawa, Sangyo and Soko. From 1989 to 1992 she worked as a textile designer for the International Wool Secretariat. Between 1991 and 1993 she worked for Tokyo apparel company Threads. She is Lecturer at Musashino Art University. Reiko Sudo now directs Nuno and has been in partnership with Hiroko Suwa since 1998. Nuno is known worldwide for its innovative and beautiful fabrics for fashion or interiors. All its employees are actively involved in the creative aspects of textile production which use traditional fibres and techniques as well as the most sophisticated synthetics and finishing treatments. Based in the Roppongi district of Tokyo with shops in Sapporo, Kokura and Aoyama, Nuno also has showrooms in Los Angeles and New York. The work of Nuno has been included in many international exhibitions and is held in permanent collections worldwide. Exhibitions include the touring Tradition and Innovation – Contemporary Textiles from the Nuno studio (2001–2); Structure and Surface: Contemporary Japanese Textiles (1998–2001) and Nuno: Sense and Skill (2001 and 2004).

Nylstar
Textile company, founded in 1994
Nylstar was formed when the French company Rhone-Poulenc (now Rhodia) and the Italian company, Snia Fibre (now Snia SpA) merged. Both companies have been involved in research and development into synthetic textiles and the merger brought together their expertise in polyamide polymers and textile fibres. Nylstar is now one of the largest European manufacturers of synthetic yarn for many applications including extreme sportswear and fashion. Fibres they manufacture include Elite, a modified polyester, and Meryl® which uses ultra-fine polyamide for a range of speciality yarns.

Jessica Ogden
b. Jamaica
Fashion designer working in London. She studied at Rhode Island School of Design, USA and Byam Shaw School of Art in London. She has worked with NoLogGo, the eco-friendly design collective, before launching her own label in 1993. She has quickly become a pioneer of salvage fashion. She uses layering, hand printing and hand-stitching often finishing with paint, needles and on

occasion nail guns. Ogden has made unconventional presentations during fashion weeks, choosing to make an installation or to have her clothing modelled by amateur ballroom dancers. She has collaborated with French label APC to create the line JO Custom and exhibited as part of the Fabric of Fashion British Council Touring Exhibition.

Omikenshi Co. Ltd
Textile company based in Osaka, Japan
One of the largest textile spinners in Japan. Has devoted much time and money to research and development. Omikenshi are known for their Crabyon yarn which uses crab shells to make a textile which is capable of destroying bacteria.

Lucy Orta
Artist, b. UK, 1966
Originally trained in fashion and textiles in the UK, Orta moved to Paris where she has been based for many years. In 2001 she was awarded the first Rootstein Hopkins Chair of Fashion at London College of Fashion, University of the Arts, London. She heads the Man & Humanity Masters programme in Industrial Design at the Design Academy in Eindhoven. Her art work comments on the role of the artist in today's world and the fragile environment in which we live; it is frequently in the form of installations or performances which use the latest technical textiles. She was commissioned in 2000 by Expofil, Paris, to create an installation Urban Life Guards. Live multi-media interactive installations and performances include Fluid Architecture Act IV (2003) and Transgressing Fashion No. 204 (2004). She has presented site-specific performances at the Venice Biennale (1995), the Johannesberg Biennale, (1997), the Museum of Contemporary Art, Sydney (2004) and the Victoria & Albert Museum, London (2004).

Outlast Technologies, Inc.
Textile company, founded USA, 1990
Co-founded by Ed Payne and Bernard Perry as Gateway Technologies Inc. The name changed to Outlast Technologies, Inc. in 1995 to reflect their successful branded product, Outlast, a phase-change material. This technology was first developed for NASA in the late 1980s. The phase-change material is very versatile and can be incorporated into a textile as a fibre, fabric or foam. Outer surfaces or linings can use Outlast for different appearance, handle and performance. Outlast is used for many applications including sportswear and activewear.

Palmhive Technical Textiles Ltd
Technical textile manufacturer producing a range of Raschel and Tricot warp knitted fabrics primarily for high performance and industrial and military applications.

Plaspack USA Inc
Established for over a decade, Plaspack USA Inc. produces a range of High Density Polyethylene Mesh materials for packaging, presentation, and protective hortifabric applications.

J. Morgan Puett
Artist, b. Hahira, Georgia, USA, 1957
Graduated from the Art Institute of Chicago with a BFA in Painting and Sculpture and an MFA in

Sculpture and Filmmaking. She has exhibited in group and solo shows in USA and in London at Give and Take, Serpentine Gallery, Victoria & Albert Museum, 2001. She collaborates with Mark Dion on the creation of art works.

Prada
Fashion company, established Milan, Italy, 1913
Mario Prada founded the company for luxurious leather goods by selling products all exclusively designed and manufactured in luxury materials using sophisticated techniques. Miuccia Prada, who gained a PhD in Political Science, began working within the company in 1970 when she ran the Galleria store in Milan and produced exclusive products. She took over the company in 1978 and transformed the label with her use of innovative fabrics. Her collections have attracted a cult following. She introduced womenswear in 1988 for their Autumn/Winter 1988/89 collection and menswear in 1993 for their Spring/Summer 1994 collection. There is also a diffusion line called Miu Miu and a separate sports-inspired line within the Prada brand. Prada became famous for its use of lightweight nylon, black in particular, and their bags with the triangular metal stamp became much sought after accessories. The collections use the very latest techno textiles as well as the finest naturals and the look of their garments and accessories is always a very contemporary aesthetic. Established the Fondazione Prada in Milan in 1993 to show fine art.

Nicholas Pryke
Trained in furniture design at Parnham College in Dorset. Specializes in furniture design as well as interiors and architectural installations. Exhibitions include Hitec-Lotec and clients Heal's, Muji and Apicella Associates.

Paco Rabanne
Fashion designer, b. Spain, 1934
Moved to France in 1939 and studied Architecture at the Ecole Nationale Supérieure des Beaux-Arts, Paris (1963). In the mid-1960s he started to create dresses from plastic discs and squares linked together and opened his showroom in Paris in 1966. Created costumes for two Jean-Luc Godard films in 1966 and Casino Royale in 1967. He started making paper clothes in 1967; his paper has a fine polyamide backing to make it stronger and the garments were joined using adhesive tape, not seamed in the conventional sense by sewing. He used lozenges of metal to create a kind of chainmail inspired by butcher's protective wear to create garments and accessories, linking the metal together using pliers. He is a craftsman and his methods unite his architecture training with his interest in new technology. Paco Rabanne researches into new materials and has used iridescent rubber, laser-treated reflective textiles, optical fibre, plexiglass, aluminium, chromium-plated steel and even experimented with moulded garments using liquid plastic. His cut is very clean and refined with simple shapes which gives full attention to his materials. Paco Rabanne has influenced many of today's fashion designers.

Dorothea Reese-Heim
Textile artist, b. Germany, 1943
Studied Drawing, Painting, Tapisserie, Textiles (Fibre Art) at the Academy of Bildende Künste, Karlsruhe and Munich, Germany 1964–72. Qualified in 1972 with a Diploma at the Academy of Munich, Germany. She has worked as a freelance artist and has been Professor of Textiles at the Univerity of Paderborn in Germany. Her artworks use handmade papers alongside technical textiles, composites, prepegs, plastics and metal. She has exhibited in Europe, USA, Korea and Japan.

RE:FORM
The Interactive Institute's RE:FORM studio investigates technology as design material. While the typical notion of form is physical shape, they believe that in considering computation as a design material, concepts of form must be fundamentally re-interpreted since time, flow, and energy and other dynamic elements become central in the interaction with computational things. In their research, they develop both methodological foundations and practical examples, exposing the experiential, social, and design implications of new technologies.

Ann Richards
Textile designer, b. UK, 1947
Trained as a biologist – BSc in Zoology/Marine Biology (1969) from University College of North Wales, Bangor, and MSc in Applied Hydrobiology (1972) Chelsea College – before studying textiles at Surrey Institute of Art and Design (1987). Her science background is evident in her textile work which frequently looks at form and function in nature. Interested in biomimetics, she observes the interplay between material and structure, for example in her use of high-twist yarns and high-tech metallics and reflectives. She is Lecturer in Woven Textiles at Surrey Institute of Art and Design, Farnham, since 1995 and has lectured in the UK, Sweden, Denmark, the Netherlands, Canada and USA. Her work is in several public collections including the Crafts Council, London, and the Fashion Foundation, Tokyo. Exhibitions include On Growth and Form: Textiles and the Engineering of Nature at The Textile Museum of Canada, Toronto, From the Shadow to the Light, Contemporary Applied Arts, London (2002) and Artists at Work: New Technology in Textiles and Fibre Art, Prato (2003).

Vibeke Riisberg
Textile designer, b. Denmark 1951
Studied at Art and Craft School, Copenhagen. Works as a textile artist and designer for print, but also designs weaves and knits. Co-founded Tastemain & Riisberg design studio, Paris, where she worked 1982–92. Has made pioneering use of digital tools and specialized printing techniques like flock, dévoré and cloqué.

Rival
Sportswear company established in Sydney specializing in performance and active lifestyle swimwear. Produces UV- and chlorine-resistant as well as competitive swimwear. They sponsor a number of events such as the Kellog's Nutri-Grain Ironman/Ironwoman series and the Accenture Triathlon series.

Richard Rogers Partnership
International architectural practice responsible for a number of landmark buildings such as the Pompidou Centre in Paris and Lloyd's of London. Clients include the Canary Wharf Group, British Airport Authority, New York City Economic Development Corporation and Daimler Chrysler. Richard Rogers is Chief Advisor on Architecture and Urban Design to the Greater London Authority, and a member of the Mayor of Barcelona's Urban Strategies Advisory Council.

Sophie Roet
Textile designer, b. Australia, 1970
Studied for her BA in Woven Textile Design at the University of Brighton (1991) and MA in Woven Textile Design at the Royal College of Art (1995). Finalist of Hanae Mori International Textile Competition, Tokyo, 1994; Winner of Woven Textile Designer Prize, TexPrint, London, 1995 and Winner of the Lea & Bullukian Textile Competition, Lyon, 1996. She has worked as a freelance stylist for Studio Edelkoort in Paris (1991–98) and supplied woven textile designs to Trend Union, Paris (1991–98). She works freelance as a textile consultant and designer – clients include Hussein Chalayan, Romeo Gigli, Mandarina Duck for textile, colour and trend research, Willow as co-designer for its lingerie label, Cerruti and Nicole Farhi. She has worked as textile designer and textile production organizer for Eskandar, a Persian-born fashion designer based in London. Her textiles have been shown in group and solo exhibitions in Europe, USA, Canada and Australia. Textiles have been purchased by the Textile Arts Gallery, New Mexico, the Victoria & Albert Museum, London, the Wellcome Trust, London, and the Berlin Technical Museum.

Julie Ryder
Textile artist and designer, b. Australia, 1960
She has studied both applied science and textiles, graduating with a masters in visual arts textiles from Canberra School of Art in 2003. She specializes in printed textiles for interiors and homeware. Postgraduate investigations have included chemical resist dye-printing onto cotton, degumming and direct digital printing onto silk. Inspirations for designs come from scanning electron micrographs of her own fabrics that are then colour-enhanced and manipulated using digital software.

Jakob Schlaepfer
Textile design company, founded 1960, Switzerland
Based in St Gallen, known for embroidered textiles, the fabrics of Jakob Schlaepfer combine the latest technologies with traditional aspects. Their innovative fabrics for fashion and interiors use many advanced materials such as new synthetics, metallics and fibre optics together with finishing treatments, for example laser-cutting, ink-jet printing and emboidery. Jakob Schlaepfer show various collections each year – haute couture, prêt-à-porter, dimensional woven fabric and interior. They supply leading fashion designers such as Christian Lacroix and John Galliano with glamorous and extravagant fabrics. In 2004 they had an exhibition at the National Museum in Zurich, Bling Bling. Art Director Martin Leuthold compiled Blenwerk with Bernhard Duss, which demonstrates their inspiration and creativity for fabrics and fashion, also launched in Summer 2004.

Schoeller Textil AG
Textile company, established 1868
Family-run company that has created many technically inventive fabrics and concentrates on the development of speciality textiles for sport at all levels, leisure, safety and industrial design. They use synthetics and advanced finishing treatments to create fabrics which satisfy high-function needs while also looking and feeling good. Schoeller are committed to environmental concerns and carefully consider the waste created in their textile production. Their innovative fabrics are also used by many leading international fashion designers including Donna Karan, Prada and Armani. Schoeller have won many awards, including the Design Prize in Switzerland, 1997.

Lesley Sealey
Textile designer, b. 1970, UK
Studied textiles at Nottingham Trent University, graduating in 1992, then at the Royal College of Art, for her MA Textiles (1996). She spent her final year at the Royal College of Art studying print and beading techniques in India which made a strong impression on her work. In 1997 i.e. uniform was established with Roger Lee, fashion designer, and Chris Connors who managed the business side. They received New Generation sponsorship in 1999–2000 and put on their first catwalk show at Atlantis 2 Gallery, London. Both high technology and hand craft are employed for a contemporary look. The designs of i.e. uniform were included in the British Council touring exhibition Fabric of Fashion (2000–2) and also in 2002 in Planning, Design & Construction at Barcelona Museum of Contemporary Arts. The last collection of i.e. uniform was called Botanik for Autumn/Winter 2002/3 and was shown in February 2002. Lesley Sealey now works as a freelance textile designer. Clients include DKNY and Diane von Furstenberg.

Pēteris Sidars
Textile artist, b. Latvia, 1948
Graduated from the Latvian Art Academy, Textile Department, Riga, Latvia, 1978. He has had many solo and group exhibitions which include 2010: Textiles and New Technology, curated by Sarah Braddock Clarke and Marie O'Mahony for the Crafts Council, London (1994); 9th International Lace Biennale – Contemporary Art, Brussels, Belgium (2000); International Fibre Art Exhibition, Beijing, China (2002) and Artists at Work: New Technology in Textile and Fibre Art, Prato (2003). His materials include glass fibre fabric, copper wire, synthetics, fibre optics and hot-melt glue; he has also used weaving and lamination techniques. His work has won many awards – the Prize of From Lausanne to Beijing – 2002 International Tapestry Art Biennale, China and the Annual Prize for Innovation in Visual Art, the Culture Capital Foundation of Latvia (2003). His work is in public collections in Latvia, Germany, Russia, Hungary as well as in numerous private collections.

Malgorzata Skuza
Textile artist and graphic designer, b. Poland, 1959
Studied at the Academy of Art in Lodz for her MA, 1985. She has participated in international and national exhibitions in France, Germany,

Holland, Hungary, Israel, Bulgaria, Slovakia and Japan in the 6th International Textile Competition '99 in Kyoto. An expert in many computer programmes, she also works as a photoeditor and graphic designer at Polskapresse, Dziennik Lodzki newspaper since 1992. She uses her experience of software such as Photoshop to create layers of imagery for digitally printed one-off art works. Won the III Prize Grand Font 2003 – Polish Press Editors Competition.

SmartSlab Ltd
Developed and produced the SmartSlab digital display system for walls, floors, billboards and buildings. The patented technology uses a digital tile intended to provide an ultra-strong canvas for design and communication including moving images. The product has won numerous awards including a NESTA Innovation Award and reached the final of the Saatchi & Saatchi Innovation in Communication Award 2003.

Grethe Sørensen
Textile artist and designer, b. Denmark
Studied textiles at the College of Art and Design in Kolding. Works on shaft, damask and a digital loom with single thread control. She has worked with Georg Jensen Damask as a freelance textile designer of Jacquard woven tablecloths and has started designing interior fabrics for Kvadrat. Exhibitions include the 5th and 6th International Textile Competition 1998 and 1999, Kyoto.

Karen Spurgin
Textile designer, b. UK, 1955
Brought up partly in USA, returned to UK and studied Textiles at Goldsmiths College, University of London, 1979. She has worked as freelance textile designer in fashion, interiors, advertising, stage and theatre and for film and television. Clients include Shirin Guild, Richard James, Deborah Milner, Bruce Oldfield, Debenhams, Laura Ashley and Marks & Spencer. Her main client is the Los Angeles-based company dosa (Christina Kim). She taught on Constructed Textiles and Mixed Media Textiles at RCA for seven years. She is currently developing embroidered wallpaper.

Norma Starszakowna
Textile designer and artist, b. UK, 1945
Studied at Duncan of Jordanstone College of Art and Design, University of Dundee (1966), where she has been head of Textiles and Fashion (1984–95) and Chair of Design (1994–99). Since 1999 she has been Director of Research Development, University of the Arts, London. She established her own design studio in 1966 and gained an Arts Council Research Award in 1977. Her textile work involves innovative print processes, the development of heat-reactives and experimental print media to create fabrics where the image is integral to the structure of the cloth. She has had many exhibitions including Artists at Work: New Technology in Textile and Fibre Art, Prato (2003) and a solo exhibition, Transmutations, Textile Museum, Tilburg (2004). She has worked in collaboration with Issey Miyake Design Studio, Nuno Corporation and the fashion designer Shirin Guild. Her work is in numerous private and public collctions including the Arts Council and the German Textile Museum, Krefeld.

Naoki Takizawa
Fashion designer, b. Japan, 1960
Naoki Takizawa attended the Kuwasawa Design Institute (1982) to train as a painter/sculptor. Joined the Miyake Design Studio in 1982 to create wearable work. He has collaborated with many practitioners working alongside Issey Miyake, including fine artists, musicians and architects. He worked with William Forsythe of Ballet Frankfurt on the costumes for Eidos Telos in 1995. Fascinated with new textile technologies, he creates ultra-modern collections but at the same time is often inspired by nature. He is Chief Designer at the Issey Miyake fashion house for the label Naoki Takizawa for Issey Miyake.

Sarah Taylor
Textile artist and designer, b. UK, 1969
Studied Textile Design at Winchester School of Art (1991) and a Postgraduate Diploma in Textile Design at the School of Textiles, Heriot-Watt University, Galashiels (1992). Undertook MPhil research at Heriot-Watt, investigating fibre optics in woven textiles (1995). Since 2002 she has been Reader and Lecturer at the School of Textiles, Heriot-Watt University. Taylor has collaborated with British fashion designer and artist Helen Storey for the exhibitions Primitive Streak and Mental. She has shown her work in numerous group exhibitions including Addressing the Century: 100 Years of Art and Fashion, Hayward Gallery, London (1998–99), Coming to Our Senses, a nationally touring exhibition organized by Craftspace Touring, Birmingham (2000–2), Jerwood Applied Arts Prize: Textiles, at the Crafts Council Gallery, London (2002), and Artists at Work: New Technology in Textile and Fibre Art, Prato (2003).

Tecknit
Incorporated in New Jersey in 1958 as Technical Wire Products, the original facility consisted of 10,000 square feet. The company now occupies over 150,000 square feet of manufacturing and office space in the USA, Europe, South America and China. Tecknit products have been designed for thousands of highly advanced commercial and military applications. Products include knitted wire mesh, conductive silicone elastomers, Fabric-Over-Foam gaskets, conductive coatings, adhesives, vent panels, windows and beryllium copper EMI gaskets.

Technical Absorbents Ltd (TAL)
Established in 1993. Manufacturer of the Oasis PolyAcrylate Super Absorbent which is listed in the FDA Inventory of Effective Premarket Notifications for Food Contact Substances. Member of the European Disposables and Nonwovens Association (EDANA). Manufactures nonwovens, yarns, woven fabrics and finished consumer products, all containing the Oasis SAF.

Tensar International Ltd
Founded in 1952 as Netlon Ltd. The group has three main business streams, providing solutions that combine both products and associated applications technology to civil engineering, industrial and turf reinforcement customers. Specializes in a high performance range of innovative geogrid and geotextile products for roads, rail, runways, embankments and many other applications across the world.

Tissue + Culture
Oron Catts, b. Finland, Ionat Zurr, b. UK
Catts is a tissue engineering artist living and working in Western Australia. Co-founder and Artistic Director of SymbioticA, the Art & Science Collaborative Research Laboratory, School of Anatomy and Human Biology, UWA. Founder of the Tissue Culture & Art Project/TC&A (1996). Research Fellow at the Tissue Engineering and Organ Fabrication Laboratory, Harvard Medical School (2000–1). Trained in product design and specialized in the future interaction of design and biological derived technologies.
Ionat Zurr is a Wet Biology Art Practitioner living and working in Western Australia. Artist in residence/PhD candidate in SymbioticA. Co-Founder of the TC&A Project. Research Fellow at the Tissue Engineering and Organ Fabrication Laboratory, Harvard Medical School (2000–1). Studied art history, photography and media studies. Specializes in biological and digital imaging as well as video production.

Toray Industries Inc.
Textile company, founded Japan, 1926
Originally founded as Toyo Rayon Co. Ltd, renamed Toray in 1970. Produces fibres, textiles, plastics, chemicals and advanced composites. Active in research and development and produce textiles based on the three main synthetics, polyamide, polyester and acrylic. Manufactures high-performance textiles for many applications including sportswear and fashion. Worldwide outlets in the Far East, Europe and USA.

Machi Ue
Textile designer, b. Japan, 1972
Studied for Diploma in Textile Design at Art Studio Fuji, Florence, Italy, and General Art Studies at Okanagan University College, British Columbia, Canada. Lives and works in Florence as a freelance textile print designer with clients including Kariyamokuzai Co. Ltd and Sony Plaza Co. Ltd. Exhibited in Artists at Work: New Technology in Textile and Fibre Art, Prato (2003).

Eugène van Veldhoven
Textile designer, b. the Netherlands, 1964
Studied Fashion Design at the Rotterdam College of Art and Architecture, 1993. Since 1998 he has taught at the Royal College of Arts in Den Haag. He has also given lectures at various institutions throughout Europe and at the RCA in London. Worked as a fashion designer for a few years for Marithe and François Girbaud specializing in textile design. Since 1996 he has worked as a textile designer, first for trend agencies and magazines such as Li Edelkoort's Trend Union, Promostyl and Textile VIEW. He is now working full-time for the textile industry. All his recent textiles are intended for interior application. His clients are producers and editors of interior or fashion textiles or for the automotive industry, mostly at the higher end of the market. His specializations are coatings and combinations of print techniques. He works together with Stork Printing systems in Boxmeer, the Netherlands.

Irene van Vliet
Textile designer, b. the Netherlands, 1965
Studied at the Academy of Industrial Design, Eindhoven, specializing in Product and Textile Design (1989) and then at the Atelier National d'Art Textile in Paris (1991) postgraduate study specializing in weaving and textile design for interior and fashion markets. In 1992 she set up Weaving Studio Irene van Vliet in Amsterdam and had own label Future & Fabrics. Wide range of materials used in her woven fabrics, particularly synthetics, metallics, reflectives and iridescents. She has created fabrics for fashion designers and companies including Calvin Klein, Esprit and Missoni. Since 2001 she has worked for Philips Design as a Visual Trend Analyst, creating colour palettes and material finishes for domestic products and is Creative Director for Packaging Design. She started Studio CIT in 2000 working in the areas of colour concept and forecast.

Verosol
Develops and produces fabrics for blinds and curtains. Specializes in metallized fabrics used in sunshades to protect against solar heat and glare. Many offer a view and provide additional insulation. The company's sunscreening products are marketed in many countries throughout the world by appointed licensees and fabricators.

Marcel Wanders
Designer, b. the Netherlands, 1963
One of the founding members of the Droog collective of Dutch conceptual designers. In 1992 he founded the 'WAACs', in 1995 'wanders wonders'. Wanders is an independent industrial product designer working in Amsterdam. He designs for companies such as British Airways, Boffi, Cappellini, Droog Design, Flos, Mandarina Duck, Cassina, Magis, and Moooi (where he also is art director). He has won various national and international awards, attending numerous collections and exhibitions. His products are presented at MoMA in New York, SFMOMA, Stedelijk Museum in Amsterdam and at Vitra Design Museum.

Junya Watanabe
Fashion designer, b. Japan, 1961
Avant-garde fashion designer of futuristic-looking collections. Graduated from Tokyo's Bunka Fashion Institute in 1984 and then joined Comme des Garçons. After three years he was working on the Comme des Garçons Tricot (knitwear) line. In 1992 supported by Rei Kawakubo, the Junya Watanabe-Comme des Garçons label was launched. Has complete creative freedom to design and make his own collections, independent of her label. In 1993 he won the Mainichi prize for young creators and also had his first catwalk show in Paris which now follow with twice-yearly collections. Well known for his use of the latest materials, sophisticated synthetics and advanced finishes.

Sonja Weber
Artist, b. Germany, 1968
Studied at the Textile School, Münchberg, Germany, 1983, then at the Art Academy, Nurnberg, 1998, and Graduate Studies with Professor Gerd Winner at the Art Academy Munich, 2002. She has had several exhibitions of her textile art work – both solo and group – including Artists at Work: New Technology in Textile and Fibre Art, Prato (2003), Augenblicke, a solo show at Constance, Germany (2002) and

since 1996 many throughout Germany. She is interested in the effect of light across a surface, water for example, and evokes light and shade with her textiles. Her work combines photography, painting, computer techniques and weaving. Using the Jacquard loom she is able to control the lifting of each individual thread to allow for complex imagery. Sonja Weber has won several awards for her work including the Award for Young Artists, Düsseldorf, 2003.

Carol Westfall
Textile artist, b. USA, 1938
Trained at Rhode Island School of Design,1960 and at the Maryland Institute College of Art at Masters level, 1972. She has held many lecturing positions and was Professor at Montclair State University, New Jersey 1972–2002 where she taught in the Fine Arts Department. She is now a freelance artist. She explores cultural roots and contemporary imagery of textiles/fine arts. She works with computer-aided Jacquard looms to achieve complex imagery. Her work Aids is included in the 4th International Fiber Art Biennial Trame d'autore in Chieri, Italy, which toured to St Gallen's Textile Museum. Her work has been exhibited throughout the world including Japan, USA, the Philippines, India, Switzerland and Germany. In addition, she has won many awards for her work. Carol Westfall's textiles are in international collections including Kawashima Textile School, Angers Museum and Delaware Museum of Art.

Grethe Wittrock
Textile designer and artist, b. Denmark, 1964
Studied Textiles at the Danish Design School, 1992 and spent a year at Kyoto Seika University College of Fine Art 1990–91. Set up her own studio in 1991 and in 1993 established Project Papermoon with fashion designer Ann Schmidt-Christensen. For many years they created sculptural garments using paper yarn in textile which was imported from Japan. They showed their experimental clothing as art in galleries and museums. Grethe Wittrock has worked for Creation Baumann, Switzerland as a designer for interior textiles. Received a 3-year grant from the Danish State Art Foundation 2001–4. Her work was selected for the Danish Biennale 2004. She has exhibited her designs and art work internationally including Artists at Work: New Technology in Textile and Fibre Art, Prato (2003).

Linda Worbin
Currently a Doctoral Candidate in Smart Textiles and Interaction Design at the Swedish School of Textiles in cooperation with the Department of Computer Science and Engineering, Chalmers University of Technology, Sweden. She is a formal textile designer and researcher from the Interactive Institute in Sweden, where she has been working within the research project 'IT and Textiles'. She is designing dynamic textile patterns using Smart Textiles to enlarge the understanding and the usage of aesthetics in the area of Smart Textiles.

Hideo Yamakuchi
Textile artist, b. Japan, 1962
Graduated from Bunka Fashion Institute, Tokyo, 1988. The son of a weaver, his grandfather was the founder of a weaving company in Yonezawa, Yamagata Prefecture, well known for its textiles. Studied electronic engineering and later worked as a computer engineer at Fujitsu Company which included the development of personal computers. Joined father's textile company, Yamasho Orimono as textile designer, combining interests in computers and textiles, initially for textile designs for interiors. He uses the computer to design and manufacture Jacquard woven textile pieces with complex imagery which often have a photographic realism. In 1993 he established his own company, Orimoto Yamakuchi Co. Ltd. In 1996 he was winner of the Grand Prize, Tokyo Textile Contest for Jacquard woven art works and in 1997 won the Grand Prize, International Textile Competition, Kyoto. His work has appeared in several group and solo exhibitions including Defining Craft at the American Craft Museum, 2000, and Plants at the Digital Art Gallery, Tokyo, 2000. His work is in the permanent collections of the Metropolitan Museum of Art and the American Craft Museum, New York.

Yohji Yamamoto
fashion designer, b. Japan, 1943
Initially studied law at Keio University in Tokyo and then travelled to Europe, visiting Paris.

Studied Fashion at Bunka Fashion College in Tokyo, graduating in 1969 and set up his own studio in 1972, launching his own label in Tokyo in 1977. He had his first catwalk show in Paris in 1981 where the Press slated his work as being too experimental. He began by creating womenswear and now also shows menswear collections; his first collection was shown in Paris in 1984. His work fuses Japanese and European cultures and is well documented in German film director Wim Wenders' film Notebook on Cities and Clothes, 1989. In 1994 he was nominated Chevalier de l'Ordre des Arts et des Lettres by the French Ministry of Culture. Designed costumes for opera, namely Madame Butterfly and Tristan und Isolde. He frequently selects unusual materials and has a unique approach to cutting.

Ryoko Yamanaka
Textile artist and designer, b. Japan, 1940
Studied Woven Textile Design at Tama Fine Art College, Tokyo and Printed Textiles with textile artist and designer Hiroko Watanabe. Teaches Textiles and History of Decoration at Tohoku University of Art and Design. Designs textiles and lighting for interior design and creates textile art works. Explores new synthetic materials and uses techniques such as bonding. Recent work uses polyurethane with electro-luminescent fibres. Group exhibition Material-ism at the Ozone Gallery in Tokyo, 2004.

Directory of Addresses

3M Center
Ceramic Materials Department
St Paul, MN
USA
——— United Kingdom plc
3M House, 20 Jackson Street
Manchester M15 4PA
UK

Helle Abild
Gustav Johannsensvej 5
2000 Frederiksberg
Denmark

Machiko Agano
2-30-6 Yokogi Otus Shiga
520-0063 Japan

Mitsuko Akutsu
90-2-301 Iwase
Matsudo-shi
Chiba 271-0076
Japan

Akzo Nobel Fibers SAS
164, rue Ambroise, Croizat
France

Akzo Nobel Faser AG
D-42097, Wuppertal
Germany

Akzo Nobel Nonwovens
PO Box 9300 6800 SB
Arnhem
The Netherlands

Alpha
Westbury
Sherborne
Dorset DT9 3RB
UK

Amalgam
Morelands
5-23 Old Street
London EC1V 9HG
UK

Apple Computer USA
3565, Monroe Street
Santa Clara CA 95051-1468
USA

Jun'ichi Arai
PO Box 9, 1-1-228 Sakaino-cho
Kiryu 376
Gunma Prefecture
Japan

Helen Archer
30C Glover Road
St Heliers, Auckland 1005
New Zealand

Architects of Air
Oldknows Factory
Egerton Street
Nottingham NG3 4GO
UK

Aspen Aerogels Inc
30 Forbes Road
Northborough
MA 01532
USA

Nigel Atkinson
4 Camden Square
London NW1 9UY
UK

August Herzog Maschinenfabrik
GmbH and Co. KG
Am Alexanderhaus 160
26127 Oldenburg
Germany

BFF Nonwovens
Bath Road, Bridgewater
Somerset TA6 4NZ
UK

Savithri Bartlett
29 Tretawn Gardens, Mill Hill
London NW7 4NP
UK

Bekaert Asia
934 Shin Building, 3–1 Marunouchi
3-Chrome Chiyoda-ku
Tokyo 100
Japan

Bekaert Corp
1395 South Marietta Parkway
Building 500
Suite 100
Marietta GA 30067
USA

Bekintex NV
Industriepark Kwatrecht
Neerhonderd 16
9230 Wetteren
Belgium

Eva Best
Syster Estrids Gata 2
413 25 Gothenburg
Sweden

Bidim Geosynthetics SA
9 rue Marcel Paul – B.P. 80
95873 Bezons Cedex
France

Maria Blaisse, Flexible Design
Bickersgracht 55
1013 LG Amsterdam
The Netherlands

Ulla E:son Bodin
Mansagarden
523 98 Hokerum
Sweden

Bonar Technical Fabrics
Waverslaan 15
9160 Lokeren
Belgium

Niels Bonde
Adelgade 55, 2TV
DK – 1304 Copenhagen
Denmark

Boudicca
Unit 16D King's Yard
Carpenters Road
London E15 2HD
UK

BAe (Systems and Equipment) Ltd
PO Box 55 Gunnels Wood Road
Stevenage
Herts SG1 2DB
UK

Liza Bruce
9, Pont Street
London SW1X 9EJ
UK
———
80 Thompson Street, SoHo
New York, NY 10012
USA

Carrington Performance Fabrics
Calder Works, Thornhill Road
Dewsbury
W. Yorks WF12 9QP
UK

Caruso GmbH
Garnstadter Strasse 38/39
96237 Ebersdorf/Cob.
Germany

Cellaris, Ltd
Bar-Lev Industrial Park
PO Box 15
D.N. Misgav 20179
Israel

Celltran Limited
The Innovation Centre
217 Portobello
Sheffield S1 4DP
UK

Luisa Cevese
via Bramante 39
Milan
Italy

Simon Clarke
Mill House
Nancledra, Penzance
Cornwall TR20 8NA
UK

Clothing +
Jämintie 14
FIN-38700 Kankaanpää
Finland

Comme des Garçons
59 Brook Street,
London W1Y 1YF
UK
———
16 Place Vendôme
75001 Paris
France
———
5-2-1 Minami-Aoyama, Minato-ku
Tokyo 107
Japan

Corpo Nove
Karada Italia Srl
Via Leonardo da Vinci 190
50059 Sovigliana-Vinci (Fi)
Italy

Courtaulds Tencel Fibres Europe
72 Lockhurst Lane
Coventry CV6 5RZ
UK

Simon Conder Associates
8 Nile Street
London N1 7RF
UK

Critz Campbell
B9 Furniture
PO Box 12387
Chicago, IL 60612
USA

**D.L.M.I. Département Mailles
Techniques – Technical Knits**
Avenue Paul Chartron
F-26260 St-Donat
France

Diesel
Headquarters - Staff International SpA
via del Progresso 10
36025 Noventa Vicentina
Italy

Mark Dion
517 Plank Road
Beach Lake, Pennsylvania 18405
USA

**DLMI (Dorures Louis Mathieu
Industrie)**
15 rue Louis Malle
69616 Villeurbanne cedex
France

Isabel Dodd
102 Wormholt Road
London W12 0LP
UK

Hil Driessen
Amsteldijk 26 A-II
1074 HT Amsterdam
The Netherlands

Droog Design
Rusland 3
1012 CK Amsterdam
The Netherlands

ECOTEXTIL, Ltd.
CZ - 277 11 Hornatky u Neratovic
Czech Republic

Emily DuBois
12-168 Kipuka Street
Pahoa
Hawaii 96778
USA

Dunne & Raby
Pegasus House
116–120 Golden Lane
London EC1Y 0TF
UK

DuPont Tactel
Industrie Strasse 1
Werk Ostringen
76684 Ostringen
Germany

——— 94 Regent Road
Leicester LE1 7DJ
UK

Rebecca Earley, b.earley
58 St Stephen's Gardens
London W2 5NJ
UK

Eley Kishimoto
215 Lyham Road
London SW2 5PY
UK

Ellis Developments Ltd
The Clocktower
Bestwood Village
Nottingham NG6 8TQ
UK

European Space Agency
8-10 rue Mario Nikis
75738 Paris Cedex 15
France

Fairey Arlon Ltd
2920-99th Street
Sturtevant, WI 53177
USA

Fairey Industrial Ceramics Ltd
Filleybrooks
Stone
Staffs ST15 0PU
UK

Serge Ferrari SA
B.P. 54, 38352 La Tour-du-Pin, Cedex
France

Fibertex A/S
Svendborgvej 16
DK-9220 Aalborg Øst
Denmark

Ford Motor Company
Customer Relationship Center
P.O. Box 6248
Dearborn, MI 48126
USA

Foresight Institute
PO Box 61058
Palo Alto
CA 94306
USA

Fothergill Engineering Fabrics
PO Box 1, Summit
Littleborough
Lancs OL15 9QP
UK

Shelley Fox
Flat 2, 131 Amhurst Road
London E8 2AN
UK

Katharine Frame
Middleton House, Farnhill
Nr Keighley
N. Yorks BD20 9BW
UK

Frances Geesin
Headrest, Street End Lane
Broadoak, Heathfield
East Sussex TN21 8TU
UK

W.L. Gore & Associates
P.O. Box 729
Elkton, MD 21922
USA

Grado Zero Espace
Via del Lazzeretto 109
59100 Prato (PO)
Italy

Grafil Inc.
5900 88th St,
Sacramento CA 95828
USA

Julie Graves
8 Rochester House
Rushcroft Road
London SW2 1JR
UK

Green-Tek Inc
407 North Main Street
Edgerton
WI 53534
USA

Griffin
Elvis Rocks Ltd. T/A Griffin
Graceland
Edington Road
Edington
Wiltshire BA13 4NW
UK

Grimshaw
1 Conway Street
Fitzroy Square
London W1T 6LR
UK

Sue Gundy
6537 Sunnyside Avenue North
Seattle,
Washington 98103
USA

Zaha M. Hadid Architects
Studio 9
10 Bowling Green Lane
London EC1R 0BQ
UK

Jane Harris
135 Coburg Crescent
Streatham Hill
London SW2 3HU
UK

Kyoko Hashimoto
6-24-21, Matubara
Setagaya-ku
Tokyo 156 0043
Japan

Ane Henriksen
Ourøgade 40, 2th
2100 Copenhagen Ø
Denmark

Herman Miller Ltd
149 Tottenham Court Rd
London W1P 0JA
UK

Herman Miller Inc.
855 East Main Avenue
Zeeland
Michigan 49464-0302
USA

Hexcel Composites Ltd
Duxford
Cambridge CB2 4QD
UK

Hexcel Corporation
281 Tresser Boulevard
Stamford, Connecticut 06901-3238
USA

Ainsley Hillard
5/203 Cambridge Street
Wembley, Perth 6014
Western Australia

Yoshiki Hishinuma, Hishinuma
Associates Co. Ltd
3-12-12-2F Higashi
Shibuya-ku
Tokyo 150 0011
Japan

Hoechst High Chem
(Hoechst Aktiengesellschaft)
Postfach 80 03 20
D-6230 Frankfurt-am-Main 80
Germany

Hoechst UK
Beech Croft House, Ervington Court
Meridian Business Park
Leicester LE3 2WL
UK

Michael Hopkins and Partners
27 Broadley Terrace
London NW1 6LG
UK

Hybrids + Fusion
Poortdijk 34d
3402 BS Ijsselstein
The Netherlands

ICI plc
9 Millbank
London SW1P SJF
UK

ICI Polyurethanes
6555 Fifteen Mile Road
Sterling Heights, MI 48077
USA
——— Everslaan 45
B 3078 Everberg
Belgium

Immersion Corporate Headquarters
801 Fox Lane
San Jose
California 95131
USA

Inoue Pleats Inc.
4-2-17 Jingumae, Shibuya-ku
Tokyo
Japan

Institute for Molecular Manufacturing
555 Bryant Street
Suite 354
Palo Alto
CA 94301 USA
USA

Institut für Textiltechnik, Aachen
Department of Textile Technology (ITA)
Eilfschornsteinstrasse 18
D-52062 Aachen
Germany

International Cellulose Corporation (ICC)
PO Box 450006
12315 Robin Blvd
Houston
Texas 77245-0006
USA

International Fashion Machines Inc.
1205 East Pike Street, Suite 2G
Seattle, WA
98112
USA

Jakob Müller Forschung AG
CH-5262 Frick
Switzerland

Janis Jefferies
29 Alderney Road
London E1 4EG
UK

JongeriusLab
Eendrachtsweg 67
3012 LG Rotterdam
The Netherlands

Kanebo Ltd
410 Maekawa 3F, 4-/ Kobune-cho
Nihonbashi
Chumoku, Tokyo 103
Japan
———(Research) Akasaka Centre
Building 3-12
Motoakasaka 1 chome
Minato-ku, Tokyo 107
Japan
——— 13–14 Woodstock Street
London W1R 1HJ
UK

Anish Kapoor
c/o The Lisson Gallery
52–54 Bell Street
London NW1 5DA
UK

Christine Keller
Ernst-August Strasse 7
D-22605, Hamburg
Germany

Koch Hightex
Stuart House, The Back
Chepstow,
Gwent NP6 5HH
UK

Koit Konstruktive Membranen
Herbert Koch GmbH and Co. KG
Nordstrasse 1, D-8219 Rimsting
Germany

Michiko Koshino Japan Co. Ltd
74 Salusbury Road
London NW6 6NU
UK
www.michikokoshino.com

Kyoko Kumai
1-3-10 Sumiyoshi-cho
Oita-city 870 0032
Japan

Yayoi Kusama
c/o Robert Miller Gallery
524 W. 26th Street
New York
NY 10001
USA

Kuraray Co. Ltd
1-12-39 Umeda, Kita-ku, Osaka 530
Japan
——— Immermannstrasse 33
4000 Düsseldorf 1
Germany
——— US office, Clarino America
Corporation
489 Fifth Avenue
New York, NY 10017
USA

Kuraray International Corp.
30th Floor, Metlife Bldg, 200 Park Ave
New York, NY 10166
USA

Lang and Baumann
Lyssachstrasse 112
3400 Burgdorf
Switzerland

Lee Lapthorne
Doll
1st Floor, 3 Percy Street
London W1T 1DE
UK

Koko Toshima Larson
1452 Orange Grove Avenue
Santa Barbara,
California 93105 2130
USA

Barbara Layne
4334 Avenue Laval
Montreal, Quebec H2W 2J5
Canada

Jürgen Lehl
3-1-7 Kiyosumi, Koto-ku
Tokyo 135 8421
Japan

Lenzing Lyocell AG, Lenzing
Aktiengesellschaft A-4860 Lenzing
Austria

Maccaferri Ltd
4b The Quorum Business Park
Garsington Road
Oxford OX4 2JY
UK

Anja Madsen
4 Impasse Molin
75018 Paris
France

Benoît Maubrey/Die Audio Gruppe
Bahnhofstrasse 47
D-1821 Baitz
Germany

Mayser GmbH and Co
Bismarckstrasse 2,
D-88161 Lindenberg/Allgäu
Germany

Meadowbrook Inventions Inc.
P.O. Box 960
260 Mine Brook Road (Rt. 202)
Bernardsville
New Jersey 07924 0960
USA

Melton Corporation
133 Frances Avenue
Cranston, RI 02910
USA

Microthermal Systems Ltd
Tregonce Cliff, St Issey, Wadebridge
Cornwall PL27 7QJ
UK

Johanna Mills Rose
35 Lawford Road
London NW5 2LG
UK

Issey Miyake UK Ltd
270 Brompton Road,
London SW3 2AW
UK

Miyake Design Studio
1-23 Oyama-cho, Shibuya-ku
Tokyo 156 0065
Japan

Masako Mizumachi
5-23-3 Kyodo, Setagaya-ku
Tokyo 156 0052
Japan

Mitsubishi
Mitsubishi Shoji Building
6-3, Marunouchi 2-chome
Chiyoda-ku
Tokyo 100-8086
Japan

Montefibre, Enimont Group
via Pola 14
20124 Milan
Italy

Helen Murray
Unit 12
5 Durham Yard
London E2 6QF
UK

NASA Headquarters
Washington, D.C. 2054
USA

N.V. Schlegel SA,
European Industrial Products Division
Rochesterlaan 4
B-8470 Gistel
Belgium

Netlon Ltd
New Wellington Street
Blackburn BB2 4PJ
UK

Nexia Biotechnologies
1000 St-Charles Avenue,
Block B
Vaudreuil-Dorion, QC
J7V 8P5
Canada

Karen Nicol
Friel House, 18 St Mary's Road
East Molesey, Surrey KT8 0ST
UK

NIKE Inc.
1 Bowerman Drive
Beaverton
Oregon 97005
USA

Nuno Corporation
B1F Axis Building
5-17-1 Roppongi
Minato-ku, Tokyo 106 0032
Japan
——— Second Floor, Suite A, D & D
Building,
979, Third Avenue, 58th Street
New York, NY 10022
USA

Nylstar Headquarters
via Friuli 55
20031 Cesano Maderno
Milan
Italy

Omikenshi
4-25, Awaji-machi, Higashi-ku,
Osaka 541
Japan

Lucy Orta, Studio Orta
42 boulevard de Bercy
75012 Paris
France

Outlast Technologies Inc.
6235 Lookout Road
Boulder, CO 80301
USA

Ove Arup and Partners
13 Fitzroy Street
London W1P 6BQ
UK

Palmhive Technical Textiles Limited
NTG House
Willow Road, Lenton
Nottingham NG7 2TA
UK

Parabeam
Hoogeindsestraat 49
5705AL Helmond
The Netherlands

Plaspack USA Inc.
753 Amron Ave
Antigo, WI 54409
USA

Prada
via A. Fogazzaro 28
20135 Milan
Italy

Nicholas Pryke
25 Hayfield Road
Oxford
OX2 6TX

J. Morgan Puett
517 Plank Road
Beach Lake, Pennsylvania 18405
USA

Dorothea Reese-Heim
Mainzer Str. 4
80803 Munich
Germany

RE:FORM Studio
Hugo Grauers Gata 3
SE-412 96 Gothenburg
Sweden

Ann Richards
16 Albany Road
Southsea
Hampshire P05 2AB
UK

Vibeke Riisberg
J.M. Thielevej 6
1961 Frederiksberg
Copenhagen
Denmark

RIVAL
Unit 1-2/26-34 Dunning Ave
Rosebery NSW 2018
Australia

Sophie Roet
Clockwork Studios
38B Southwell Road
London SE5 9PG
UK

Richard Rogers Partnership
Thames Wharf, Rainville Road
London W6 9HA
UK

Julie Ryder
PO Box 104
Jamieson Centre
A.C.T. 2614
Australia

Jakob Schlaepfer
Fürstenlandstrasse 99
9001 St Gallen
Switzerland

Schoeller Textil AG
Bahnhofstrasse
9475 Sevelen
Switzerland

Schuller GmbH
Faserweg 1
97865 Wertheim
Germany

Lesley Sealey, i.e.uniform
9, Portland Mansions
Addison Bridge Place
London W14 8XL
UK

Shape 3 – Innovative Textiltechnik
GmbH
Friedrich-Engels Allee 161
42285 Wuppertal
Germany

Pēteris Sidars
11 Novembra
Krastmala 35
Riga 1050
Latvia

Malgorzata Skuza
Wyszynskiego 58 M 69 A
94 046 Lodz
Poland

SmartSlab Ltd
42A Charlotte Street
London W1T 2NP
UK

Grethe Sørensen
Bastrup Skolevej 24a
6589 Vamdrup
Denmark

Speedo International Ltd
Pentland Centre
Lakeside
Squires Lane
London N3 2QL
UK

Karen Spurgin
39 Sundorne Road
London SE7 7PR
UK

Norma Starszakowna
102 Royle Building
Wenlock Road
London N1 7SH
UK

Stelarc
4 Dorset Place
West Melton
Victoria
Australia

Stomatex Ltd
Treasure House
19-21 Hatton Garden
London EC1N 8LF
UK

Stork Screens BV
PO Box 67
5830 AB Boxmeer
The Netherlands

Stretch Ceilings (UK) Ltd
Whitehall Farm Lane
Virginia Water
Surrey GU25 4DA
UK

Sarah Taylor
1 Broomhall
Mertown Estate
St Boswells
Roxburghshire TD6 0EA
UK

Technical Absorbents Ltd
PO Box 24
Great Coates
Grimsby
UK

Tecknit USA (EMI Shielding)
129 Dermody Street
Cranford
NJ 07016
USA

Tencel Limited
The Acordis Group
Sager House
50 Seymour Street
London W1H 7JG
UK

Tess Trend SRL, Gruppo Bonazzi
Viale dell'Industria
European distributors for Sunfit
5-37036 S. Martino Buon Albergo (VR)
Italy

Tecknit USA (EMI Shielding)
129 Dermody Street
Cranford
NJ 07016
USA

Tensar Corporation
1210 Citizens Parkway
Box 986
Morrow
Atlanta
GA 30260
USA

Tensar International
New Wellington Street
Blackburn BB2 4PJ
UK

Tess Trend SRL, Gruppo Bonazzi
Viale dell'Industria
5-37036 S. Martino Buon Albergo (VR)
Italy

Tissue + Culture
SymbioticA
Image Analysis and Acquisition Facility
Department of Anatomy and Human
Biology
University of Western Australia
35 Stirling Highway
Nedlands 6009
Western Australia

Toray Industries Inc.
Toray Building
2-1 Nihonbashi-Muromachi
2-chome, Chuo-ku
Tokyo 103 8666
Japan
——— 3-3-3 Nakanoshima, Kita-ku
Osaka 530
Japan
——— 3rd Floor, 7 Old Park Lane
London W1Y
UK
——— 5th Floor, 600 Third Avenue
New York, NY 10016
USA

Machi Ue
Via Don Milani 54
50011 Antella
Italy

Walter van Beirendonck
Bvba big
Henri van Heurckstraat 5
2000 Antwerp
Belgium

Eugène van Veldhoven
Dunne Bierkade 29
2512 BD Den Haag
The Netherlands

Veech.media.architecture
Berggasse 21/2
a-1090 Vienna
Austria

Verasol Fabrics BV
PO Box 15
7150 AA Eibergen
The Netherlands

Virtual Technologies Inc.
2175 Park Boulevard
Palo Alto, CA 94306
USA

Irene van Vliet
W.G. Plein 10 bg
1054 RA Amsterdam
The Netherlands

Marcel Wanders Studio
Jacob Catskade 35
1052 BT Amsterdam
The Netherlands

Sonja Weber
Arcisstrasse 43
80799 Munich
Germany

Carol Westfall
208-17 West Shearwater Court
Jersey City
New Jersey 07305
USA

Westwind Composites Inc.
7701 Monroe
Houston
Tex. 77061
USA

Suzanne Whitehead
Birchall Moss, Hatherton
Nr Nantwich
Cheshire CW5 7PJ
UK

Grethe Wittrock
Sopassagen 14, 3th
2100 Copenhagen
Denmark

Linda Worbin
Textilhögskolan i Borås
School of Textiles
SE-501 90 Borås
Sweden

Hideo Yamakuchi
1790-1, Yanazawa, Yonezawa-city
Yamagata 992 0077
Japan

Yohji Yamamoto
Aoyama Honten
5-3-6 Minami-Aoyama
Minato-ku, Tokyo 107
Japan

Ryoko Yamanaka
25-19 Honmoku-Hara, Naka-ku
Yokohama-city 231 0821
Japan

Exhibitions

Artists at Work: New Technology in Textile and Fibre Art
Textile Museum, via Santa Chiari 24
59100 Prato, Italy
18 September–24 November 2003

Bling Bling
National Museum in Zurich
Museumstrasse 2
80001 Zurich, Switzerland
August 2004
Fabrics by Jakob Schlaepfer

Contemporary Textile Art
Ormeau Baths Gallery
Belfast,. Northern Ireland, UK
12 December 2002–11 January 2003

Digital Creativity (online exhibition, 2002)
www.axisartists.org.uk

e-Textiles – Ventures in Jacquard Weaving
Ivan Dougherty Gallery
UNSW College of Fine Arts, Sydney
Australia
19 July–18 August 2001

Edge: The Influence of Sportswear
Oksnehallen, Halmtorvet 11
1700 Copenhagen, Denmark
4–31 January 2002

Extreme Textiles
Cooper Hewitt National Design Museum
Fifth Avenue at 91st Street
New York
New York, USA
8 April –30 October 2005

Fabric of Fashion
British Council exhibition co-curated by Sarah
Braddock Clarke and Marie O'Mahony
Crafts Council Gallery, 44A Pentonville Road
London N1 9BY, UK
8 November 2000–14 January 2001 and
toured Europe until 25 August 2002
Included work by Shelley Fox, Eley Kishimoto
and Hussein Chalayan

Fashion at Belsay
Belsay Hall, Castle and Gardens
Belsay, Newcastle upon Tyne
Northumberland NE20 0DX, UK
29 May–30 September 2004
Art works by international fashion designers

Fashion Creation in Fabrics 1960–2000
The Galliera Museum
10 avenue Pierre Premier de Serbie
75116 Paris, France
March–July 2000

Fashions by Jurgen Lehl
Fashion Gallery
Gemeentemuseum Den Haag
The Netherlands
8 April–1 October 2000

Fluid Architecture IV
www.fluidarchitecture.net
26 February 2003
Live installation by the artist Lucy Orta

Future Textiles: Fast Wear for Sport & Fashion
The Hub
Sleaford
Lincolnshire
UK
13 August–23 October 2005
Curated by Sarah E. Braddock Clarke and
Marie O'Mahony
Included work by Maharishi, Eley Kishimoto
and Griffin

Great Expectations
Vanderbilt Hall
Grand Central Station New York
New York, USA
14–28 October 2001
Hosted by the Design Council, UK. Showed
100 examples of the best of British design
from fashion to architecture. Included work
by textile and fashion designers Savithri
Bartlett, Deborah Milner and Karen Spurgin.
Touring international exhibition.

Hitec-Lotec
Crafts for Now Touring exhibition
Curated by Marie O'Mahony. Venues included:
Brewery Arts, Devon Guild of Craftsmen,
Black Swan Guild, Walford Mill and the Crafts
Council of Ireland.
Included work by Sophie Roet and Nick Pryke.

Intersecting Traditions, recent textiles by Cynthia Schira
Robert Hillestad Textiles Gallery
University of Nebraska
Lincoln
Nebraska, USA
19 April–21 May 2004
Touring USA until June 2005

My Favourite Dress
The Fashion and Textile Museum
83 Bermondsey Street
London SE1 3XF, UK
12 May–November 2003

NEST
Stedelijk Museum of Modern Art
Amsterdam
The Netherlands
18 February–16 May 2005
Included work by Hil Driessen and
Maria Blaisse.

The New Knitting
Fashion Space Gallery
20 John Princes Street
London College of Fashion, University
of the Arts
London W1G 0BJ, UK
23 March–7 April 2000

Nuno: Sense and Skill
Curtin University of Technology
Perth, Western Australia
April 2004

Out There
Sainsbury Centre for Visual Arts
University of East Anglia
Norwich NR4 7TJ, UK
3 July–29 August 2005
Included outdoor work by Machiko Agano

Rapture: Arts Seduction by Fashion Since 1970
Barbican Gallery
London EC2, UK
10 October–23 December 2002

RN: The Past, Present and Future of the Nurse's Uniform
The Fabric Workshop and Museum
Philadelphia
Pennsylvania, USA
3 October 2003–14 February 2004
Included work by Mark Dion and J. Morgan
Puett

The Soft Machine, Design in the Cyborg Age
Stedelijk Museum of Modern Art
Amsterdam
The Netherlands
28 November–10 January 1999
Curated by Marie O'Mahony

The Space Between
Curtin University of Technology
Perth, Western Australia
April 2004
Exhibition to coincide with symposium
included Maria Blaisse, Jane Harris, Nuno
and Lucy Orta

Structure and Surface: Contemporary Japanese Textiles
The Museum of Modern Art
11 West 53rd Street, New York
New York 10019, USA
12 November 1998–26 January 1999
and at the Saint Louis Art Museum, USA
18 June–15 August 1999

Through the Surface
Originated through the Surrey Institute of Art
and Design University College
Sainsbury Centre for Visual Arts
University of East Anglia, Norwich, UK
6 April–13 June 2004
Contemporary textile artists from Britain and
Japan. Included the work of Machiko Agano
and Frances Geesin

Transgressing Fashion No. 204 (Nexus
Architecture)
Victoria & Albert Museum
London SW7 2RL, UK
Live installation by the artist Lucy Orta
www.showstudio.com
25 June 2004

Collections and Galleries

AUSTRALIA
Art Gallery of Western Australia
Perth Cultural Centre, Perth, WA 6000
Canberra School of Art Gallery
Canberra Institute of the Arts, PO Box 801,
Canberra 2601
**The Powerhouse, Museum of Applied Arts and
Sciences**
500 Harris Street, Ultimo, Sydney NSW 2007
Sydney Textile Museum
172 St John's Road, Glebe, Sydney NSW

AUSTRIA
Österreichisches Museum für Angewandte
Kunst, Stubenring 5, 1010 Vienna

BELGIUM
Flanders Fashion Institute
Nationale Straat, 2000 Antwerp
Galerie Philharmonie
7 bis rue des Bénédictines, Liège

CANADA
Musée d'Art Contemporain
Cité du Havre, Montreal, Quebec
Museum for Textiles, Contemporary Gallery
55 Centre Avenue, Toronto, Ontario M5G 2H5

COLOMBIA
Museo de Arte Contemporaneo
Plaza de Banderas, Bogotá

CZECH REPUBLIC
Musée des Arts Décoratifs
17 Listopadu 2, 11000 Prague

DENMARK
Oksnehallen
Halmtorvet 11, 1700 Copenhagen

FINLAND
Galleria 25
Kasarmikatu 25, 00130 Helsinki

FRANCE
Musée d'Art Moderne de la Ville de Paris
11 Avenue du Président Wilson, 75016 Paris
Musée de la Mode
11 La Canebière, 13001 Marseille
Musée de l'Impression sur Étoffes
3 rue des Bonnes Gens, 68100 Mulhouse, Alsace
Musée de Tissus
30–34 rue de la Charité, 69002 Lyon
Musée des Arts de la Mode et du Textile
Palais du Louvre, 107–109 rue de Rivoli, 75001,
Paris

Musée National d'Art Moderne
Centre Georges Pompidou, 75004 Paris
Musée National des Arts et Traditions Populaires
6 Avenue du Mahatma Ghandi, 75116 Paris

GERMANY
Bauhaus-Archiv
Klingerhöferstrasse 14, 1000 Berlin 30
Deutsches Textilmuseum
Andreasmarkt 8, 4150 Krefeld-Linn
Museum für Kunsthandwerk
Schaumainkai 15, 6000 Frankfurt-am-Main
Museum für Kunst und Gewerbe
Steintorplatz, 2000 Hamburg 1
Stuttgart Design Centre
Landesgewerbeamt Baden-Württemberg,
Willi-Bleicherstraße 19, 70174, Stuttgart

HUNGARY
Museum of Applied Arts
Ulloi, utca 33–37, 1146 Budapest
Szombathelyi Képtár Textilcollection
Rákóczi Ferenc, utca 12, 9700 Szombathely

ICELAND
Textile Guild
Öldugata 30A, 101 Reykjavik

IRELAND
Craft Council of Ireland Gallery
Kilkenny Design Centre, Kilkenny

ITALY
Design Gallery
Via Manzoni 46, 20121 Milan
Galleria del Costume
Palazzo Pitti, 50125 Florence
Museo del Tessuto
via Santa Chiari 24, 59100 Prato

JAPAN
City Museum of Contemporary Art
Hiroshima
Crafts Gallery, National Museum of Modern Art
Kitanomaru-Koen, Chiyoda-ku, Tokyo, 102
Fashion Foundation
Hanae Mori Building, 3-6-1, Kita-Aoyama,
Minato-ku, Tokyo, 107
Gallery Gallery
Kyoto International Contemporary Textile Art
Center (KICTAC)
Kotobuki Building 5F, Kawaramachi,
Shijo-Sagaru, Shimogyo-ku, Kyoto 600 8018
Gallery Ma
Toto Nogizaka Building 3F, 1-24-3 Minami
Aoyama, Minato-ku, Tokyo 107 0062

Gallery Maronie
Kawara-machi, Shijo Agaru, Nakagyou-ku, Kyoto
Gallery Space 21
Watanabe Building BF, 1-1-18, Higashisinbashi,
Minato-ku, Tokyo
International Textile Fair
Horikawa Imadegawa, Kamigyo-ku, Kyoto, 602
Kanebo Museum of Textiles
1-5-102, Tamabuchicho, Miyakojima-ku, Osaka
Kobe Fashion Museum
2-9 Koyocho-naka, Higashinada-ku, Kobe 658
Kyoto Costume Institute
Wacoal Corporation, 29 Nakajimaco Kisshoin,
Minami-ku, Kyoto 601
Museum of Modern Art
Okazaki, Enshoji-cho, Sakyo-ku, Kyoto, 606
National Museum of Modern Art
Kyoto, Okazaki Enshoji-cho, Sakyo-ku, Kyoto, 606
National Museum of Modern Art
1 Kitanomaru-Koen, Chiyoda-ku, Tokyo 102
Nishijin Textile Museum
Imadegawa, Kamigyo-ku, Kyoto

LATVIA
Museum of Decorative Applied Arts
Skárnu Street 10-16, 1050 Riga

MEXICO
Museo Palacio Las Bellas Artes
Paseo de la Reforma y Gandhi, Mexico City

THE NETHERLANDS
Centraal Museum
Agnietenstraat 1, 3512XA Utrecht
Galerie Lous Martin
Nieuwstraat 11, 2611HK Delft
Gallery Ra
Vijzelstraat 80, 1017 HL, Amsterdam
Gemeentemuseum
Stadhouderslaan 41, 2517 HV The Hague
Nederlands Textielmuseum
Goirkestraat 96, 5046 GN, Tilburg
Stedelijk Museum
Paulus Potterstraat 13, 1071 CX, Amsterdam

NEW ZEALAND
Canterbury Museum
Roleston Avenue, Christchurch 1
Crafts Council of New Zealand
22 The Terrace, Wellington, PO Box 498, Wellington 1

NORWAY
Kunstindustrimuseet
St Olavsgate 1, 0165 Oslo
Kunstnernes Hus
Wergelandveien 17, 0167 Oslo

POLAND
Central Museum of Textiles
Piotrkowska 282, Lódz, 93034

SPAIN
Museo Textil
Parc de Vallparadis, Salmeron 25,
08222 Barcelona
Museo Textil y de Indumentaria
Calle de Montcada 12, 08003 Barcelona

SWEDEN
Nordiska Museet
Djurgardsvagen 6-16, 11593 Stockholm
Röhss Museum of Arts and Crafts
Vasagatan 37-39, 40015 Göteborg
Textile Museum
Druveforsvagen 8, 50256 Boras

SWITZERLAND
Musée Bellerive
Hoschgasse 3, Zürich
Musée des Arts Décoratifs
4 avenue Villamont, 1005 Lausanne
Textil Museum
Vadianstrasse 2, 9000 St Gallen

UK
Barbican Art Gallery
Barbican Centre, Silk Street
London EC2Y 8DS
Bonington Gallery
Nottingham Trent University, Dryden Street
Nottingham, NG1 4FX
Castle Museum
Nottingham NG1 6EL
The Challenge of Materials Gallery
Science Museum, Exhibition Road
London SW7 2DD
**The Constance Howard Resource and Research
Centre in Textiles**
Department of Visual Arts, Goldsmiths College
Deptford Town Hall, New Cross
London SE14 6NW
Contemporary Applied Arts
2 Percy Street, London W1P 9FA
Crafts Council Gallery
44A Pentonville Road, London N1 9BY
Design Museum
28 Shad Thames, London SE1 2YD
The Fashion and Textile Museum
83 Bermondsey Street, London SE1 3XF
Fruitmarket Gallery
29 Market Street, Edinburgh, EH1 1DF
Ikon Gallery
58–72 John Bright Street. Birmingham B1 1BN

James Hockey Gallery
West Surrey College of Art and Design
The Surrey Institute, Falkner Road
Farnham GU9 7DS
Holburne Museum and Crafts Study Centre
Great Pulteney Street, Bath BA2 4DB
Horniman Museum
100 London Road, Forest Hill, London SE23 3PQ
The HUB
Navigation Wharf, Carre Street, Sleaford
Lincolnshire NG34 7TW
Laing Art Gallery
Higham Place, Newcastle-upon-Tyne
Livingstone Studio
36 New End Square
London NW3 ILS
Museum of Costume
The Assembly Rooms, Bennett Street
Bath, Avon BA1 2QH
Royal College of Art
Henry Moore Gallery, Gulbenkian Hall

Kensington Gore, London SW7 2EU
Sainsbury Centre for the Visual Arts
University of East Anglia, Norwich NR4 7TJ
The Ulster Museum
Botanic Gardens, Stranmillis Road
Belfast BT9 5AB
Victoria and Albert Museum
Cromwell Road, South Kensington
London SW7 2RL
Whitworth Art Gallery
University of Manchester, Oxford Road
Manchester M15 6ER
The Winchester Gallery
Park Avenue, Winchester
Hants, S023 8DL

USA
American Craft Council
72 Spring Street, New York NY 10012
American Craft Museum
44 West 53rd Street, New York NY 10019 and

77 West 45th Street, New York NY 10036
Art Institute of Chicago
Michigan Avenue, Adams Street
Chicago IL 60610
The Brooklyn Museum USA
Eastern Parkway, Brooklyn, New York NY 11238
Computer Museum
Museum Way, 300 Congress Street
Boston MA 02210
Cooper-Hewitt National Design Museum
Smithsonian Institution, 2 East 91st Street
New York NY 10128-9990
The Costume Institute, Metropolitan Museum of Art
1000 Fifth Avenue, New York NY 10028
Costumes and Textiles Department
Los Angeles County Museum of Art, 5905
Wilshire Boulevard, Los Angeles CA 90036
The Fabric Workshop
1315 Cherry Street, Philadelphia PA 19107
The Museum at the Fashion Institute of Technology

West 27th Street at 7th Avenue, New York, NY 10011
Museum of Contemporary Art
237E, Ontario Street, Chicago IL 60611
Museum of Modern Art
11 West 53rd Street, New York NY 10019
San Francisco Museum of Modern Art
151 Third Street, San Francisco CA 94103
Paley Design Centre, Philadelphia College of Textiles and Science
4200, Henry Avenue, Philadelphia PA 19144
Philadephia Museum of Art
26th Street and Benjamin Franklin Parkway
Philadelphia PA 19130
Rhode Island School of Design Art Museum
2 College Street, Providence RI 02903
Saint Louis Art Museum
Fine Arts Drive, Forest Park
Saint Louis MO 63100
The Textile Museum
2320 South Street. Washington, D.C. 20008

Illustration Credits